U∅ 7∅8∅∅∅∅9

5—

LOVE POTIONS

LOVE POTIONS

A Guide to Aphrodisiacs and Sexual Pleasures

CYNTHIA MERVIS WATSON, M.D.

WITH ANGELA HYNES

JEREMY P. TARCHER / PERIGEE

A portion of the author's proceeds from the sale of
this book will be donated to projects for the homeless.

Jeremy P. Tarcher/Perigee Books
are published by
The Putnam Publishing Group

This book contains information on aphrodisiacs. Prior to implementing any exercises or pharmacological or homeopathic regimens, the reader may wish to consult with a health care professional. The publisher and the author expressly disclaim any liability resulting from the use of this book.

Requests for such permissions should be addressed to:
Jeremy P. Tarcher, Inc.
5858 Wilshire Blvd., Suite 200
Los Angeles, CA 90036

Library of Congress Cataloging-in-Publication Data

Watson, Cynthia Mervis.
Love potions: A guide to aphrodisiacs and sexual pleasures
Cynthia Mervis Watson with Angela Hynes.
p. cm.
Includes bibliographical references and index.
ISBN 0-87477-724-0 (pbk. : acid-free paper)
1. Aphrodisiacs. I. Hynes, Angela. II. Title.
RM386.W35 1993
615'.766—dc20   92-35363 CIP

Design by MaryJane DiMassi
Cover design and illustration © by Lee Fukui
Author photo © by David D'Angelo

Printed in the United States of America
1 2 3 4 5 6 7 8 9 10

This book is printed on acid-free paper.
∞

This book is lovingly dedicated to
Ryan Watson, my son; Bill Wilson, my life partner;
and to the memory of my
father, Abe Mervis.

ACKNOWLEDGMENTS

I am grateful to the many people who have helped me to write this book and to expand my vision throughout the years.

I especially wish to thank Daniel Kaufman and Jeremy Tarcher, who believed in me enough to put this project together.

Thank you to those who generously shared their experience and knowledge to make this book possible: Roger Hirsh, O.M.D., C.A.; Laura Paris, C.A.; Nalini Chilkov, C.A.; Janet Zand, C.A.; Tim Ray, C.A.; David Frawley, O.M.D.; Amanda McQuaid Crawford, B.A., M.N.I.M.H.; James Green; Patricia Kaminski; Kathryn McCarthy; Alexandria Carrington-Lake; and Charles Yaksic.

Thank you to the members of Bios Study Group who have supported my practice and contributed to my knowledge of nutritional medicine: Murray Susser, M.D.; David Allen, M.D.; Allen Green, M.D.; Hyla Cass, M.D.; Jesse Hanley, M.D.; Michael Rosenbaum, M.D.; Jay Goldstein, M.D.; Joan Priestly, M.D.; and Mel Werbach, M.D.

Thank you to the practitioners of Women's Medical Group who have taught me more gynecology than I learned in my training: Karen Blanchard, M.D.; Marki Knox, M.D.; Allison Leong, M.D.; Carolyn Kaplan, M.D.; Jackie Snow, N.P.

Thanks to Rosalyn L. Bruyere for teaching me about chakras.

Thanks to the friends who offered books and personal knowledge: Michel Citrin, Nik Boyd, Janet DiGiovanni, Michael Shields, and Charles Yurchack.

Thanks to my friends who gave me a willing ear and emotional support during the process of completing this project: Barbara

Cleland, Diane Stillwell, Deirdre Wilson, and Hayden Schwartz.

Thanks to Robert Ratner, who assisted in tedious library research and photocopying.

Thanks to Kristen McCann for helping with the bibliography.

Thanks to Carol Spier, who patiently was available to print my discs into the early hours.

Thanks to T.C. and David Barr for being willing to be guinea pigs and for the back cover.

Thanks to Cheri Briggs for Bali.

Thanks to Lisa Nash, M.D., and Rick Romano, M.D., who provided a peaceful environment for the completion of several chapters.

Thanks to Diane Ladd for creating a spiritual haven in Sedona when I needed it most. And to Stefanie Hurcos for getting me there.

Many, many thanks to Angela Hynes, my co-writer, and Mary Ellen Strote, my editor, who poetically translated my thoughts into words.

Thanks to my son, Ryan, who graciously spent nights at home with me while I sat at the computer.

Thanks to my partner in life, Bill Wilson, who loved me and believed in me with his heart and helped to open mine.

And most of all I thank my family: my father, the late Abe Mervis; B. J. Zatman, my mom; Jana Kahn, Ph.D., my sister; and Scott Mervis, my brother, who accepted and loved me despite my choosing a different path.

CONTENTS

AUTHOR'S NOTE

In 1971, at the age of twenty-one, I ran away from the urban life to a remote corner of rural Norway. There I found work as a mother's helper—I, a sheltered, middle-class young woman who had never learned any of the domestic arts. Raised in Pittsburgh by a father who expected achievement and a protective mother who went so far as to iron the family's underwear, I was acting out the final stage of a long rebellion. As an adolescent, I'd embraced Zen, macrobiotics, and the works of Alan Watts; now I'd alienated friends and family by dropping out of college to earn this trip to Europe.

My Norwegian employers were farmers with seven children and a variety of farmhands; suddenly I was cooking and cleaning for twenty people. I worked the fields and learned to milk cows, bake bread, can fruit, knit, and sew. The owners of this "biodynamic" farm followed the teachings of Rudolf Steiner, Ph.D., a turn-of-the-century architect and metaphysician. The farming was based on soil treatments Steiner had developed, including homeopathic remedies intended to increase the power and energy of the soil itself. Soon I developed an interest in homeopathy and herbal medicine; I'd take my plant guide and go into the incredible fertility of the Norwegian woods to find different plants and herbs.

A year and a half later I took a new job, this time as a nurse's aide at a small homeopathic hospital in Germany's Black Forest.

I noticed that European physicians used conventional medicine along with "naturopathic" remedies. I returned home determined to finish college and become this kind of doctor.

From the beginning, I combined traditional allopathic medicine with the more controversial alternative methods, including homeopathy. Many of my patients needed drugs and surgery, but others benefited from herbal cures, nutrition supplements, hypnotherapy, or psychological counseling.

My practice was booming, but by 1988, overworked and exhausted, I ran away again, this time to Bali. All around me were vital and graceful people who expressed a reverence for the earth. The Balinese women were extraordinarily feminine; I learned that after childbirth they use special tonics to adjust their hormones. Looking deeper for an approach toward medicine that would nourish me spiritually, I realized that the rejuvenative powers of these herbal tonics were a key. I decided to use this invention for myself and for others to achieve my goals of maintaining vitality, longevity, and good health. I left Bali with a deeper understanding of the connection between vitality and sexual energy.

I had long believed that sex plays a major role in health. The basic medical-history questionnaire I asked my patients to complete had always included the question, "Are you having any problems with sex?" The patient's answer, or non-answer, allowed me to broach this delicate subject and offer whatever help I could. Now I realized that the Western medical approach to this issue was far too limited. I needed to do more study; in the long history of aphrodisia I found many of the answers I sought.

Some of the world's first physicians understood the link between sex and health, and many of them incorporated aphrodisiacs into their medical practices. A professor of classics at the University of Cincinnati has translated from the Greek a medical manuscript written by a sixth-century female gynecologist called Metrodora. Her remedies included this aphrodisiac: "Take the womb of the hare and fry it in a rusted bronze frying pan. Throw in three pounds of rose oil, then grind smooth with good-smelling myrrh. Add four drams of fat, one dram crocodile dung, two drams juice of garlic, germander, and of bloody flux and four drams of honey. Some also blend in a small amount of sparrow fat."

This ancient recipe includes substances that medical science now knows to be efficacious. How Metrodora arrived at her list of ingredients is lost in the fog of history. More important, she and many other ancients accepted aphrodisiacs as an integral part of medicine.

The word aphrodisiac means something different to almost everyone who hears it. Some believe an aphrodisiac should strengthen the libido, increase sexual stamina, provide better performance, be the fountain of youth. There are those who condemn aphrodisiacs as drugs or potions you give to some innocent for an easy seduction. This approach, akin to slipping a Mickey Finn to an unsuspecting victim, is exploitation, and it is not what this book is about. If you need to drug and trick someone into having sex with you, something inside you is amiss and needs to be treated before you look to aphrodisiacs for help, for only when you are comfortable with yourself can you fully enjoy the pleasure of making love. Which is what this book is about.

Why You Need This Book

Today's lovers, at least as much as yesterday's, desperately want to believe claims made about products that promise to fuel the libido. Why inhabitants of this enlightened era should be intrigued by aphrodisiacs is not surprising, for many factors have combined to take the mystique—and the fun—out of lovemaking.

We live in an age in which low sex drive has its own medical name: hypoactive sexual desire (HSD). According to the clinical definition of HSD, those who become aroused or have sexual thoughts less than twice a month fall into a growing category of men and women for whom eroticism is becoming a casualty to the twentieth-century rat race. Lack of interest in sex is one of the main reasons unhappy couples go to counselors.

Stress, fatigue, prescription medication, junk food, excess weight, smoking, overuse of recreational drugs and alcohol, a toxic environment, and poor general health are endemic. Alone or in combination, those factors take a devastating toll on the libido.

This is also an aging civilization. More people are living longer than ever before. No evidence exists that desire need diminish with age. To the contrary, a wealth of biological evidence supports the notion that lust lives on in spite of the subtle functional changes that occur over time.

Lastly, sex has been getting bad press. With more people baring the intimate details of their lives in public, daily news broadcasts are rife with child abuse, incest, sexual harassment, and rape. And now that sexually transmitted diseases (STDs) have entered the everyday lexicon, sex is also closely associated with illness, even death. The cumulative effect is insidious: An act that should be synonymous with love and ecstasy is acquiring an aura of anxiety and even fear.

AIDS has wrought other changes. Therapists report that couples who previously might have given up on shaky partnerships are working through problems and re-energizing the intimate side of their relationships. The more promiscuous are discovering the joys of monogamy. These people are learning what sexual masters of both the West and the East have long taught—that uniquely beautiful and profound sexual experiences occur between couples in committed and trusting relationships. After the initial incandescent passion has dimmed and a couple has settled into a stable partnership, they have the time and confidence to explore the subtleties and complexities of sexual union. Aphrodisiacs can help them ascend the blissful peaks of "higher sex."

Paradoxically, the public that is being urged to limit its sexual partners, to have only safe sex or even *no* sex, is also being bombarded with erotic stimuli. Popular music and X-rated videos contain unprecedented doses of raw, explicit sex. Television and films are more graphic than ever. Advertising becomes more aggressive in its use of blatant erotic imagery. Faced with this never-ending barrage of trim young models engaging in frenetic, stylized lovemaking, who among us has not felt inadequate at times?

But sexual satisfaction should be a reasonable expectation in the life of everyone: female, male, young, old, healthy, physically disadvantaged, or even chronically ill. If we "regular folks" can restore or bolster our sexual confidence with safe aphrodisiacs, then why not?

This book will introduce you to aphrodisiacs that really work, and will steer you away from ones that are useless or harmful. I took my information from both contemporary traditional medicine and from what are often called alternative practices. In the course of researching and writing the book I was not at all surprised to find how very often "hard" science and ancient wisdom converge.

LOVE POTIONS

1

WHY APHRODISIACS WORK

The moon is nothing
But a circumambulatory aphrodisiac
Divinely subsidized to provoke the world
Into a rising birth rate.
　　　—CHRISTOPHER FRY

Human beings have gone to fantastic lengths and done strange things to enhance sexual pleasure. Or, for that matter, to make sex happen at all. Cleopatra is said to have seduced Mark Antony in a scented bedchamber knee-deep in rose petals. North American Indian girls combined *panax quinquefolius,* a local species of ginseng, with snake meat, gelatin, mica, and wild columbine, then secretly added it to the meals of the young men they wanted as husbands. Before venturing into a lady's bed, Casanova fortified himself with oysters and a cup of chocolate. Fifteenth-century Englishmen who suffered from impotence drank a potion brewed from wormwood and the left index finger of a hanged man. . . .

　　Inhabitants of the Age of Science might chuckle at these methods of inducing ecstasy, but modern techniques have more in common with these archaic machinations than one would at first think. Hold up a mirror to the scenarios described above and what is reflected back might be—

- A newly liberated divorcée who delights her lover with a sexual ritual that includes subtly perfumed baths, candlelight, and soft music.
- A young woman who writes to *Cosmopolitan*'s advice column asking how she can make a lover of a platonic friend.
- A single man who, before arriving for a late-night rendezvous, smokes marijuana.
- An overworked, overstressed executive who visits an impotence clinic when his wife's complaints of neglect can no longer be ignored.

All these people are seeking—in the broad sense of the word—an aphrodisiac. Any woman who has worn lacy black lingerie for a romantic tryst, any couple who has leafed through an adult magazine together or shared a bottle of champagne before making love, anyone who has used a recreational drug to enhance sex, has used aphrodisiacs as surely as did Lady Jane Grey in the 1550s when she employed an herbal love philter to win the affections of King Edward VI.

The quest for the ultimate aphrodisiac is timeless. Lovers through the centuries have turned to alchemists, witches, and physicians in the search for sexual fulfillment.

One mythological goddess came to be associated with this search. Called Ishtar by the Babylonians and Astarte by the Phoenicians, she is known best by her Roman name, Venus, or her Greek name, Aphrodite. Aphrodite was said to have emerged fully formed from the sea, a naked maiden ready to take her place in the divine social register as the goddess of beauty, desire, and fertility. She was a goddess of contrasts. Ever virginally appealing, she had numerous lovers. She was the patroness of fertility and mother of Eros, the winged god of love. Aphrodite embodied the best aspects of sexuality. She combined desire with tenderness; she was gifted in the physical aspects of love. The ancients prayed to her, but modern man pays her homage with the substances that bear her name: aphrodisiacs.

What Is an Aphrodisiac?

Most people think of an aphrodisiac as a substance that excites or prolongs passion. Actually, the subject is far more complicated— as complicated as men and women and love itself.

Throughout the centuries, aphrodisiacs have been called upon to inspire devotion, enhance allure, bring back an errant lover, increase fertility, improve vitality, promote longevity, even to identify a future mate. There are anti-aphrodisiacs said to cool the fires of sexual addiction and obsession and, primitive as it sounds, to "cure" such "abnormal" behavior as homosexuality and nymphomania.

Aphrodisiacs have taken the shape of food or drink, herb or spice, charm or ritual, drug, homeopathic remedy, flower essence or aroma. Although they varied in form, aphrodisiacs were among the ancient cultures' great common denominators: Remedies promising similar results have been found in the traditions of China, Egypt, Mesopotamia, India, Europe, Africa, South America, and Polynesia.

Unfortunately, the modern Western medical establishment has usually regarded substances or rituals said to enhance sexual desire or prowess as swindles perpetrated by charlatans. Most contemporary doctors worry about their patients harming themselves with dangerous methods and as a result warn them away from aphrodisiacs. The U.S. government feels likewise. As recently as 1982, an advisory panel to the Food and Drug Administration investigated and declared it could find no evidence to support the claims of a number of over-the-counter aphrodisiacs.

Sex experts seem to follow the same line of reasoning. In his classic book *Male Sexuality: A Guide to Sexual Fulfillment,* clinical psychologist Bernie Zilbergeld quoted research pharmacologist James Woods as saying: "In reality there are no known drugs that specifically increase libido or sexual performance, and every chemical taken for this purpose, without medical advice . . . poses the danger of drug interaction or overdose to the user."

But, as evidence of the eternal human quest for erotic fulfillment, people today are ignoring the caveats of the experts, and are putting aside their own skepticism, to experiment with aphrodisiacs. The use of these enhancers is slowly gaining acceptance as legitimate means to achieving sexual happiness. In spite of the resistance of some psychologists such as the one quoted above, many researchers have come up with facts about aphrodisiacs that support the wisdom of ancient cultures. Science is confirming tradition.

For example, from ancient Egypt to the present day, honey has been served at wedding feasts. This is no coincidence or mindless ritual: Honey contains B-complex vitamins and certain minerals that promote sexual health in men and women as well as providing the easily absorbed sugar needed to replenish semen. Sea horses, used by the Chinese for centuries in the treatment of male infertility, recently have been shown to contain vital proteins and amino acids that can increase semen production. Early American colonists who recommended dandelion weed for impotence were unaware that the plant's leaves contain an astronomically high amount of vitamin A, essential to the production of sex hormones in both men and women.

The more we doctors learn about the sexual physiology of the human body, the better we understand the underlying truth of so many ancient remedies, a truth that is largely a matter of chemistry.

Sexual Chemistry

The "chemistry" or "electricity" between two people refers to an inexplicable mutual magnetism. Those terms are apt because our bodies are biochemical and bioelectric organisms, and sexual chemistry evolves from the substances that control arousal and reproduction as well as the complex communication system between the brain, organs, and cells.

Many physical reflexes—including sexual arousal—are activated in much the same way as the "fight-or-flight" syndrome: that sweaty-palm, thudding-heart feeling you get when faced with, say, a snarling dog or a near miss in traffic. When that happens, the brain perceives danger and alerts the autonomic nervous system: the command center that controls unconscious activities. A subbranch—the sympathetic system—triggers stepped-up heartbeat and breathing, sweating, pupil dilation, and muscle tension. This sympathetic system also floods the body with hormones, including, in the case of fight-or-flight, the stress hormone epinephrine.

TABLE 1

SYMPATHETIC SYSTEM	PARASYMPATHETIC SYSTEM
epinephrine/norepinephrine	acetylcholine
constriction of blood vessels	dilatation of blood vessels
increased heart rate	decreased heart rate
blood pressure increases	blood pressure decreases
pupils constrict	pupils dilate
palms sweat	generalized sweating
ejaculation	erection

The sympathetic branch, which operates during times of tension, works in conjunction with the parasympathetic branch, which dominates on less stressful occasions and dilates blood vessels, contracts pupils, tempers heart rate, and regulates digestion, learning, and memory. Most of the time, these systems balance each another out. When, for whatever reason, there is an increase in sympathetic muscle tone, there is a decrease in parasympathetic muscle tone, and vice versa.

Both branches play a vital role in sex. When a person becomes aroused, his or her parasympathetic system prevails: then, during orgasm, the sympathetic takes over and dominates. The communication between the various branches of our autonomic nervous system and our organs that triggers these events takes place via our brain's output of chemical messengers called hormones, neurotransmitters, and neuropeptides.

The Hormone Factor

Hormones (the word derives from the Greek "to excite" or to "urge on") are better known than neurotransmitters and neuro-peptides, probably because they have been publicized longer and also because people are more aware of them. They wreak havoc on emotions and sensations during physical changes such as adolescence, pregnancy, and menopause. Sex hormones are members of the steroid group, using cholesterol as a base. They are responsible for these and many other more subtle changes. Levels of sex hormones circulating in our bodies at any given time affect spatial and motor skills, mood, skin condition, hair growth, fertility, and our capacity for sexual enjoyment. So important are they for sexual pleasure that hormone-replacement therapy, for both impotent men and postmenopausal women, has long been the one "aphrodisiac" given the medical stamp of approval.

The endocrine system secretes three types of sex hormones: androgens (male) and estrogens and progestins (female). Men and women alike produce these hormones in amounts that vary with age and gender. It is the androgen, testosterone, that largely fuels libido in both sexes, although men have much more—some reports suggest that as much as thirty times more—since they manufacture it in their testes as well as in the adrenal glands. It is a surge of testosterone that seems to account for adolescent boys' unrelenting interest in sex.

Many women experience a peak in testosterone levels around the time they ovulate. The testosterone and libido of a smaller group peak shortly before the onset of menstruation. Published studies have shown that some monogamous couples achieve a strange synchronicity: Every month the couple's levels of testos-terone peak simultaneously, suggesting that the body has a built-in mechanism that encourages arousal at the most likely time for conception.

A medical colleague discovered all too well how effective male hormones are as aphrodisiacs for women. She prescribed an an-drogen-like drug called Danocrine for a patient suffering from endometriosis, a condition in which the uterine lining usually expelled during menses backs up through the fallopian tubes and into the pelvic cavity. As a side effect, the drug tremendously increased the patient's sex drive. Unfortunately she was a nun, so the doctor had to find an alternative therapy.

Estrogen is also present in both sexes, but women have more, as it is secreted by the ovaries as well as the adrenal glands. Estrogen is responsible for maintaining the vaginal lining, producing lubrication, and preserving tissue elasticity, especially of the breasts and vagina. High levels also affect mood, and very high levels may lower the sex drive in men. A study conducted among imprisoned male sex offenders found that estrogen reduced the frequency of their sexual thoughts and activities.

Progesterone—a progestin—is another sex hormone secreted by both genders. Levels of progesterone are highest in women during the second half of their menstrual cycles because it stimulates the uterine lining in preparation for a pregnancy. Too little is thought to cause premenstrual syndrome, while too much causes a decrease in sexual desire. In 1982 the World Health Organization Task Force on Contraception tested male contraceptives containing progestins. The drugs inhibited fertility; unfortunately they also squelched the men's desire for sex.

DHEA, dihydroepiandrosterone, a steroid hormone produced in the adrenal gland, is now being researched for its potential anti-aging, anti-cancer, and immune-boosting effects. Blood levels of DHEA fall as aging occurs, and low levels are found in patients with AIDS and cancer. At present, chemical replacement is still experimental, however it is being used in patients with AIDS, cancer, and Alzheimer's. Further research looks promising in the areas of maintaining sexual vitality and overall health. The most common side effect is the appearance of facial hair in women. Long-term effects are still unknown. A natural form of DHEA suspended in vitamin E is being studied and produced by Raymond Peats, Ph.D., from a wild yam root extract.

Neurotransmitters and Neuropeptides

Neurotransmitters, made of amino acids, are generated in nerve cells, and in some instances have hormone-like effects. They control emotions such as love, combativeness, apathy, animosity, and sociability, and affect the basic drives of hunger, thirst, sleep, and sex. The sympathetic nervous system functions through the release of the neurotransmitters epinephrine and norepinephrine, while the parasympathetic system largely relies on acetylcholine. Two other neurotransmitters, dopamine and serotonin in particular, are directly linked to libido and sexual functioning. As you read forthcoming chapters, you will see these substances come up time and again in explanations of how various aphrodisiacs work.

Dopamine, produced in the brain, is the alertness neurotransmitter. It is what is missing at four in the afternoon when concentration wavers. When present in the correct amounts, dopamine plays a key role in reasoning, memory, learning, and emotional balance, and—most pertinently—in desire and excitement; you need dopamine to become aroused. Some prescription drugs, such as L-dopa taken for Parkinson's disease, increase the brain's production of dopamine. The connection between dopamine and libido was discovered when many Parkinson's patients reported that their sex lives perked up as a side effect of these drugs. Too much dopamine, however, is thought to be a contributor to schizophrenia.

Serotonin, synthesized in the brain from tryptophane, is dopamine's counterpart; the right balance is needed to trigger orgasm. Clearly related to mood, serotonin is generally regarded as a calming substance. Maintaining the right balance is critical; studies have shown that people with too little serotonin can become anxious, depressed, or subject to violent behavior. But you don't want too much, either. Some prescription drugs—particularly antidepressants like Prozac which boost serotonin—have a side effect of anorgasmia.

Neuropeptides are a relatively recent discovery. Made up of chains of amino acids in specific sequences, neuropeptides are more complex than neurotransmitters and often work hand-in-glove with them. Additionally, although they differ in the way they are synthesized and released by the cells, some neuropeptides act as neurotransmitters and others act as hormones. Cocaine, morphine, codeine, and heroin were the first neuropeptides to be identified. We manufacture various neuropeptides in our own bodies, and there are more than fifty substances responsible for, among other feelings, those of pleasure and arousal. Perhaps the most well-known of those that we self-produce are the endorphins (coined from the words *endogenous morphine* and meaning "the morphine within"). Often called natural opiates, they are pain blockers and can make you feel euphoric. If you have ever experienced runner's high, you were running on high-octane endorphins. The following two neuropeptides are thought to play a major part in sexual arousal and fulfillment.

Vasoactive intestinal peptide (VIP) is believed to work on the dilation of blood vessels that cause an erection, while the neurotransmitter, acetylcholine, helps maintain the erection by keeping the muscles in the arteries relaxed. A deficiency of VIP is quite possibly responsible for organic impotence, the impotence that has a physiological rather than a psychological or emotional basis. Currently, VIP is being studied for its potential use in treating this type of impotence by direct injection.

Oxytocin, the other important neuropeptide, produced in the pituitary gland, has been utilized during childbirth because it stimulates uterine contractions. Researchers now think it is involved in the contractions of orgasm, because it is secreted in the brains of both men and women during sexual climax. Animal studies have found that oxytocin causes females to respond to their babies in a more motherly way. When oxytocin was blocked, rats mistreated their offspring. The chemical is credited with promoting romance and nurturance in humans because it helps elicit loving emotions.

So what does all this have to do with aphrodisiacs? When our endocrine glands are properly fueled and working at maximum capacity, we should have no physical difficulties in secreting hormones, thus becoming sexually aroused and responsive to those feelings. But a stress-plagued life, combined with the typical American diet and heavy use of nicotine and alcohol, can seriously weaken glandular functioning. Many traditional aphrodisiacal substances specifically nourish the endocrine system.

Other aphrodisiacs support the nervous system. Both neuro-transmitters and neuropeptides need specific amino acids and vitamins for their manufacture. To make epinephrine and norepinephrine and to keep its dopamine in perfect balance, your body needs vitamins C and B-6 along with tyrosine or phenylalanine, two of the essential amino acids. (An "essential" amino acid is one that the body does not manufacture but must get through diet.) Like dopamine, serotonin also depends on an essential amino acid, in this instance tryptophan. And acetylcholine is dependent for its existence upon the presence of choline, a member of the B-complex vitamin family.

A number of aphrodisiacs also work by altering levels of neuro-transmitters and neuropeptides. The drug MDMA—known on the street as Ecstasy and used by some people as an aphrodisiac—causes the release of huge quantities of serotonin. This influx can produce a sense of euphoria and empathy, but Ecstasy is not an ideal aphrodisiac because the drug can inhibit orgasm. Further, large doses of MDMA can kill the nerve fibers that produce serotonin.

Aphrodisiacs can affect levels of neuropeptides by another method. When nerve cells release neurotransmitters, some of the substance is taken up by the nerve cell to be reused, a recycling effort that saves energy for the body. This re-uptake and the breakdown of the remaining substance is orchestrated by an enzyme called monamine oxidase (MAO). Some aphrodisiacs—certain drugs, herbs, and foodstuffs—act as MAO inhibitors, reducing the degradation of neurotransmitters and increasing their concentrations in the body.

One of the newest and most exciting developments in this field is the discovery of nitric oxide as a neurotransmitter. Nitric oxide (NO) exists as a gas under atmospheric conditions. It is a very chemically reactive substance, active only about six to ten seconds. It is also quite noxious. Nitric oxide has been found in bacteria, but until recently was not believed to be active in mammals. It is now known that nitric oxide not only has multiple roles, but it also behaves like no other neurotransmitter.

Nitrates have been studied extensively in the treatment of cardiovascular disease and are a standard for the treatment for angina. They work by causing the blood vessels to dilate, thus reducing hypertension and allowing better blood flow into the heart. Other studies show that nitric oxide assists the body in killing tumor cells and bacteria.

The primary mechanism for its release is an enzyme, nitric oxide synthetase, which frees nitric oxide from arginine, an amino acid. With recent techniques, scientists have been able to isolate release of nitric oxide in the brain. Its role appears to be protective; it reduces damage to nerve cells. As a side effect of this unusual research, scientists noted an increase in erections in laboratory animals. Research on how nitric oxide can be used to treat impotence is now under way. One method under investigation is use of a topical cream. The use of arginine as an amino acid supplement may also be studied.

This aspect of aphrodisiacs is really as simple as high school chemistry. The body is able to manufacture hormones, neuro-transmitters, and neuropeptides only when fed certain essential ingredients. Many traditional aphrodisiacs are high in amino acids and the required vitamins and enzymes, which is why they really do work.

The Mind/Body Connection

Most people were taught, and many still believe, that the mind and the body are separate entities. One of the first inklings of scientific doubt came in connection with studies of the fight-or-flight syndrome, and since then researchers around the world have accumulated an impressive amount of evidence that postulates a direct link between our thoughts and feelings and our physical state. Observation of the fight-or-flight syndrome clued scientists in to the concept that the body does not actually have to be threatened to elicit the responses that it does—the brain has only to *think* danger. In the case of aphrodisiacs, it is entirely

possible that as long as your brain *thinks* that any given substance
or ritual will work, it will trigger the appropriate chemical responses and your body will experience all the physical signs of
arousal. For centuries, without knowing any of the scientific bases
of their practices, witches and wizards, voodoo priestesses, medicine men and snake oil salesmen have all made, if not good
medicine, at least a good living from the mind-over-matter, or
placebo, principle. Their success gives credence to aphrodisiacal
spells, charms, rituals, and prayers.

The Psychology of Desire

Body chemistry is a critical element in arousal, but we cannot
ignore the psychology of sexuality: How we feel about ourselves
is equally important. If you say you feel little or no desire but are
otherwise healthy, it is likely that you have a habit of avoiding or
rejecting your sexuality. Feelings of anxiety, anger, guilt, shame,
and low self-esteem often show up in the bedroom. People who
feel hostile toward their partners will distract themselves from
amorous feelings. Those who fear aging or are self-conscious
about their bodies may also distance themselves from their sexuality. And those who suffer setbacks at work or worry inordinately
about money may feel their self-confidence deteriorate, which in
turn causes sexual indifference. If these feelings go on too long,
the victims may succeed in convincing themselves that they are
devoid of any sex urge—that they are "asexual."

No aphrodisiac or combination of aphrodisiacs will effect a
quick fix for emotionally rooted sexual dysfunction. It is first
necessary to identify, by way of therapy or resolute self-examina-
tion, what is causing the blockage.

Eastern Sexual Secrets

Concurrent with greater knowledge of the biochemistry of the
human body and an understanding of the psychology of sexuality,

there is a wider acceptance in the West of the ancient wisdom of Eastern philosophies. These traditions have always sought to achieve a union of the body, mind, and spirit. They view the mastery of sexuality as a legitimate and necessary starting point for personal and spiritual growth. Unlike institutionalized Judeo-Christianity, which usually associates sex with either procreation or sin, the Eastern view acknowledges sex as a gift that allows humanity to experience pleasure, intimacy, and a heightened sense of self-awareness. Because of the importance they placed on sex for healing and energizing, Eastern philosophers spent centuries studying the subject. There is much to learn from them about the aphrodisiacal power of foods, herbs, flowers, barks, meditation, and yogic exercises.

Over the last few decades, for example, many in the West have become familiar with Tantra, a spiritual method of yoga that was developed in northern India and Tibet centuries ago and unites individual with cosmic consciousness. A new magazine called *Tantra* was inaugurated recently. Students of Tantra, both hetero- and homosexual, now have classes, seminars, and workshops available to them nationwide. In Tantric teaching, the body is perceived as a system in which energy moves via an arrangement of energy vortexes called *chakras,* each related to specific emotions and organs. *Kundalini,* also called the "serpent power," is the force that moves through the body during meditation or sex and creates the experience of rapture. Practitioners of Tantra experience that this kundalini force can be activated with specific disciplines and exercises. When making love, the energy rises to the top chakra—in other words, to the brain—where the hypothalamus releases the neurotransmitters that induce ecstasy. One of my patients, a woman who knew nothing about Tantric beliefs, told me that recently, during a particularly enjoyable session with her lover, she felt a tingling on top of her head and laughed out loud. Her partner was upset by this. She confessed to me that she was worried about being "a bit crazy," but when I explained about chakras she laughed again, this time in relief.

In Eastern forms of lovemaking, orgasm is much less important than in the West. Intercourse is slow and often with limited

movement. The teachings suggest taking time to give each partner intense pleasure. Often the body can become so relaxed that
whether or not either partner reaches orgasm isn't really important, since the awareness of pleasure is so concentrated.

Science now understands some of the physiology behind this
philosophy. Orgasm makes demands on both the sympathetic
and parasympathetic systems. The parasympathetic system relaxes
the muscles and sends blood into the sex organs. The body then
must switch to the sympathetic system to create the tension and
muscular contraction of orgasm. When you are in a deepened
state of relaxation, the second stage may not be desirable; it may
be more pleasurable to coast in the first state.

Taoism is an ancient Chinese doctrine that predates Tantra and
quite possibly gave birth to it. Taoist principles are similar to
those of the Tantra, though based more on philosophy and less
on religion. The Taoist way teaches that energy flows through
channels in the body by way of meridians, the same channels and
meridians used by acupuncturists. Specific exercises that concentrate the movement of energy along these channels can enliven
the body's organs. The Chinese deer exercise, for instance, is an
ancient practice to keep the pelvic muscles strong and move
energy up the body. The exercise is strikingly similar to the Kegel
exercises prescribed by many gynecologists, although Western
doctors focus solely on the muscular benefits of the exercise, not
its ability to energize.

These ancient exercises were said to return vital sexual energy
to the pituitary, hypothalamus, and pineal glands in the brain,
keeping them healthy and active and so able to continue secreting
the hormones we need to feel sexy. In Taoism, the sex glands are
known as the stove that heats the mind/body house; through
exercises and lovemaking, the stove is continually fed, which
keeps the house warm and full of life. This belief parallels the
results of recent scientific research. In studies conducted at the
University of Pennsylvania and Stanford, women who made love
weekly had nearly twice as much circulating estrogen as those
who had sex sporadically or not at all. Postmenopausal women
who are sexually active secrete more estrogen than those who are

not, which reduces the need for estrogen-replacement therapy to treat side effects of menopause such as vaginal dryness.

Alternative Views of Aphrodisiacs

Along the spectrum that separates science from philosophy are a number of alternative medical disciplines that may enlighten those in search of the ideal aphrodisiac. Herbalism, which provides natural alternatives to synthetic drugs, has been practiced for thousands of years on all continents and is thriving today. Aromatherapy, an ancient practice that uses substances obtained from perfumed flowers, is also enjoying a renewal of interest. Researchers are discovering that certain sounds, even certain colors, can affect both the psyche and body chemistry.

Then there is a group of disciplines that could be called "vibrational" medicine. Vibrational, or energy, medicine are terms recently coined to describe the application of the principles of electrical and magnetic forces to healing. We know that the earth emits electromagnetic waves, that electromagnetic radiation beamed at us from the moon and sun influence our internal rhythms, and that the human body and all other living things have their own magnetic fields. In fact, every cell has its own electromagnetic field which, when disrupted, can result in disease. This magnetic field is what is often referred to by metaphysicians or psychic healers as the body's aura or etheric body.

The science of acupuncture, which dates back 4,000 years, is based on the principle of electromagnetics. A number of other healing traditions work on equalizing the flow of energy, which is variously called the "life force" or "vital force." They include homeopathy, which uses remedies derived from plants and other natural substances to balance mind and body and can improve one's sex life in the process. Flower essences, first developed by British physician Edward Bach in the 1920s, are also vibrational medicines said to heal or unblock emotions, to act as catalysts to spiritual transformation, and to enhance lovemaking.

Proof that the body is electromagnetic is seen in the measurement of the heart's electrical impulse with an electrocardiograph (ECG) machine. It is seen also in magnetic resonance imaging, which essentially measures the release of energy when the protons in the body's water molecules are stimulated by a magnetic field. Research in applying electrical and magnetic energy for therapeutic treatments is ongoing, and already in use with such instruments as the Electroacuscope, Alpha-Stim and Tens machine used in healing injuries. A number of other instruments developed as potential diagnostic tools have not yet passed muster with the Food and Drug Administration.

Although a great deal of research into electromagnetic fields is being undertaken around the world, including at NASA, apart from the applications mentioned above, little information has yet been integrated into mainstream medicine; the potential is virtually untapped. Yet these ancient healing therapies have long contended that they interact with the body's magnetic field rather than with its chemistry.

Whether you place your faith in scientific data or are guided by spiritual beliefs, whether you refer to the endocrine system or to Kundalini, it all comes down to one thing: When you strive for health and well-being, your natural vitality will bring more ecstasy into your sex life.

2

SETTING THE STAGE FOR SEX

Is not music the food of love?
—RICHARD BRINSLEY SHERIDAN

One of my patients told this story.

At a party, she was introduced to a nice but unimpressive man. As she was leaving, he invited her for a drink at his nearby apartment. She didn't find him particularly attractive, but his conversation was lively, so . . . she went, and found herself in the most delightful place she had ever seen. Lights were low, Mozart was playing on the stereo, the art was unobtrusive but carefully selected. He handed her a crystal glass of fine wine, lit the log in the fireplace, and sat there smiling while he listened to her talk.

Little by little she began to find him more attractive. By the time he said goodnight at the door an hour later, her view of him had changed. The reason she came to me for treatment? Elated by the highly charged environment—and by him—she had run and danced on concrete sidewalks the ten blocks to her car, resulting in a moderately painful case of shin splints, a condition that healed in time for the two of them to begin an affair. She had been seduced, in part by the stage setting.

Aphrodisiacs are not just something you "take." The lights, colors, and sounds with which you surround yourself can be as effective as any mood-altering drug. Desire can be ignited by any one of the five senses—sight, hearing, touch, taste, and smell—

as well as by mental processes such as fantasy. And when all are stimulated at once, look out!

Sight

Men seem to react more strongly to visual sexual stimuli than do women. You don't need to be a researcher to know this—an attractive woman walking down the street elicits more overt reactions from male observers than when the passerby is a good-looking man and the observers female. Evolutionary biologists explain this phenomenon as a reproductive survival strategy. Men must be able to fairly quickly assess a woman's ability to conceive; the visual indications that she is young and healthy (and thus beautiful) are important keys to her fertility. Female sexual response depends more on the sense of touch than on sight, and when it comes to seeking a mate for reproductive purposes, women tend to look for the less visual cues of money and power. Still, both sexes use their eyes in other aspects of sexuality.

THE FACTS OF LIGHT

The life of primitive man was governed by the sun. He slept when the world was dark and cool and awakened when the sun provided light to see by and warmth for his body. Natural light is still the most important regulator of the daily ebb and flow of our cell growth, glandular secretions, intestinal contractions, kidney output, blood sugar, pulse rate, blood pressure, and body temperature. For instance, after dark the kidneys cut back on urine production to allow an uninterrupted night's sleep.

Scientists are trying to harness the power of light. Experiments are under way on how light can be used to treat autoimmune diseases such as lupus, to regulate menstrual cycles, and to combat the effects of jet travel or the night shift by resetting biological clocks.

Doctors are already using light therapy to treat a form of depression known as seasonal affective disorder (SAD), which affects its victims by changing their bodies' use of serotonin during long, dark Northern winters. Anyone who loses interest in sex during chronic depressions that occur during the fall and winter might benefit from light therapy. Two hours a day of exposure to 10,000 lux of white fluorescent light that re-creates early-morning sunlight often does the trick.

Sunlight also governs a biological timekeeping substance called melatonin, secreted by the pineal gland in the brain, and, some scientists believe, in the retinal cells of the eye. Melatonin mediates the sleeping/waking cycle, with levels of the hormone being four to six times higher at night than during daylight hours. Because we now live under self-selected lighting and are able to manipulate our own light/dark cycles, many of us no longer conform to natural rhythms and can be roughly divided into night owls and early birds.

The impact of different sleep habits on relationships was studied in 150 couples from three states; the Brigham Young University researchers found that a startling 55 percent of the couples—whose average age was thirty—were mismatched in their sleep rhythms. Of those mismatched couples, 33 percent had marital problems, compared to only 8 percent of the couples who were in tune with each other's cycles. The out-of-sync husbands and wives reported less-frequent sex, less time spent in joint activities, and more frequent arguments. A satisfying liaison between a night person and a day person is not impossible, of course, but it does take more work.

Each can surrender an hour a day to get closer together. The night person can wake a little earlier: Many people exercise that ability when they change jobs or residences and have to rise early to get to work on time. The early bird can fit in a short nap during the day so that he or she is able to stay up later to play. A more effective way to get in sync is to spend a lot of time outdoors; strong sunlight's suppression of melatonin is one of the most important components in establishing sleep rhythms.

SEX IN THE RIGHT LIGHT

Indoor lighting is a vital component of an intimate atmosphere. With the right light, even the dingiest room can be transformed into a place that encourages lovemaking. Architects and interior designers place great importance on a building's lighting schemes because they know how light affects perception, not to mention mood. Technology can now mass-produce the low, indirect, and diffuse illumination that has long been regarded as provocative.

Many lighting experts believe that soft, pink light bulbs are easiest on the eyes and most flattering to the skin. Using an "up" light from the floor with colored bulbs can create dramatic effects. Another ploy is to position a lamp behind a palm tree, an oriental parasol, a rattan screen, or a lace curtain; it will cast a subtle, shadowy, and very sexy light.

When it comes to designing lighting to make love by, sometimes the old ways are best; humans still respond powerfully to flickering firelight. The language of eroticism is permeated with references to fire. We call a passionate person "fiery," and talk of "burning desire" or "blazing passions." Words such as "torrid," "sizzling," "inflamed," "hot," and "smoldering" all have a place in the jargon of sexuality. Everyone looks more alluring or heroic in the glow of firelight. Many couples report that their most intense lovemaking has taken place in front of a fire, whether a pile of incandescent embers in the home hearth or a blazing campfire in the outdoors. One of my patients counts her winter woodpile as one of her most potent aphrodisiacs. Her lover knows that when she strikes the match and lights the kindling she means business. Fire juxtaposes the comfort of light and heat with an element of danger. Unlike man-made light, which is static and constant, flame is mobile—seemingly alive—ever changing in intensity, color, and mood.

If lighting a fire is impractical or impossible, candles are an excellent substitute. A single taper or a roomful of votive candles artfully arranged can provide much the same effect. Use scented candles for double impact.

MOONSTRUCK

If fire is the leading light of aphrodisiacs, a full moon is not far behind. The moon's cool, silvery light has become almost a cliché in romantic literature; it also has a long history as a source of power and inspiration to the love-struck. An ancient Greek cere-mony that survives to this day involves the goddess Hecate, who is associated with both the moon and sorcery. The Greeks fashion a clay figure of the goddess said to have the power to draw the desired object or person to the petitioner; hence the name of the ceremony, "drawing down the moon." Elements of the ritual found their way into witchcraft, voodoo magic, and even modern Christianity, with its images of saints that are believed to have the power to grant requests and answer hearts' desires.

Because of the moon's changing aspects, and its gravitational effects on the planet and our bodies, mankind has imbued it with arcane powers. Even skeptics must acknowledge that the men-strual cycle is closely aligned with the 29.5-day lunar cycle. Next time the moon is full, throw open your windows, or, if possible, arrange a tryst in a secluded garden and make love by the light the moon sheds. You'll have difficulty resisting its age-old mys-tique.

COLOR YOURSELF SEXY

People use color consciously and unconsciously every day of their lives when, for example, they make choices about what to wear, opting for bright, vibrant colors when they correspond with a mood or, conversely, to get a lift when they feel down. Manufac-turers spend millions of dollars in research to make sure they package their products in colors that are appropriately appealing, and interior designers decorate with colors believed to be condu-cive to the activities conducted in buildings such as libraries or restaurants. I've seen conventional medical practitioners who scoff at the notion of color therapy choose pastel shades for their office suites because such colors are considered soothing.

Colors speak to us on different levels. We have learned associa-tions with many colors. Black, for instance, though representative of mourning in our society, is also considered chic and sexy when it comes to clothing. Blue is associated with sadness, red with anger, and yellow with cowardice, although these colors have quite different meanings in other societies.

Some psychologists have used color as an assessment tool. In the 1940s, Dr. Max Luscher devised a color-based personality test based on studies that linked people's color preferences with their psychological state of health. More recently, however, color researchers have come to the realization that color has possibilities beyond being a simple visual stimulus to provoke psychological reactions.

Inherently and regardless of culture and personal taste, some colors have a physiological effect. Red excites, while its soft pastel cousin, pink, calms. Colors also influence perception of temperature. A room decorated in blue or gray can seem chillier than one furnished in orange or brown. Studies have shown that colors affect perception of time and even the ability to concentrate, memorize, and learn.

Like light, color can actually create physical changes; the two often work together as light, of course, has its own spectral colors. In tests at Cambridge University in England, exposure to red light caused changes in heart rate, skin resistance, and the electrical activity of the brain to the point of provoking extreme distress in patients with certain pathological disorders of the brain. Both red and blue light affect the autonomic nervous system. Red provokes the sympathetic system and blue the parasympathetic system, which means red arouses and blue calms.

Disciples of the alternative medical practice of color healing go even further; they believe color is another form of vibrational medicine. Dinshah P. Ghadiali, a physician from India, developed an extensive system for healing with color that he called Spectro-Chrome Therapy. His work was extremely controversial; before he died in 1966, he engaged in a running battle with the American Medical Association, the Food and Drug Administration, and the Postal Service. Color expert Wallace McNaughton, M.D., claimed to have recorded many cases of healing with colored lights.

This radical theory is that body cells take into themselves certain color rays when they need them. Too much, too little, or the wrong color—just as could be said about food—disrupts the natural order, setting off a chain reaction that concludes with illness or dysfunction. Therapists beam colored lights on the affected body part or organs with a view to bringing them back into balance and a state of health. According to this belief, different shades of green rays applied to the sex organs tone and stimulate them, and have aphrodisiac properties. Again, all this was very controversial, even in its time, but it *is* known that color can influence our sexual appetite.

Following is a look at some colors, their associations, a little on their use in healing, and their impact when used in the environment.

RED

In Tantra, red is associated with the first, or lowest, chakra. In Western culture red denotes passion, anger, danger, blood, and fire. (Brothels are found in "red-light" districts.) From a biological standpoint, red stimulates the sensory nerves benefiting smell, sight, hearing, touch, and taste. (If you've ever wondered why so many restaurants have red banquettes or table linens, it's because red is thought to pique the appetite and encourage faster eating.) Red also activates blood circulation and causes the pulse to race.

In color therapy it is used to stimulate circulation, as a strengthener for the musculoskeletal system, and for listlessness. Of the different shades of red, scarlet is most closely associated with aphrodisia.

Decorators consider red a good color for people who entertain because it stimulates conversation, and most people look good in its reflected glow. However, those with emotional disturbances or an aggressive temperament should avoid red. Red is an excitory color: sexy and vibrant. To inspire passion, burn red candles in your bedroom.

ORANGE

The second chakra is associated with orange. This color is associated with feelings and emotions. Golden orange is the color of vitality. Orange light can relieve muscle cramps and can be helpful in cases of extreme exhaustion.

Related colors from the orange side of the color wheel, such as golden orange, salmon, and peach, will create warmth in a room.

YELLOW

Yellow is associated with the third chakra and the adrenal glands. It is the most eye-catching color, which is why it is used so often for traffic signs. Yellow is the color of regeneration and stimulation. Edgar Cayee described that when golden yellow is in the aura, it indicates a state of health and well-being. We associate sunlight, cheerfulness, and happiness with the color yellow.

Decorators recommend yellow to enliven a dark room, but do not suggest it for the bedroom because of its association with sunlight. While yellow uplifts some people, others find it provokes anxiety. One study revealed that babies cry more frequently in a yellow room.

GREEN

Green is associated with the fourth, or heart, chakra in Tantra. Although the color of nature and harmony, green also connotes envy—the "green-eyed monster"—and immaturity. In all its shades, green is thought to build muscles, bones, and cells, lower blood pressure and act on the sympathetic nervous system. Like blue, it is soothing both physically and mentally. Color healers use green as an aphrodisiac, to tone sex organs, and as a curative for sexual diseases. Green decor can have a cooling and calming effect; designers report that it makes people feel "at home."

BLUE

Blue, the color of the throat, or fifth, chakra, is the most universally popular hue, perhaps because of its pleasing association with the sky and sea. Blue is a good color for a room in which to meditate or engage in spiritual practices. Surveys show that blue is a favorite color for decorating bedrooms, which is fine if all you want to do there is sleep; this calm color will not inspire much passion. Too much unrelieved blue literally can give some people the blues.

PURPLE AND INDIGO

Like blue, purple is conducive to meditation. The color of the sixth chakra, purple puts you in a psychic, ethereal mood, which may not be what you want in an aphrodisiac. Indigo is associated with the seventh chakra at the crown and is considered a spiritual color that controls psychic currents. Healers characterize this color as cooling and astringent.

To create a sexy environment with light, it is better to stay with the warm colors of red, orange, and yellow. If using purple, use a warmer, redder shade rather than indigo or violet since it is a combination of red and blue. One of my patients reported that her boyfriend had taken charge of the lights in the bedroom; he chose orange and yellow because they resembled firelight. One day, just for a change, he bought a blue bulb. They found that the blue light killed the sexy ambience, creating what they called "a cold and distant feeling."

Sound

Sit still, and listen. Unless you live in a cave, chances are your ears will be assaulted by a cacophony of noises: airplanes, street traffic, ringing telephones, a neighbor's television, barking dogs, voices, music, machinery. . . . Noise, commonly defined as unwanted sound, is the most pervasive of all urban pollutants. Nature has its own loud sounds—thunder or crashing waves, for example—but it is man-made din that jangles nerves. Experts believe that the level of noise most city dwellers are exposed to on a regular basis may result in hearing loss, high blood pressure, suppressed immunity, learning disabilities, stress, and antisocial behavior—none of which are conducive to a healthy love life.

Ironically, it is on the home front and in leisure activities that most people are exposed to the highest noise levels. Federal regulations have reduced occupational clamor, but many people flip on a blasting television, radio, or stereo system as soon as they walk in the door. These same people tend to conduct most of their activities—including lovemaking—in a raucous environment.

THE SOUNDS OF SILENCE

Silence can be a potent aphrodisiac. Cutting out external noise allows you to tune in to the subtle sounds and rhythms of your own body, and to your partner's. In total silence you can virtually hear your heart beating and the blood pulsing through your veins. Quiet also encourages communication between you and your lover. Even if you do not speak while making love, you can still hear the sighs and murmurs of ecstasy more clearly and use them as auditory guidelines. And if you are given to fantasizing, quiet also allows your imagination to soar without distraction.

Many people, however, have become so accustomed to noise that silence actually disquiets them. They may prefer to make love with a background of music. There is nothing wrong with that, since music can be a powerful aphrodisiac in itself.

MUSIC AND MOOD

The belief that music can alter moods and expand levels of awareness—music as a drug, if you like—is timeless. It doesn't take a scientific degree to understand that upbeat music will quicken the heart rate, while slow, andante sounds will soothe. Every ancient culture used some form of music as stimulants and balms. Native American tribes, for instance, psyched themselves up for battle with certain songs and dances; they also performed healing ceremonies that involved different chants, songs, or dances with different rhythms.

Plato linked music with the welfare of society; he believed that a change in prevailing musical fashions could undermine the State. Musicologists have proposed that certain composers precipitated changes in an era's political and moral timbre. Was Handel's balanced, formal music in some obscure way responsible for English society's switch from promiscuity to relative restraint in the early eighteenth century? And did Beethoven, in turn, set emotions free once more? Did rock and roll contribute to the change in sexual mores of the 1960s?

It says something about our own time that so-called new-age music is booming. Today's mood music has its roots in "cosmic" rock of the late sixties and early seventies, in Indian ragas and other ethnic forms, folk music, and certain forms of contemporary jazz. Strangely, the sum is much more mellow than the parts. It is easy to hypothesize that this soothing music is an antidote to a strident world that leaves senses assaulted and nerves raw. According to musician and author Lee Underwood, this music "provides us with emotional, psychological, and spiritual nourishment. It offers peace, joy, bliss, and the opportunity for all of us to psycho-acoustically rediscover in ourselves our own highest nature. It does not attack or intoxicate us."

Not everyone is turned on by this type of music. Some prefer, say, classical works, the transcendental sounds of Gregorian chants, the excitement of rock, the emotional stir of blues, the throbbing rhythms of African drumming. Rather than confine yourself to one type of music, give your lovemaking a fillip by trying something of a different tempo and mood.

There is also no need to limit yourself to music. You can score your lovemaking with any imaginable sound. Tapes can bring nature—waterfalls, rustling leaves, a tropical rainstorm, animal calls—right into your bedroom. Or consider the esoteric sounds of Tibetan bells or Japanese gongs. The resonating notes they produce can transport you and your lover on waves of vibrating tone.

Touch

The body has different types of nerve endings, including some called exteroceptors, that process tactile information originating outside the body. The skin has literally thousands of these ex-teroceptors, with particularly large concentrations around the lips, the tip of the tongue, and the finger pads. Exteroceptors, in turn, are broken down into two main types that allow perception of myriad different sensations from a tickle to an itch to a pain to a caress.

Sensual touch is critical to foreplay and lovemaking, and many, many books have been written on the subject of touching techniques. The feel of another's skin on yours has to be one of the most sensational of sensations. It surely is one of this earth's pleasures to explore the textures of your lover's body: the skin, the hair, the muscles—each has its own sensuality.

The touch that can act as an aphrodisiac by releasing stress, helping the body to heal what ails it, and boosting various bodily functions such as the endocrine or circulatory systems is the touch of sensual and therapeutic massage. There are two main schools of thought on massage. Western massage tends to concentrate on the body's structure and the manipulation of muscle and joints. This includes Swedish massage and the types of massage athletes might get to help them prepare for or recover from competition. Eastern approaches—and there are many including acupressure, shiatsu, Ayurvedic, and reflexology—help keep the vital energy force that flows through the body vigorous and unimpeded.

If you want to learn specific techniques, there are many books available that will teach you. In the meantime, here is a look at some methods of massage that will help add spice to your love life.

SENSUAL SWEDISH MASSAGE

The ancient Greeks and Romans were convinced of the benefits of massage. The Greek physician Galen wrote a lengthy treatise on the subject, and massage has gone in and out of fashion in Western medicine ever since.

The currently popular technique of Swedish massage, created about two hundred years ago to help Swedish athletes prepare for competition, was synthesized from ancient Chinese massage techniques. You can just as easily adapt this method to help you prepare for making love. A massage can provide exquisite intimacy and a delightful physical high that lasts for hours.

There are five types of body manipulation used in Swedish massage:

- *Effleurage* or stroking. Long, smooth strokes either glide over the surface of the skin or are applied with heavier and deeper pressure. Stroking boosts circulation and increases the blood supply to the immediate area being worked on.
- *Petrissage* or kneading. Muscles are grabbed, pulled gently away from the bone, and manipulated: twisting, squeezing, and rotating. This increases circulation to deeper blood vessels and stimulates the muscle tissue.
- Friction: A deep, rolling movement is applied to particularly sore spots and around bones and joints, dissolving stiffness and warming the area.
- *Tapotement* or percussion. Hands are used to tap, chop, or slap with cupped palms to stimulate the muscles and nerves.
- Vibration. The whole hand or just the fingers are lightly fluttered so that the tissue beneath them trembles, stimulating nerves and internal organs.

You do not have to be an expert to employ these techniques, although you will improve rapidly with practice. Even an "amateur" attempt at massage can be delicious as long as you follow a few simple guidelines. Never put direct pressure on bones, especially the spine—work with the surrounding muscle and tissue. Whenever possible, keep your fingers together and massage with the entire flat of your hands, use finger pads only for deep work on particularly tight spots. Try to maintain a consistent rhythm, which can have a sensually hypnotic effect. From the time you commence until the time you finish, always maintain contact with your partner. Keep one hand on him or her even when changing positions or replenishing your supply of massage oil.

Make a few preparations before you begin so that you don't have to interrupt the process. First, the room should be comfortably warm because when the partner being massaged starts to relax, his or her metabolism slows down, resulting in a chilly feeling. Turn down the lights or simply light a fire or a couple of candles for illumination, and put on soothing but not distracting music.

You will need a massage oil or cream to use as a lubricant and prevent your hands from pulling your partner's skin. I like Nadina's Scented Cremes, made from natural ingredients and packed in ceramic pots (available by mail order; see resources section). But you can also use a light vegetable oil, slightly warmed and scented with aphrodisiac essences. Go to the aromatherapy section of chapter 3 and to chapter 7 for ideas. The most efficient way to handle the oil is to pour it into a plastic squeeze bottle for ease of application and to avoid spills.

Now have your partner lie facedown on a firm bed or on a sheet on the floor. Begin your massage with the back, work your way down to the buttocks, then down each leg in turn all the way to the feet. Come back up to the shoulders and massage them, the neck, and the upper arms. Gently ask your partner to turn over. Massage the fronts of the shoulders and down each arm in turn to the fingertips. Massage the chest, abdomen, and fronts of the legs. Take cues from your partner about points of enjoyment and discomfort. Sighs and moans likely indicate that what you are doing is giving pleasure, and you can linger over the spot for further enjoyment. A flinch or shudder means you have found a place that needs work, and with verbal guidance from your partner, you can gently knead out the tension.

Such a massage can stand alone as a refreshing and blissful experience or can be a prelude to intercourse. In this case, once you have finished your full body massage, you can begin to turn your ministrations toward your partner's genitals. (Chapter 8 will show you how you can use various flower essences to enhance the energy of the body's seven chakras, and this may be the sexiest way to finish your massage.)

ACUPRESSURE

Acupressure is an ancient Chinese therapeutic art in which the practitioner uses the fingers to exert pressure on key points on the subject's skin to stimulate the body's natural self-healing abilities. (The Japanese technique of Shiatsu works on similar principles.) When any of these 365 points—called potent points—are pressed, they release muscular tension and promote the circulation of blood and the body's vital life force. When a point is at the actual site of the pain or tension, it is called a *local point;* when it is some distance from the area needing work but is on the same energy meridian, it is called a *trigger point.* The Chinese gave graphic and romantic names to each point, as you will see below. The idea is to maintain a proper distribution of life energy along the body's meridians to keep the body in perfect, healthy balance.

Acupressure works on the same principles and points as acupuncture, but the advantage is that you can perform acupressure on yourself. In fact, many unknowingly have done just that when they massaged their temples while in the grips of a headache. Professionals use a number of different techniques, but by simply exerting a steady, penetrating pressure on the point—usually, but not exclusively with your fingers or knuckles—for two to three minutes, you can achieve remarkable results.

You can practice acupressure on another person to help relieve a specific problem, but you can also perform the technique on yourself as a health-maintenance program. There are a number of trigger points that you can work on for boosting sexual energy. The Chinese believe that sexuality is governed by the kidneys, and so a number of acupressure points for sexual issues are on the same meridian as the kidneys. Others help relieve congestion and increase energy flow in the abdominal area. For optimum results the following exercises should be done daily, even after you begin to see some results from the process, in order to keep toned and healthy. At the very least, fit them in three times a week, perhaps as an adjunct to your exercise regimen.

Sea of Vitality. These four points are located in the lower back at waist level in line with the navel, two and four finger widths on either side of the spine. Manipulating them is said to help with impotence, premature ejaculation, reproductive problems, vaginal discharge, and fatigue. Many believe this can also boost the immune system.

Sit upright but comfortably in a chair with a couple of inches space between you and the chair back. Make a fist with both hands and use the backs of your hands to briskly rub the points for one minute. The area will feel warm. Now use your fingers or knuckles to press each point in turn for one minute. You can do one side at a time, or the corresponding points on each side simultaneously, depending on your strength and energy.

Sea of Energy.   This point is in the middle of your abdomen, three fingers widths below your navel. Working on it is said to strengthen the reproductive system, relieve PMS and menstrual cramps, and help with impotence.

Lie on your back with your knees bent and your feet flat on the floor. Locate the point and, using the fingers of one hand, press in firmly at least an inch and hold for one to two minutes.

Gate Origin.   This point is close to the previous one, being *four* finger widths under the belly button. It is supposed to relieve problems of the urogenital tract, vaginal discharge, incontinence, and help with impotence.

Find the spot, then follow the direction above. You can combine these two exercises, using one hand on one point and the other hand on the remaining point.

REFLEXOLOGY

Reflexology is similar to acupressure in that it is based on a principle of manipulating certain spots on the body to energize or heal other places and organs. In this technique, all the relevant points are on the hands or feet. This system was documented early this century by an American doctor, William Fitzgerald, who found it was based on oral traditions passed down for thousands of years. In reflexology, the body is broken down into ten vertical divisions. Each hand and each foot is similarly divided into five sections, together making up ten that equate with the ten areas of the body. By massaging the relevant section of the foot, you affect the organs that lie in that corresponding section of the body. For instance, the reflexology spots for the heart are in the second-from-the-outside sections of the left hand under the ring finger, and the left foot under the second-smallest toe.

You can perform reflexology on yourself, but a foot massage concentrating on trouble spots is a wonderful gift to offer your lover, too. Working on the following reflex spots will help with sexual health. You can do this anytime you have a free hand, but reflexology is most effective for health maintenance when done on a daily basis.

The Gonads.   These reflex spots are the same for both genders: On men they relate to the testicles, on women to the ovaries. The hand points are on the outer (under the little finger) edge of the wrists at the bases of the palms; the foot points are in the hollows under the outer ankle bones. Stimulating these points balances hormonal flow and helps keep these glands healthy. Massaging these points is said to keep the prostate and uterus healthy.

> Hold one palm facedown and gently grasp your wrist with the other hand so that your forefinger hits the spot. Press firmly for five seconds, release for a second, then press again. Repeat seven times. Now do the same with the other hand. Use exactly the same technique on your feet, while gently holding the heel in your hand with your thumb on the inside of the ankle.

The Pituitary.   Pituitary points are on the pads of both thumbs and the pads of both big toes. The pituitary secretes a number of the hormones that have a bearing on growth and reproduction and also instructs the gonads to produce sex hormones. Working on these points is believed to keep the gland healthy and relieve menstrual discomfort, impotence, and infertility.

Place the right thumb, nail down, into the left palm so that the left index and middle finger can easily massage the thumb pad. Exert pressure in a circular motion for five seconds, release for one, then repeat seven times. Do the same with the other hand. Perform the same technique on your feet, using your thumbs to press the center of the big-toe pads.

AYURVEDIC MASSAGE

Massage is an integral part of the Indian healing practice of Ayurveda. However, it is individualized—tailored to your body type and physical problems—and its effectiveness depends on the use of specific herbal oils. Thus it is difficult to adapt this kind of massage for home application. You can find an Ayurvedic massage specialist through the resources section in the back of this book.

However, Ayurvedic practitioners do recommend a brisk, ten-minute, head-to-toe body massage with sesame oil as a prelude to your morning shower. It is said to help balance the *doshas,* tone the endocrine and nervous systems, and rejuvenate the skin.

The senses of smell and taste, both of which play key roles in sexuality, are dealt with in separate chapters. Meanwhile, it is important to remember how your state of mind can play a role in an erotic encounter.

The Erotic Imagination

Once you have set the exterior stage for lovemaking, it is time to create the interior setting, based on fantasy. Fantasy is probably the most common form of human sexuality. Its content varies from person to person. Some people describe their fantasies as merely brief fragments of daydreams or as vague, formless sexy musings. Others have told of elaborate erotic scenarios with entire casts of characters. There are numerous books on the subject—Nancy Friday has written several excellent works dealing with fantasies. Your erotic imagination can be a rich source of sexual pleasure and can help to heighten intimacy as long as the thoughts do not become obsessive. If you do, however, find yourself unable to control obsessive thoughts, it is best to seek professional help to resolve any inner conflicts.

Fantasies can act as aphrodisiacs in several ways. They can bring insight into your sexual conflicts and problems and help you overcome them. They can allow you to mentally rehearse sexual situations that you find inhibiting. Finally, and most obviously, they inspire arousal. They do this by actually provoking changes in body chemistry, releasing messenger hormones and neurotransmitters as your brain accepts the reality of the fantasy.

Fantasy comes easily to most people. Conjuring up salacious daydreams is such a basic human function that most of us do it automatically. But if you believe—which is unlikely—you have no imagination, or have been raised to repress erotic thoughts and find it difficult to become absorbed in flights of sexual fantasy, or simply want to expand your enjoyment, you may need to learn how to tap into the brain's erotic, intuitive energy by actively engaging your right brain.

The brain's left hemisphere controls logical, analytical thought; the right works by intuition and emotion. For example, when you hear someone speak, the left hemisphere makes literal sense of the words while the right hemisphere reads between the lines and interprets the intonation and emotional shadings of the words.

Arousal and orgasm are right-brain experiences, and sex is most ecstatic when that hemisphere is engaged. When the left brain dominates during sex, you become overly critical of technique and performance, and as a result have difficulty surrendering and reaching orgasm. Giving free rein to fantasy is an excellent way to minimize the left brain's analytical chatter. Like any other activity, doing so can be learned and practiced.

   • Set aside at least a half hour when you won't be interrupted. Relax by stretching, taking a warm bath, or sipping a glass of wine: whatever works best for you.

• Make sure the room is comfortably warm and your clothing is not binding. If you wish, put on some music or a tape of environmental sounds like waves or wind through the trees. Some people prefer white noise such as an air conditioner or fan, as these block outside sounds without being distracting. Make yourself comfortable lying on your back or sitting in a chair that supports your whole body.

• Spend five minutes progressively relaxing your body. Start with your toes and work your way up to your scalp, consciously tightening, then slackening each muscle group. Breathe deeply while you do this, relaxing even more deeply with each exhalation. While relaxing your body, let your mind wander where it may—allow thoughts to drift in and out. As you become more and more relaxed, your body will start to feel heavy. Respiration and heart rate decrease and tension leaves your muscles.

• Direct your thoughts to some pleasing but nonsexual event. Remember—or imagine—a time when you felt happy or particularly successful, perhaps a wonderful vacation or a time you looked particular great, or a triumph at work. Go over the minutiae of the scene as though you were writing about it in a journal or relating the event to a trusted friend.

• Now ease yourself into a sexual situation. Neither inhibitions, nor pressures, nor rationalizations have any place in your fantasy. Your imagination will give you a harmless opportunity to act out situations you may be unable or unwilling to experience in real life. It offers a way to change the way you look, the way you act, and the way you speak. Change gender if you want to. When you feel uncomfortable with any part of your story, you can rewrite it instantly. In a fantasy, give yourself the freedom to be and do whatever you wish without fear of criticism.

Make your erotic escapade as detailed as possible, using all your senses. Imagine the scent, the skin and hair texture, the taste, the sounds and sighs of your imaginary lover. Feel the cool breeze or the warmth of a fire, relish the awareness of silk or satin, or—why not?—the restraints on your wrists or the sting of a slap. Remember, nothing is taboo: Sexual fantasies are often not pretty, frequently bizarre, and sometimes anatomically impossible.

Practice as often as you like. Before long you will skip the nonsexual scenario and go straight to the sexually explicit fantasy, which may change from day to day. Once you are thoroughly familiar with the relaxed, dreamy state that involves your right brain, you can introduce your fantasizing into lovemaking, either by using it to arouse yourself beforehand or to enrich the sexual experience.

You can either keep your fantasies to yourself or you can share them with your partner—that is your decision. Sharing fantasies can open up new channels of communication and revitalize relationships that have bogged down in everyday routine. A word of caution, however: If you decide to go this route, do not pass judgment on your lover's flights of fantasy. After all, if you are capable of creating scenarios such as ones that include rape, or pain, or multiple participants, or exhibitionism—all common themes, incidentally—then you should not be offended or critical if your partner does the same.

LIVING OUT A FANTASY

A major appeal of sexual fantasy is that you can indulge in the most aberrant or outlandish behavior without following through in reality. But there may come a time when you want to expand your experience by living out fantasies such as bondage, dressing in costume, or enacting scenarios. As long as both partners consent and are comfortable with the idea, and no one gets hurt either physically, emotionally, or in a legal sense, there is no real reason why you shouldn't strut around in a tight French maid's uniform or tie your lover to the bedposts with silk stockings.

One essential pact to make is that should either of you want to back out of the situation—at any time—the other will agree to it. When one partner wants to stop and the other does not comply, you are in the area of sexual abuse, even sexual assault or rape. This is important to consider when thinking about actualizing fantasies: In your imagination you have total control over the situation, in reality you might not.

Some couples indulge in mild exhibitionist fantasies by taking instant photographs of each other naked or using video equipment to film themselves making love. If you like to pretend that you are a centerfold model or a movie star, there's no reason why you shouldn't incorporate such playacting into your intimate life. But you need to establish an atmosphere of mutual trust so neither your actions nor the material come back someday to haunt you. An unscrupulous former lover or spouse could embarrass you by showing photographs or video footage to others, or use them as a lever to blackmail you.

Erotica

Beyond your own fantasies, you can always turn to other people's lustful imaginings that have been set down for public consumption in the form of erotica. The problem with recommending its use as an aphrodisiac is that for some people erotica equals pornography. In my mind there is a difference: Erotica is any writing, film, photograph, or other art form that I find sexually stimulating. Pornography, on the other hand, signifies sexuality presented as exploitation, such as sex with children. The problem is that what excites one person may horrify another; one person's erotica is another person's pornography. Pornography is subjective; you know it only when you see it.

Back in the distant 1940s, Kinsey reported a vast difference in what men and women said they found stimulating. Men said they reacted more to graphic eroticism, while women claimed they were turned on most often by romantic images. More recent studies conducted in the U.S. and Europe have shown the sexes coming closer together in this respect. Women now respond—or at least now admit to responding—more to commercial eroticism, and more and more women are becoming consumers of it.

Consequently, the manufacturers of such material are tailoring more of it toward women's tastes. Even the producers of X-rated movies are softening their focus, literally and figuratively, to make their films palatable for viewing by couples rather than just in "stag" situations. Both *Playboy* and *Penthouse* sell lines of pretty, soft-core videotapes that many couples have reported have given their love lives a fillip. Many videos are available for rental at video stores or by mail.

There is also a wealth of classic erotica available right from your library or bookstore. A little D. H. Lawrence, James Joyce, or Henry Miller read aloud to your lover at bedtime may get the pot boiling. There are wonderful books of Tantric and Taoist art depicting lovemaking positions and Eastern erotica that many couples find stimulating to look through.

Erotica notwithstanding, romance will probably never go out of style with women. Tens of millions of copies of paperback romance novels are sold in the U.S. each year, overwhelmingly to women. Contrary to the conventional notion of these readers being either naive, uneducated young girls or very elderly ladies, a poll conducted a couple of years ago revealed that women who regularly read romances seem to have happier sex lives, and, if married, report having sex more frequently with their husbands than those who don't read romances.

Setting the stage for sex is a little like planning a party, producing a play, or preparing a celebratory feast; getting ready is half the fun. The more you enjoy putting it all together, the more fun you will have when the guest of honor arrives.

3

HOW PHEROMONES AND PERFUMES EXCITE DESIRE

In bed her heavy resilient hair—a living censer, like a sachet—
released its animal perfume, and from discarded
underclothes still fervent with her sacred body's form,
there rose a scent of fir.
—BAUDELAIRE

In the course of her examination for sinus problems, one of my
women patients described an important use for the sense of smell.
She had met a man who immediately rushed her; trying to schedule a series of dates that would keep her busy for weeks. His
presumption made her cautious; instead she invited him to her
home for a dinner with friends and family where she observed him
charm her guests. At the end of the party, she saw him to the
door and did something she'd never done before. She stood on
her tiptoes and put her nose to the place just under his right ear.

"What are you doing?" he asked with a grin.

"Finding out what you smell like," she answered, much to her
own surprise.

My patient instinctively was trying to collect information she
needed in order to decide whether to accept this eager man as a
suitor.

The First Aphrodisiac

Body odors are one of nature's most potent aphrodisiacs—not the obvious, unpleasant smells such as nervous sweat, which usually put people off, but rather those imperceptible fragrances called *pheromones.* These scents, which cannot be perceived consciously, are as unique to each individual as his or her fingerprints. Humans share the pheromone phenomenon with other animals, but to a much more subtle degree.

Some animals will identify another by sniffing its pheromones and will mark the boundaries of its territory by depositing its own scent. Pheromones also trigger the desire to mate, and the animal-husbandry business has learned how to manipulate this knowledge. Pig breeders, for instance, have developed an aerosol spray containing the pig pheromone androstenone, which, when sprayed on the sow, makes her instantly ready for the boar.

Human pheromones become active at puberty. Like hormones, they are secreted by glands and circulated in the bloodstream. While hormones come from the endocrine glands, pheromones are produced by the apocrine glands in the armpit and around the genitals, where underarm and pubic hair is designed to trap the odor. They can also be smelled around the nipples, face, and on the soles of the feet. (There is a theory that the fabled American Indian trackers had the ability to detect the pheromones left on the ground by the feet of their prey.)

Whereas hormones influence internal organs and tissues, pheromones are external agents. They don't affect the person who secretes them, but rather the person who smells them. In the 1980s, studies revealed that female pheromones cause women who live or work closely together to menstruate at the same time.

Female pheromones also apparently operate as powerful aphrodisiacs. Winnifred B. Cutler, Ph.D., a renowned biologist and author, conducted a double-blind experiment in which young women were exposed to either female pheromones or a placebo. During the first three weeks of the test, 36 percent of those receiving the pheromones reported having weekly sex, while only 11 percent of those on the placebo did so. Between the fourth and fourteenth week, the discrepancy became even greater: Seventy-three percent of women exposed to the pheromones were now having sex on a weekly basis, while the figure for those on the placebo remained at 11 percent.

Male pheromones contain about three times more of the active ingredient, dehydroepiandrosterone sulfate (DHEAS), than do female pheromones, and according to Dr. Cutler's findings, seem to have more impact on fertility than on libido. It appears that a woman's pheromones incite a couple to make love. When they are close together, she receives concentrated doses of *his* pheromones and her endocrine system is stimulated to optimum fertility.

Pheromones are the source of the "chemistry" between two people who are instantly attracted to each other without knowing why. Pheromones of potential mates are received through sensors in the ceiling of the nasal cavity. They convey the message to either pursue or avoid a romantic encounter. Most people are unaware of pheromones; the passions they arouse begin on a subconscious level. We may be convinced that any number of other factors are the source of the attraction we feel to someone, when instead we are being bewitched by his or her unique sexual scent. Natural body odors—in conjunction with proper personal cleanliness, of course (deodorants don't affect pheromones)— can be extraordinarily powerful aphrodisiacs.

Cave dwellers almost certainly became aware of perfume about the time they discovered fire. Smoke that wafted up into heaven was revered as a messenger that carried prayers to the gods. When smoke was aromatic and therefore pleased man's sensibilities, it was assumed that the gods would be equally gratified, hence the probable origin of incense in religious ceremonies. Hence also the word "perfume," from the Latin *per,* meaning "through," and *fumus,* meaning smoke.

The Influence of Scent

The perfumes humans *can* detect are also powerful aphrodisiacs. For centuries people have used intoxicating fragrances to excite the object of their affections and enhance lovemaking.

The human sense of smell is both less and more acute than that of other animals. Because they were bipeds, instead of walking on all fours, early humans came to rely more on their eyesight and binocular vision than on the sense of smell, which is therefore less developed. But with the development of the imagination and the long-term memory, humans gradually grew to appreciate the sense of smell for its sensuous and aesthetic rather than its survival qualities.

Smell remains the least-understood of the human senses, a situation that is changing as research begins to show the powerful influence of scents over minds, moods, and bodies. Studies at the University of Cincinnati revealed that workers receiving occasional wafts of peppermint or lily of the valley performed given tasks 25 percent more efficiently than those breathing regular air. In Japan, office workers whose environment was pleasingly scented showed fewer signs of stress than their colleagues. European airlines are using aromatherapy to reduce jet lag in their employees. Research also confirms that the response to smell continues during sleep. Tests conducted at the sleep laboratory at Bowling Green State University found that subjects' heart rates and brain waves quickened when they were exposed to perfumes.

The medical profession is finding practical applications for scents. Patients who undergo magnetic resonance imaging (MRI) by lying motionless for an hour or more inside a small cylinder often experience claustrophobia or even panic attacks. Doctors have discovered they can reduce anxiety in about 63 percent of those patients by introducing the smell of heliotrop, which has a pleasing fragrance something like a combination of vanilla and almond.

So it should not be difficult to accept the concept that scents can affect the libido. Most people believe that their reactions to others are dominated by the visual, auditory, or kinesthetic senses. In actuality, the sense of smell is the strongest tie to most emotional experiences. The sense of smell is controlled by the limbic system, one of the innermost parts of the forebrain. This system is a "mini-brain" that handles emotions, behavior, appetites and some memory functions. Parts of the limbic system are older in evolutionary terms than other areas of the brain. Known as the "primitive" or "old mammalian brain," it is not that different than the brains of primitive mammals.

The most basic sensations—hunger, fright, rage, joy, love, hate, sexual arousal—are moderated by the limbic brain, where impulses speed through first the internal pathways, then along routes to other forebrain regions and the cerebellum. Whereas the sensations of sight, sound, and touch must cross many synapses to reach the limbic core of the brain, the sense of smell is the most direct link to the limbic center. Because of this close connection between the nose and the limbic system, people may unknowingly make a decision to either embrace or retreat from an experience based on olfactory information. The following two case studies clearly show how scent rekindled memories, which in turn evoked sexual responses.

My patient Elaine disliked the reek of cigars until she fell passionately in love with a man who smoked them. For years afterward, cigar smoke was, to her, an erotic scent. Whenever she perceived the unmistakable pungency, Elaine would become aroused. In fact, even before her mind had registered the scent, her body would respond to it with a jolt of excitement and longing.

Ted was married for years to a woman who used Jean Naté toiletries. A year after he and his wife divorced, Ted met a woman who had all the qualities he'd been looking for. Their budding romance progressed perfectly until they went to bed and Ted got a whiff of a distressingly familiar perfume. His new love had splashed herself with Jean Naté cologne after showering in happy anticipation of the night ahead. What should have been an agent of arousal became in this instance an immediate turnoff. Rudyard Kipling said it well: "Scents are surer than sights and sounds to make your heartstrings crack."

Most people have experienced the impact of "involuntary memory" upon encountering a familiar scent. The sensation of being catapulted into the past can be overwhelming. This unique ability of scents to excite sexual desire via our strong "scent memory" is just one of the many ways aromas can be used as aphrodisiacs. Scents can stimulate sexual pleasure directly; they can undo physical inhibitions or act as psychological relaxants; or they can be used to create a romantic mood.

Scenters of Civilization

Only now is science understanding how scents work, but almost every ancient civilization put great stock in the power of perfume. In Babylon, Carthage, Phoenicia, China, and India, the importance of scents in everyday—as well as love—life is well documented. Egypt, however, held the record for extravagant use of perfume. As far back as 5000 B.C., Egyptians were exploring all manner of aromatic substances for use in medicine, religious ritual, and, of course, embalming. Ancient papyri contain references to aromatic cures for illness, aging, and allergies. Fragrance assumed divine status in the myth of the goddess Isis; she anointed Osiris with her precious oils and made him immortal. As part of their worship of the sun god, Ra, Egyptians burned aromatic incenses as he moved across the sky.

The Egyptians made little distinction between religious, ceremonial, and private use of fragrances. In their view, the corporeal and the spiritual were one. High priests mastered the art and science of creating perfumes that were used in incense and drugs as well as body lotions. Kyphi, a blend of scented herbs and resins, achieved renown; in the words of Plutarch, it engendered a heightened dream state because it was distilled from "those things that delight most in the night."

But it was in the area of sensuality that they perfected the use of scent. Cleopatra, notoriously well versed in the art of seduction, used scent freely to create an aura of mystery and irresistibility. In her case beauty was in the nose of the beholder. Reputedly far from ravishing, Cleopatra made up in aromatic impact what she lacked in looks. According to legend, she would drift down the Nile on a barge that was enveloped in a cloud of perfume, her body glistening with rare and exotic oils and the sails of her vessel permeated with heady aromas.

When the Jews fled Egypt they took with them the scentual

secrets of the Egyptians. The Queen of Sheba, whose Arabian kingdom exported spices and perfumes, used exotic fragrances to conquer the heart of King Solomon. The ancient Greeks and Romans regarded perfume as divinely inspired.

Aphrodite herself was said to include aroma in her bag of sacred tricks. According to the *Iliad,* her blend of rose-sweet oils protected Hector's body from disfigurement at the hands of Achilles. Venus, Aphrodite's Roman equivalent, slipped Helen of Troy the perfume recipe that endowed her with legendary powers of attraction. And Circe, the enchantress, ensnared the freedom-loving Odysseus with her irresistible perfume. Gods had spears and arrows, but the goddesses of Greek and Roman mythology had a more potent weapon, proving that once the nose succumbs, the heart is sure to follow.

For Greek and Roman mortals, daily life was filled with scent. Guests at Greek banquets received their own scented sachets; the events culminated with a shower of rose petals falling from the ceiling. Inheriting this reverence for the rose from the Greeks and Egyptians, the Romans imported rose petals by the boatful for their feasts and bacchanalia. The floor would be strewn and cushions stuffed with rose petals. Guests feasted on rose pudding, and after overindulging would sip rosewater to soothe digestion. Rosewater perfumed Rome's public baths and fountains, and, of course, was a featured ingredient in love potions.

The Greeks were masters of the art of aromatherapy and sexual arousal. Records show that Athens teemed with perfume shops, where the rich could buy expensive concoctions and the poor could get cheap imitations. The Greeks used fragrance for sensual pleasure, but they also considered it a prerequisite of health, believing that scented air purified the body. They went so far as to prescribe a different perfume for every area of a woman's body. This luxury had its drawbacks, as it took considerable time and effort to find scents that wouldn't collide in an olfactory offensive. Men as well as women followed the trend. One Greek gentleman rubbed his jaws and chest with palm oil, his arms with mint, his eyebrows with marjoram, and his knees with thyme. The Romans found the custom intriguing enough to adopt, and Roman women had all manner of perfumes in solid, liquid, and powder forms.

Through the centuries, attitudes toward personal hygiene swung from one extreme to another. By the Elizabethan era, the ancients' insistence on personal cleanliness was long forgotten; people relied on perfume to cover up natural body odors. The age of stench brought with it plenty of disease and personal discomfort; herbs and flowers were used as medicines, insect repellents, room deodorizers, and fumigators. Nosegays—small, fragrant bouquets—were carried under the nose to counteract the all-pervasive stench of unwashed humanity and garbage.

Many of the stately English homes built during Elizabethan times had formal herb gardens. Almost every home also had a "stillroom," a pantry area where herbs and flowers were hung out to dry, and exotic spices were stored. The sixteenth-century housewife was adept with the mortar and pestle, and in her stillroom concocted recipes and made potpourris that sweetened home and hearth. Some of her combinations dated from ancient Grecian times. Although the Elizabethans did not link bad hygiene, bad smells, and ill-health, they nevertheless were aware of the ancients' belief in the healing and erotic power of fragrant plants. The Elizabethan housewife scented clothes and bedding with orris powder, strewed sickrooms with bay leaves, and burned heavily perfumed candles to make the stale air conducive to romance.

Today's Perfumes

Perfumes have always been endowed with magical qualities, and to the present day they carry an aura of the erotic. The perfume industry hasn't become so huge only because of good marketing and beautiful models. Every woman knows from either instruction, instinct, or experience, that scent conveys a subliminal invitation to sexual pleasure. Today's perfumers can thank Avicenna, the eleventh-century Arab physician, philosopher, and scientist who invented the process of distillation and bottled the first rosewater perfume. Earlier attempts at making long-lasting perfumes had ended in disaster, and the scents of antiquity were usually packaged as solids and powders. Centuries after Avicenna's discovery, colognes, or perfumes distilled from alcohol, appeared. The earliest recorded recipe included grain alcohol, attars of rosemary, lemon peel, lemon-scented balm and mint, and extracts of rose and orange blossom. It was given to the Queen of Hungary in 1370 as a beautifier, and apparently was still working effectively when, at the age of seventy-five, she married the King of Poland.

The art of perfume making underwent a marked evolution in the twentieth century. Thanks to the development of synthetic oils, today's perfumer deals in over two thousand substances, which he or she can mix into an infinite variety of fragrances. However pleasant, these synthetic oils lose much of the magic of pure, essential oils. The difference is similar to that of a silk rose and the real thing. While both flowers are enchanting to look at, the vitality of the natural flower cannot be duplicated.

The Art of Aromatherapy

Certainly man-made perfumes cannot be used in the practice of aromatherapy. When nineteenth-century French chemist R. N. Gattefosse coined the term *aromatherapy*, he defined it as "the therapeutic use of odiferous substances obtained from flowers, plants and aromatic shrubs, through inhalation and application to the skin." Today this venerable practice of restoring the balance between body, mind, and spirit through the use of aromatic essential plant oils—the psychoactive nature of scent, if you will—is enjoying a renaissance. While its use still lags in the United States, aromatherapy is widely practiced and accepted in England, France, Belgium, Germany, and Switzerland.

Used correctly, essential oils can help promote balance between the sympathetic and parasympathetic nervous systems. They also can help accelerate our imagination, restore peace to our mind, and create heightened self-awareness. Many essences are natural remedies for managing stress, an old enemy of love; others have long histories as aphrodisiacs. These oils act directly on the limbic portion of the brain, which, in addition to acting as our storehouse for emotion and memory, is also responsible for regulating sexual conduct. Sexual dysfunction or disharmony between lovers often stems from stress or fear. Scents can create an atmosphere of intimacy to help overcome these barriers. Some essences can be absorbed by the bloodstream and have the ability to rejuvenate sluggish reproductive glands and revive flagging ardor.

Here are a few—but by no means all—of the essential oils that have a place in your cache of aphrodisiacs:

Rose. This native of Persia, traditionally linked with Venus and love, is the reigning queen of scents. It is thought to be particularly beneficial as a sexual stimulant to women, though the rose's scent and beauty are renowned the world over and throughout history as an inspiration to lovers of both sexes.

Jasmine. If the rose is queen, then jasmine is "King Aphrodisiac." Its warm, heady perfume is a stimulant and symbolizes passion and joy. Jasmine is thought to help with problems of depression, anxiety, frigidity, and impotence.

Ylang-Ylang. This "flower of flowers" is a native of Malaysia and the Philippines and is a common ingredient of most aphrodisiac formulas. The exquisite yellowish-green blossom has a voluptuous scent with a seductive and relaxing effect. It is also an excellent tonic for the nervous system.

Sandalwood. This was probably one of the original scented smokes that wafted up to the gods. The oil distilled from this close-grained wood inspires tranquillity and is regarded as a sexual restorative for both sexes.

Cedarwood. A native of North Africa with a pleasingly distinctive fragrance, cedarwood was used in Egypt as a cosmetic and was used in the process of mummification. Cedarwood promotes relaxation and is included in many aphrodisiac formulas. Because it has antiseptic and antifungal properties, it is used to fight infections in the skin and urinary tract.

Neroli. Named for a seventeenth-century Italian princess, neroli is extracted from the flowers of the bitter—or Seville—orange tree. It is rare and expensive. Like sandalwood, it too is a natural tranquilizer, and can also have a hypnotic effect.

Patchouli. Patchouli comes from a heavy-scented plant that grows in the Far East. For thousands of years its warm pungency has been said to be stimulating and to elicit a sexual response. It is often used as a base in commercial perfumes.

Ginger. Used as an aphrodisiac in China for three thousand years, the spicy scent of ginger is thought to be a stimulant. As a tonic, it is particularly recommended to sharpen the mind and soothe the emotions. Oil of ginger can be applied to the skin to cool fevers, soothe headaches, and relieve arthritic pain.

Cardamom. This member of the ginger family has a charming, fresh scent. Cardamom oil is known as the Fire of Venus and is considered magnetic to the opposite sex. Chewing a seed counteracts the smell of garlic and aids digestion.

Cistus. Hailing from the Mediterranean area, and also sometimes known as rockrose or labdanum, the plant yields a compelling musky scent. Some people find the fragrance mind-expanding and narcotic-like.

Clary Sage. This lavender-like plant is also native to Mediterranean regions. Clary sage is often recommended to balance menstrual problems, such as cramps, premenstrual syndrome, or irregular menses. Its powerful fragrance can banish depression and sometimes induce pleasant, almost hallucinogenic states.

Beyond Aphrodisia

Beyond aphrodisia, essential oils can help with a number of complaints that cause a lackluster libido. Working up interest in sex is difficult if you are not getting enough sleep. When you are wound tight with anxiety, arousal is almost impossible. Aromatherapists recommend the following fragrances to relieve these conditions:

- **Insomnia:** neroli, clary sage, sandalwood, basil, chamomile, lavender, orange, apple
- **Nightmares:** fennel, mint, rosemary, marjoram, orange
- **Anxiety:** basil, bergamot, coriander, hyssop, mint, rosemary, heliotrope, patchouli
- **Depression:** angelica, lemon, ginger, eucalyptus, neroli, parsley, patchouli
- **Lethargy:** rosemary, ylang-ylang, eucalyptus, lemon, pine
- **Stress:** rose, tarragon, vervain
- **Inability to concentrate:** carnation, bergamot, coriander, jasmine, lemon
- **Stale or toxic air:** basil, peppermint, pine

Using Essential Oils

These perfumed distillations can be tremendously potent, and if applied directly to your skin may cause irritation. Add about six drops of your preferred essence to ⅛ cup of a base vegetable oil such as jojoba, soy, or grapeseed. The mixture will be dilute enough to apply directly on the skin without losing any of the aroma. Also add a few drops of essential oil to creams, body lotions, or massage oils. (Massaging various essential oils at chakra points is also recommended for freeing up sexual energy.)

The bathroom is a wonderful place to fully enjoy your flower essences. As the ancient civilizations knew so well, there is nothing so soothing and luxurious as a hot bath. A few drops of the right oils swirled into bathwater can prime the body for love.

Essential oils penetrate your skin and are utilized by organs and glands as needed. Experiments have shown that lavender oil applied to the skin of guinea pigs is found in the kidneys within ninety minutes. The oils are also inhaled in the form of vapor, stimulating nerve endings in your nose that directly connect with the limbic system and hypothalamus, sending chemical messages to the pituitary and all the endocrine glands. Enhance the bathing experience even further by adding a few drops of oil to an unscented liquid soap or shower gel.

Judicious use of essential oils can make the entire environment erotically charged. Aromatherapy lamps or diffusers that waft the scents into the air are available at health and specialty shops (see resources section). Get the same effect by dabbing a drop of oil on a lamp bulb: The heat will diffuse the perfume. Another way is to moisten a sea sponge with near-boiling water and add a few drops of essential oil. Place the sponge in a dish in the room and dampen it with water daily. You only need replenish the oil weekly. Or add a few drops to a mister bottle full of distilled water and use it as a natural room refresher.

The art and practice of aromatherapy is creative and exciting, one of the most pleasing techniques in the quest for conscious, healthy aphrodisiacs. Most of the ingredients used in aromatherapy are natural and nontoxic, although care must be taken to check proportions of some essential oils and herbs, which may have irritating effects if used in the wrong quantities. Ingredients are easily obtained from health food stores, herbalists, or the manufacturers of essential oils.

Being your own aromatherapist requires some research and enough patience to obtain your materials and mix them in the proper quantities. After that, it's a question of how imaginative you want to be. As you increase your knowledge of herbs, flowers, essences, and fragrances and their many fascinating properties, you will be amazed at the role they can play. Expect to feel more alive, energized, and attractive as you tap into the inherent human response to fragrance.

Aromatherapy doesn't stop with essential oils. Don't overlook the scentual power of fresh-cut blossoms, a garden or window box planted with herbs and flowers that waft aroma through your window on the night breeze, or scented candles and incense. You can also use the dried petals, herbs, and barks in potpourris, herb pillows, padded coat hangers, sachets for scenting closets, and pomanders.

A Sampling of Love Potions

Essential oils can either stand alone or be blended into customized fragrances. To get you started on your avocation as an aromatherapy alchemist, I culled some recipes from the specialists. Experiment with different scents and discover which in particular excite you and your lover or lovers. Because emotion, the olfactory sense, and personal experiences are so tightly interwoven, reactions to the same aromas will vary with the individual. Nor do two people carry a scent the same way; a fragrance that stays on one person may quickly fade on another because of differences in body chemistry. Take time to learn the scents that your body responds to.

SENSUALITY SCENT

Aromatherapist Kathryn McCarthy created her own formula, which, she reports, invariably has a most potent effect on everyone who experiences it. To a base oil such as jojoba, add the following essential oils:

15 drops ylang-ylang
8 drops sandalwood
6 drops clary sage
6 drops geranium
6 drops cedarwood
6 drops palmarosa
6 drops rosewood
6 drops orange
3 drops elemi

JUST FOR WOMEN

French aromatherapist Danielle Ryman learned her trade from one of the pioneers of the discipline, Marguerite Maury. Ryman now runs the Marguerite Maury Clinic in London and is the author of *The Aromatherapy Handbook,* in which she has a number of recipes for scented oils. This one is for women feeling decidedly unsexy because of premenstrual syndrome. She recommends applying it to warm bath water twice a day, the baths to be followed by resting for ten minutes in a darkened room.

> 4 drops pine
> 2 drops parsley
> 3 drops neroli

VENUS OIL

In his *Complete Book of Essential Oils and Brews,* Scott Cunningham includes several recipes for fragrances that act as aphrodisiacs. This one is said to be effective in attracting love and promoting beauty.

> 3 drops ylang-ylang
> 2 drops geranium
> 1 drop cardamom
> 1 drop chamomile

ALEXANDRIA'S "ATTRACTANTS"

Alexandria Carrington Lake, a fragrance designer in the San Francisco area, prefers to call herself an alchemist of the twenty-first century. She likes to work on an individual basis, customizing scents to strengthen character, image, personality, and sexuality. But she also has a repertoire of standard fragrances with names such as The Emerald Flame, Intimacy, and The Queen's Chamber, some of them including gold or diamond dust along with the scents. The following are two scents—she calls them high-voltage attractants—she designed especially for this book.

> FOR WOMEN
> 1 ounce jojoba oil
> 15 drops rose
> 10 drops jasmine

10 drops petitgrain
5 drops oakmoss
natural progesterone
ruby dust (optional)

FOR MEN
1 ounce jojoba oil
15 drops lemongrass
10 drops sandlewood
10 drops ginger
gold dust (optional)

SEDUCTIVE POTPOURRI

Dry your own flowers and leaves or buy them by the ounce from herbalists. You'll need to combine your floral ingredients with a fixative, an agent that absorbs the other scents so that they last longer. In this case the fixative is orrisroot, which comes in powdered form. Gently combine the following flowers, tossing them together with your hands, then add the fixative. If you wish, sprinkle your blend with a few drops of essential oils in the same scents as your flower petals. Stir well after each drop. Seal and store in a dry place for one month, then display in open bowls.

2 cups lemon verbena
2 cups rose petals
1 cup lavender flowers
1 cup calendula petals
1 cup meadowsweet flowers
1 cup chamomile flowers
1 ounce angelica root
4 tablespoons orrisroot

VICTORIAN POMANDER

This easy-to-make pomander can be suspended in a closet or room and will give off a heady, exotic scent for up to a year. Push whole cloves into the skin of a firm, fresh orange. Allow about one clove's worth of space between each to allow for shrinkage as the orange dries. Roll the finished item in a mixture of equal parts orrisroot powder and ground cinnamon. Tap gently to remove excess. Tie a ribbon around the orange for hanging.

Another way to use oils is to combine them with essences of flowers and gems and apply them to the body. Anne Brawley, the originator of Path of the Heart Fragrances, created fragrances with specific gem and flower essences designed for love and pleasure. She feels that these embody the divine feminine principle, from which physical passion is created. The use of aromas for enhancing lovemaking can open us into new worlds of aphrodisia of the senses.

4

FOODS FOR LOVE

A well-fed stomach and an unclothed body breeds lust in a man.
—Chinese Proverb

Delicious, sweet, hot, spicy—many of the same words apply to lovemaking and food—two of the best things life has to offer. Nevertheless, uses for humanity's highly developed sense of taste are curiously absent from the literature of aphrodisiacs. The sense of taste *is* used indirectly, however, in the choice of foods that act as aphrodisiacs, for food and sex have been inexorably entwined since the beginning of time. Aphrodite's son, Priapus, was the god and protector of garden produce, vineyards, flocks, and bees. Artists represented him with a prominent phallus, sometimes as a phallus with a face, carrying fruit in his garment and a sickle or cornucopia in his hand. (His name was given to the medical condition priapism, a persistent erection.) The link between food and sex has been celebrated since ancient times, most notably at the Saturnalia, the mid-December Roman festival that evoked merriment, gluttony, and sexual license. Conventional wisdom has always held that we are most susceptible to seduction and sexual ecstasy after an excellent meal. "A well-fed stomach and an unclothed body breeds lust in a man," says a Chinese proverb. History's most famous madams knew that food fires lust, so they often laid out succulent aphrodisiacal suppers for their clients. It is no coincidence that some of the world's most famous lovers were also famous gourmands: Casanova was as knowledgeable about food as he was about sexual technique.

Even today, mating rituals usually require that couples exchange food, either as gifts of candy or wine or as meals taken together. Dining out is the most popular form of dating, and everyone knows that cooking a meal for a prospective lover is full of implication. A well-known restaurateur who has spent a lifetime observing mating rituals told me that in the early stage of courtship, couples eat out; but once they start making love, they will more often eat at home.

Given that the act of eating together can be deliciously sensual and intimate, almost any meal could be said to be an aphrodisiac. Slowly sucking a strand of linguini into your mouth as a lover watches, sharing a forkful of cheesecake, or licking barbecue sauce from a lover's fingers can turn those foods into aphrodisiacs, although none of them would appear on any expert's list of love foods. And anyone who saw the film adaptation of Henry Fielding's bawdy classic *Tom Jones* will remember Tom and his lover, Mrs. Waters, devouring a feast, a scene in which the meal itself becomes lascivious foreplay and explosive orgasm.

Certain foods, however, have had reputations as specific aphrodisiacs. In Renaissance Italy, an impotent man might have drunk a posset made from egg yolks, Madeira, chicken broth, butter, cinnamon, nutmeg, and sugar. Chinese and Japanese brides nibbled on ripe peaches and figs, fruits associated with female fertility. The *Kama Sutra* promised that the penis could be enlarged by eating pomegranate. European farmers' daughters wallowed naked in newly harvested wheat, some of which they baked into biscuits that would render men helpless before their charms.

Less palatable traditions included tiger penises, bear gallbladders, hands and feet of gallows corpses, roasted heart of hummingbird, and the right lobe of a vulture's lung. Australian aborigine women would swallow the raw genitals of kangaroo. And a gruesome British notion that made its way to the American Deep South ascribed aphrodisiacal properties to white moss scraped from the skull of a corpse. (The use of animal parts, especially ones taken from threatened species, is of course discouraged by most governments and every environmental organization, so please do not plan on serving your lover any concoctions brewed from kangaroos or vultures.)

The Foods of Love

Foods said to possess aphrodisiacal properties have been known to almost every age and human culture. The reasoning behind the choice of edible aphrodisiacs was often preposterous, but in a surprising number of cases the ancients somehow put their faith in the right foods. Before scientific method, the visual logic of the Law of Similarity reigned. This dictated that foods that looked like genitalia were the best erotic stimulants. The Herbal Doctrine of Signatures, expounded by Paracelsus in the sixteenth century, held that the form of a plant indicates the areas to which it will be beneficial.

The Aztecs were so impressed by the anatomical likeness of the avocado that they named the fruit *ahuacatl,* or testicle, and forbade village maidens to set one virginal toe outside the house while the fruit was being gathered. Bananas are endowed with mythical properties in Asia, Africa, and the Philippines—all places where they grow naturally. Bananas are rich in potassium, a mineral essential for the function of nerves and muscles. There are scholars who believe that a banana, not an apple, led to the downfall of Adam and Eve. The carrot has long enjoyed a special niche as the phallus of the plant kingdom. The Greek word for carrot was *philtron,* from which evolved the word philter—a synonym for love potion. A mouth-watering concoction of cooked carrots, cardamom, sugar, and milk was often served at the feasts of Arabian princesses bent on seduction.

Old English wisdom says that boiling asparagus stalks and eating them three mornings in a row will induce "bodily luste" in both sexes. Asparagus, rich in vitamins and minerals, is a tonic for the kidneys—the organs that, in the Chinese system, regulate the libido. The phallic implications of celery, cucumber, rhubarb, leeks, and ears of corn are hard to ignore. Each has had its day, somewhere, as an aphrodisiac.

Rice is considered a fertility symbol in the East, and we toss it in wedding ceremonies. Wheat has been regarded as the staff of life in many cultures, and phallic-shaped loaves and cakes baked from it were eaten with gusto at Roman orgies and were a part of fertility festivals in Europe until recently.

Some of the most fabled love foods were thought to represent both male and female sex organs, depending on your point of view. The most exalted of these is the oyster. The salty bivalve was known to almost every ancient civilization from the Chinese to the Native American, and to this day has lost none of its mystique. Some say the oyster in its shell resembles the testicle, others see in the shucked oyster a graphic and tactile likeness to female pudenda. Its lust-provoking ability is linked to high levels of zinc and mucopolysaccharides, complex molecules of sugars and proteins. The oyster's less glamorous kin, mussels and clams, have similar appeal: In Chaucerian English, the word "mussel" was a naughty synonym for vulva.

Almost as rich in lore is the sweet, luscious fig. It was featured at the Roman Saturnalia and at the Greek counterpart, the Dionysian orgies, where the fruit was deemed to resemble the testicle. To Hindus, the fig represents both the *yoni,* the vagina, and the *lignum,* the phallus. The color and texture of the split fig has lent itself to various interpretations: Turks see it as the anus, the Arabs, as female genitalia.

Guavas, passion fruit, and that humble salad bar staple, the tomato—once called the "love apple" and forbidden on Puritans' tables—all have similar histories as fruits that aid in the sport of Aphrodite. The pomegranate, with its multitude of seeds, was associated with Aphrodite, and a representation of this "apple of many seeds" was carved on the pillars of King Solomon's temple. The root of pomegranate's biblical name, *rimmon,* means to bear offspring. As a symbol of fertility, women through the ages drank its red juice to encourage pregnancy. The peach and the apricot, with their provocative cleft and velvety skin, were considered love food in China. Puritanical attitudes toward sensual foods lasted well into this century. I remember older women telling tales of boarding schools and sorority houses where, to avoid whetting the girls' sexual appetites, frankfurters and sausages were served pre-sliced.

Not all foods considered aphrodisiacs come in the shape of sex organs. The onion family—all those pungent lilies of the kitchen—has a distinguished history on the lover's menu. In South African wedding rites, the bride and groom ate an onion and sang a song before retiring to their honeymoon hut. The Greeks and Romans recommended eating as many onions as possible to improve sexual endurance. Many cultures thought garlic had miraculous curative powers, particularly for the blood. Its fame extended, of course, to its positive effect on the erection, ever-dependent on good circulation. The Greek writer Aristophanes was one of many who heartily recommended garlic for failing masculine powers. Another unlikely source of ecstasy was the radish: Ancient Egyptians swore by its aphrodisiac properties when sweetened with honey.

One of the most highly regarded aphrodisiacs of the plant kingdom is the durian fruit, a native of Malaysia, Indonesia, and Thailand. The exotic, spiked fruit has a putrid stench, but its creamy-textured interior is said to be both delicious and lust-provoking.

Peppers, cabbage, lettuce, potatoes, artichokes, almonds, apples, oranges . . . Search long enough and you will discover that almost any fruit or vegetable found in the produce section of your market has been lauded as an aphrodisiac by someone, somewhere. But certain edibles stand out because of their omnipresence in literature. Perhaps the most ubiquitous is honey: Its very name is used as an endearment. The amber, viscous gift from the bee has been called the nectar of the gods and man's first sweet. The word "honeymoon" was coined in ancient Europe, where newlyweds took their amatory stamina from drinking mead— honey wine—during the first month of married life. Honey's reputation probably stems from the fact that it is one of the most easily digested and absorbed energy sources. Honey made from the pollen of aphrodisiac flowers and herbs is revered as especially potent. Not only has honey been a key ingredient in many and varied lovers' recipes, in some cultures it is also used topically. *The Perfumed Garden,* an ancient Indian textbook on sexuality, translated by Sir Richard Burton, recommends that the sexually weak drink "a thick glass" before retiring. At another point it suggests mixing honey with goat's blood and anointing the male member to ensure a night of splendor. Should this latter application hold any appeal (minus the goat's blood, perhaps), be aware that honey is an *anti*lubricant. Royal jelly, another bee product, is held in high esteem as an aphrodisiac in the Far East. This white substance, excreted by worker bees and fed exclusively to the queen of the hive, contains virtually all elements necessary for life and is dense in vitamins and minerals.

All over the world, eggs—whether the hundred-year-old eggs beloved by the Chinese, peacock eggs revered by ancient Athenians, or the ordinary product of the barnyard hen—symbolize sex and procreation. Romans, Chinese, Egyptians, Arabs, and Europeans all have advocated the egg—a tidy package of high-quality protein and essential amino acids—as a cure for sexual ailments. Our own Easter egg tradition derives from pagan springtime fertility festivals. In parts of Africa, eggs are thought to make women receptive to sex or even promiscuous. One of the least-appetizing customs comes from the Philippines, where fertilized duck eggs are highly prized aphrodisiacs. The key is to catch the egg at just the right stage: The chick is formed and its bones are still soft, but the embryo has not yet grown feathers. This delicacy is still much in demand in Manila's red-light district, especially in the early-morning hours, when the customers are feeling weary.

Another delicacy from the East is bird's nest soup, a spicy concoction made from edible nests of sea swallows found in the dark caves of Sarawak on the island of Borneo, Malaysia. The spittle from the birds that is used for the nests is thought to have aphrodisiac qualities. This "white gold" is dangerous to harvest, which helps make it extremely expensive and a good source of income to the island.

In Mayan brothels, a handful of cacao beans was the price for a night of bliss. The Aztecs made a beverage from cacao which they drank when paying tribute to their love goddess, Xochiquetzal. Montezuma, the Aztec emperor, is rumored to have sipped the drink from golden goblets before visiting his concubines. A tantalizing version of this potion, containing cocoa, kola nut, matico, and damiana, is available from Of the Jungle and Love Potions, Inc. (see resources section). Chocolate may not have the same lengthy history in Western civilization as some other foods, but once Cortez introduced this New World delicacy to Europe, it soon became one of high society's most consuming passions. Louis XV's mistress Madame du Barry, Casanova, and the sensualist Marquis de Sade all swore by chocolate's power to excite. The complexity of chocolate, its satisfying richness and sensuous melting quality, make it irresistible, but it is not only the energy-boosting sugar and caffeine in chocolate candy that earned its reputation as an aphrodisiac. Chocolate also contains the amino acid phenylalanine, which increases the brain's levels of the neuropeptide phenylethylamine, one of the body's natural aphrodisiacs. But the widely circulated theory that chocolate induces the same feelings as "being in love" has yet to be proven.

Fish, shellfish, and other products of the sea such as turtles and seaweed also have sexual mystique. Aphrodite's reputed emergence from the foam leads to the implication that anything from the same source would be imbued with her amorous spirit. Then, of course, there is the similarity of human blood and semen to seawater, and our part scientific, part mythological affinity with our primordial home. Even the ancient landlocked would not be denied their favorite fish dinners. Roman emperors had live sturgeon relayed in pails of seawater from the Caspian Sea to Rome so that they could partake of the roe—no more trouble than many people would go to today for caviar's purported powers of aphrodisia. A similar story is told about the Aztec emperors, who had relay teams bring live fish from the ocean to the table to be shared with their harems. Caviar and lobsters have also been considered aphrodisiacs.

Fish has its fans, but in his 1930s treatise, *Studies in the Psychology of Sex,* Havelock Ellis contended that for a red-blooded male, rare beefsteak was probably the most powerful sexual stimulant. Varied meats have been found on Aphrodite's menu, but game, particularly, has long been a favorite. The Romans expected bear meat to work. Native Americans ate bear, and buffalo too, but swore by deer steaks for strength and virility. And for obvious reasons, many modern people have tried rabbit and wild hare. Equally unambiguous a choice are testicles: bulls, rams, even lions have sacrificed their masculinity to the cause. The effects of a plate of "prairie oysters," however, can only be psychological; while testicles do contain testosterone, all methods of cooking render the hormone impotent. Nor are rhino horns, tiger penises, bear gallbladders, or seal tails at all effective, even though they are still marketed—often illegally—in the Far East. With the exception of deer antlers, these fake aphrodisiacs have been banned in most countries, which unfortunately has not killed their sales. In the East, deer antlers are used to brew a traditional and very powerful tonic using the fresh tips of young deer or antlers that have been shed. In this way the deer are not harmed.

The Sensualist's Diet

Myth and legend notwithstanding, some foods definitely have a physiological role in human desire. The sex drive requires a balance between the endocrine and neurologic systems, and the foods that are the most sexually stimulating contain nutrients that support these systems. The endocrine system needs nourishment to supply the building blocks for hormones; the neurologic system needs the same for production of neurotransmitters and neuropeptides. Ideally, you should get these nutrients—vitamins, minerals, amino acids, essential fatty acids, mucopolysaccharides, and glandulars—from a normal diet. At the very least, a sexually dynamic body needs a diet rich in fresh and varied fruits and vegetables and lean animal protein or legumes.

Today's food may be nutritionally deficient because of excess processing, mineral imbalances in contaminated soil, and use of pesticides and herbicides. If you are taking drugs or are under stress, if you have been ill or use tobacco, alcohol, or caffeine in excess, your ability to manufacture, absorb, or store certain nutrients may be impaired. The Food and Drug Administration's recommended daily allowances (RDAs) are designed only to prevent extreme deficiency, which is fairly rare in this country. But many doctors are unaware of the subclinical symptoms of various vitamin deficiencies, and the RDAs were never proposed to prime the body for its sexual best.

If you want to supplement your diet with additional nutrients, you will find a bewildering array at any pharmacy or health food store. But supplementation can be tricky. For instance, vitamin C can greatly increase absorption of iron, which can be undesirable in a condition of excess iron called hemochromatosis. On the other hand, inorganic iron will interfere with vitamin E absorption. A nutritionist or nutritionally oriented doctor can advise on the correct supplements for optimum functioning; they can tailor programs for your particular needs. Following are some guidelines on nutritional substances that really do influence sexuality and mood. Not surprisingly, many traditional aphrodisiacal foods are found here.

Vitamins

Vitamins are essential to human existence; in fact, the word itself derives from the Latin *vita* for life. But the role of vitamins is often misunderstood; they do not provide energy, nor do they alone construct tissues or cells. They are organic compounds required in minute amounts to act as catalysts for enzyme reactions that occur throughout the body. Many necessary elements cannot be manufactured unless vitamins are present. Vitamins fall into two broad categories—water soluble and fat soluble. The water-soluble vitamins are the B-complex and C vitamins. They must be consumed daily because they are excreted in urine. They are also fragile and can be leeched out of food during cooking or destroyed by light and heat. The following help keep your body in top sexual form.

B-1 (thiamine) is essential for healthy muscles, heart, adrenal glands, fertility, and lactation. This vitamin also converts carbohydrates into energy. Heavy users of alcohol—that means anyone who drinks on a daily basis—should take a supplement of at least 100 milligrams of thiamine a day. Low levels of thiamine may be associated with depression and anorexia. Thiamine is often referred to as the "morale" vitamin because it has such an impact on the nervous system. Natural sources are soybeans, beans, peas, peanuts, whole-grain breads and cereals, asparagus, raw nuts and seeds, and yoghurt.

B-2 (riboflavin) is required for red-blood-cell production and growth; keeps your hair, skin, and nails healthy; and helps the body obtain energy from carbohydrates and proteins. Get your quota from those favorite aphrodisiac foods—asparagus, bananas, figs, whole grains, green vegetables, broccoli, lean meats, and eggs. Indian aphrodisiacs are often mixed with honey and milk; the dairy product is a good source of vitamin B-2.

B-3 (niacin) combats anxiety, depression, insomnia, and fatigue, and also dilates blood vessels. Most important for our purposes, it is essential for the synthesis of sex hormones. Like riboflavin, niacin helps cells generate energy from food. If you choose to get niacin via supplements, be aware that it can irritate the stomach, especially in those who suffer from gastritis or ulcers. Early on, niacin supplements can cause the skin to flush and tingle. Start with doses of 100 milligrams per day, increasing to no more than 2 grams per day. Avoid the sustained-release niacin supplements as they are associated with elevated liver enzymes. Found in fish, lean meats, peas, beans, avocados, figs, dates, whole-grain cereal products, asparagus, and broccoli.

B-5 (pantothenic acid) is known as the stress vitamin, and is important for the healthy functioning of the adrenal glands and the production of steroid hormones. Required by all the cells in the body, B-5 is especially important to combat aging and for menopausal women. The latter should try a supplement of between 500 and 1,000 milligrams a day. Found in bee pollen, nuts, grains, beef, eggs, beans, potatoes, broccoli, cabbage, cauliflower, molasses, and poultry.

B-6 (pyridoxine) has three forms and as a supplement is best taken as pyridoxal-5-phosphate. Women suffering from morning sickness, or water retention and other effects of PMS, will find it beneficial, as will those taking birth control pills or replacement estrogen. Carrots, bananas, cantaloupe, eggs, red meat, wheat germ, oats, honey, and sunflower seeds are good sources.

B-12 (cyanocobalamin) is essential for the production of red blood cells and is required for digestion, protein synthesis, and metabolism. It prevents nerve damage. Strict vegetarians may need to take a supplement; B-12 is found only in fish, shellfish, seaweed, muscle and organ meats, milk, cheese, and eggs.

Choline is required by the brain to produce the neurotransmitter acetylcholine and is therefore essential to the nervous system. Recent research suggests there may be a link between choline and Alzheimer's disease. Sources include egg yolks, seeds, grains, nuts and soybeans, meats, poultry, and green vegetables.

Lecithin is required by every living cell; it prevents cell membranes from hardening and makes up the protective sheath surrounding the brain. Found in large amounts in semen, it needs to be replaced after ejaculation. Most lecithin supplements are made from soybeans, but recently a form derived from egg yolks has been used in the treatment of AIDS patients. Other sources are brewer's yeast, whole grains, legumes, and fish.

Folic Acid is necessary for energy production and the formation of red blood cells. Because it is needed for healthy cell division and replication, pregnant women may require higher levels and should talk to their doctor about supplementation. Birth control pills and hormone-replacement therapy can also increase the body's need for folic acid. It is thought by some to be an anti-aging vitamin. Recent research has shown the need for folic acid to prevent cervical dysplasia and neural tube defects in the fetus. Found in many foods including organ meats, salmon, tuna, green leafy vegetables, root vegetables, whole grains, cheese, and oranges.

Vitamin C (ascorbic acid) promotes growth, tissue repair, and bone healing, and is important for the adrenal and pituitary glands. C is also a detoxifer that protects against free radical damage from pollutants. (The free-radical theory attempts to define one of the mechanisms thought to cause aging. "Free radical" refers to a molecule of oxygen with a free electron that destroys enzymes and membranes in the cell, causing the cell to age and die.) Vitamin C is also important for the formation of collagen, which helps keep the skin supple and elastic. Sources of vitamin C are citrus fruits, strawberries, kiwi fruit, tomatoes, bell peppers, kale, and other green vegetables. Bioflavonoids are not true vitamins, but they occur in nature with vitamin C and help with the absorption of it. They are important for strengthening collagen and enhancing the strength of capillaries. They have anti-inflammatory properties when taken in high doses of 1,000 to 2,000 milligrams a day for asthma, allergies, and injuries. There are some reports that high doses of vitamin C are associated with kidney stones. Be sure to drink 6 to 8 glasses of water or herbal tea daily and use caution if you have a history or family history of stones.

Fat-soluble vitamins are A, D, E, and K. Stored in fatty tissue and in the liver, they can build up and excessive amounts can prove toxic, though this is fairly rare. Consult your doctor before taking supplements of these vitamins. Following are the "big two" for sexual health.

Vitamin A (retinol) is necessary for new cell growth, healthy tissue, and for adequate vision in dim light. It is also an antioxidant and thus is thought to retard the effects of aging. Vitamin A is essential for healthy sperm production, and supplementation in tandem with vitamin E can help to increase a low sperm count. Vitamin A is essential for a healthy thyroid gland and for production of progesterone. Vitamin A is found in two forms. Carotene, a yellow pigment found in vegetables such as carrots, yams, and pumpkins, is converted by the body to vitamin A. Retinol itself is made from carotene by other animals and ingested by humans in certain food tissues such as liver, eggs, and milk. Carotenes are also high in broccoli, tomatoes, and green leafy vegetables.

Vitamin E (tocopherol) is often referred to as the sex vitamin. It is required for the production of hormones and prostaglandins, to repair cells, and as an antioxidant to prevent cell damage. This vitamin also improves circulation, reduces scarring, and lowers blood pressure. Supplementation with E has helped to treat women with breast cysts and to reduce hot flashes in menopausal women. Use caution when initiating vitamin E supplementation, since blood pressure may go up when vitamin E is taken in large doses. Start with 100 IU and gradually increase to 600–1,000 IU daily. Abundant sources are vegetable oils, nuts, seeds, beans, eggs, whole grains, fruits, wheat grain, spinach, and other vegetables such as asparagus and peas.

Minerals

Vitamins usually take center stage in any discussion of dietary supplements, but minerals are also essential for overall well-being. Some minerals are needed in large amounts—meaning in the range of milligrams to one gram a day. These include calcium, phosphorus, sodium, iron, potassium, magnesium, and sulfur. Others, called trace minerals, are needed in smaller amounts, and include boron, manganese, copper, iodine, zinc, cobalt, fluorine, and selenium. Some minerals such as lead, mercury, and cadmium are regarded as noxious. Even minerals that the body requires for good health can be harmful in the wrong quantities: Taking too much of one essential mineral may upset the balance and function of other minerals. For instance, excess zinc can interfere with calcium absorption and vice versa. Following are minerals that have a particular relevance to sexuality.

Zinc is a fundamental requirement for healthy male sexuality. It is needed for the production of testosterone, and semen contains large amounts of zinc. Zinc supplements have been shown to help with chronic prostatitis and some cases of impotence. In more general terms, zinc is needed for healthy skin and hair and for the immune system. Too much zinc, however, can have the reverse effect on the immune system. Zinc supplements come in various forms: zinc piccolinate in doses of 25 to 50 milligrams a day is recommended. One of the best natural sources is oysters, giving credence, perhaps, to the bivalves' aphrodisiacal reputation. Zinc is also found in legumes, pumpkin and sunflower seeds, garlic, and spinach. When taking zinc supplements be sure you have an adequate copper intake. Generally, you don't need additional copper if your diet is rich in fresh green vegetables, nuts, beans, and peas. Most processed or canned foods, however, are low in copper.

Calcium is essential for strong bones, teeth, and muscles. Concern over calcium deficiency has come to the forefront due to the problem of osteoporosis in postmenopausal women. Most women have diets low in calcium and require supplements long before menopause. In addition, caffeine, alcohol, and diuretics can cause the loss of calcium and other minerals in the urine. Women can benefit from taking 1,000 milligrams a day of calcium citrate, stepping the dose up to 1,500 milligrams after menopause. Dairy products are an excellent way to get your calcium, as are salmon, sardines, seaweed, green leafy vegetables, almonds, and molasses.

Magnesium is another mineral that contributes to the production of sex hormones. Women suffering symptoms of PMS or menstrual cramps may find some relief from taking a magnesium supplement, as it increases progesterone levels. Magnesium-rich foods include meats, fish—particularly salmon—dairy products, apples, apricots, avocados, nuts, seeds, tofu, figs, peaches, beets, leafy vegetables, and whole grains.

Chromium, acting with insulin, is required for glucose utilization. It is an essential nutrient required for anyone with hypoglycemia or diabetes. We tend to retain less chromium as we age, and many American diets are low in this mineral. Brewer's yeast and beer are good sources, as are clams, corn oil, wheat germ, and chicken.

Iron is an extremely important mineral for the development of healthy red blood cells since it is the central element in hemoglobin, which carries oxygen to the tissues. Although present in significant amounts in the liver and bone marrow, iron is mostly found in blood, and lost to the body primarily by bleeding. Menstruating and pregnant women have increased requirement for iron. Both iron deficiency and iron overload can be dangerous to your health, so take supplements only on your doctor's orders.

The best iron supplements are from organic sources such as iron gluconate or fumarate, or from the herbs yellow dock and nettles. Iron sulfate is more likely to cause stomach upset. Diets that provide enough iron must be carefully selected, because only a few foods contain iron in useful amounts. Liver is an excellent source, as are egg yolks, fish, dried fruits, especially apricots and raisins, and whole grain cereals.

Selenium is an important micronutrient often lacking in diet. Requirements for men are higher than for women since there is a high concentration of the mineral in semen, and selenium is needed for sperm production. It works together with vitamin E to reduce free-radical damage, and it protects the immune system and the heart. Ample amounts can be found in Brazil nuts, brown rice, whole milk, cottage cheese, garlic, eggs, and wheat.

Iodine is an essential mineral for the functioning of the thyroid gland and is an integral part of thyroxin. Thyroxin is one of the master hormones that regulates metabolic functioning, promotes growth, stimulates cholesterol synthesis, and regulates other glandular functioning. Although not one of the minerals directly related to sexuality, low levels of iodine can result in a sluggish thyroid and can even lead to hypothyroidism and goiters. Women with under- or overactive thyroid glands are likely to have irregular periods or severe PMS symptoms. Large doses of iodine can be harmful when given pharmacologically, but iodine-rich foods are not known to cause toxic effects. Your levels of iodine may be low if you are on a low-salt diet, or if you consume large amounts of cabbage and nuts, which interfere with the body's utilization of iodine in the making of thyroxin. Iodine is found in high amounts in seafood, seaweed, onions, and pineapple.

Manganese is a trace mineral important for the activation of many enzyme systems in your body. It is required for utilization of thiamine, fatty acids, choline, and vitamin C and for the production of thyroid and sex hormones. It also helps nourish the nerves and brain. Doctors have employed manganese to stabilize disorders of sugar metabolism in both diabetics and hypoglycemics. You can get your quota from a diet containing beets, nuts, whole grains, leafy green vegetables, apples, and apricots.

Amino Acids

Amino acids are the precursors—the building blocks—of proteins, essential for all the cells in the body. When we talk about the body's requirement for protein foods, we really are saying that we need to replenish our supply of these twenty-two natural substances. Of those, nine are called the essential amino acids, meaning they are mandatory in our diets as they are not manufactured by the body. When taken as part of meals, amino acids are metabolized in the body as proteins. But for the purpose of nurturing the nervous system and increasing neurotransmitter production, single amino-acid supplements should be taken with their cofactors between meals, washed down by juice or water.

Phenylalanine (PA) is one of the essential amino acids that is a precursor of the neurotransmitters epinephrine, norepinephrine, and dopamine, all of which are influential in sexual arousal and response. PA also increases levels of the neuropeptide phenyethylamine, which is often lacking in people with a sluggish libido. Those with high blood pressure should not take supplements of phenylalanine unless under their doctor's supervision. Others can take a supplement—they usually come in tablets of 250 to 500 milligrams—along with vitamins B-6 and C, which are required in the synthesis of neurotransmitters. You may experience an increase in levels of energy and sex drive with regular use.

DL-phenylalanine (DLPA) is another form of the above amino acid. But rather than boost the excitory neurotransmitters, this one augments formation of endorphins, our natural opiates. Often used to treat depression and chronic pain, it has also proven effective in improving mood disorders and memory. Pregnant women should not take DLPA unless on doctor's orders.

L-tyrosine can be produced in the body from phenylalanine, so it is not "essential." A lack of L-tyrosine causes norephinephrine deficiency in the brain, which leads to depression and mood disorders. L-tyrosine supplements can be substituted for phenylalanine supplements but should still be treated with caution by people with high blood pressure.

Histidine is the chemical precursor of histamines, potent vasodilators stored in many cells throughout the body. Recently, through electron microscopic techniques, it was discovered that histamines are also present in nerve endings. They are found in high concentrations in the brain, especially in the hypothalamus. They are responsible for the well-known symptoms of allergies such as hives and runny noses, which is why we take antihistamines when we encounter an allergen. Histamines are also released during orgasm. Several of my male patients have complained of the sudden onset of stuffy nose at the moment of orgasm. One female patient confided that she always knows when orgasm is imminent by changes in her sinuses. Sex researchers Masters and Johnson determined that histamines are responsible for the flush that occurs with orgasm. Histidine should be taken with vitamin B-6 to enhance its conversion to histamine.

Tryptophan was providing natural relief to many people with sleep disorders until a few years ago when this essential amino-acid supplement was implicated in causing *Eiosinophilia-myalgia syndrome,* a potentially fatal blood disease. Although an offending contaminant was found only in a brand made by a single manufacturer, all supplements were pulled from the market in the United States and Canada, and at press time were still not available over the counter. Tryptophan is a precursor of serotonin, the body's stress reducer. When it is again available as a supplement, take with vitamins B-3, B-6, and magnesium for maximum effectiveness. In the meantime it can be found in turkey, milk, cottage cheese, bananas, dried dates, and peanuts.

Essential Fatty Acids and Prostaglandins

Essential fatty acids are needed by the brain, the nervous system, the immune system, the skin, the glands, and all the vital organs. In other words, they are necessary to every cell in your body. Among other functions, they protect the cells from viruses and bacteria. They are the precursors of hormone-like substances called prostaglandins, which are important for sexual response. The two essential fatty acids that you must get from your diet are linoleic acid and linolenic acid. Deficiency syndromes are quite common and can affect the body with a wide variety of symptoms, not the least of which are sterility in men, miscarriage, circulatory problems, growth retardation, and behavioral changes. These problems are all reversible when these fatty acids are put into the diet. The most potent dietary sources are nuts and seeds, flaxseed being perhaps the richest in both linoleic and linolenic acids. Evening primrose oil, often prescribed for the symptoms of PMS, menstrual cramps, breast tenderness, and arthritis, is a good source of one type of linolenic acid, called gamma linolenic, found in mother's milk, and one of the most important substances for the production of prostaglandins.

Prostaglandins are so vital to the sexual response that they are administered by local injection to impotent men. There are three types of prostaglandins—known as series 1, 2, and 3—produced in the body, some of which have opposing effects. Series 1, made from linoleic acid, are referred to as the "good" prostaglandins and have been studied the most extensively. Of these, prostaglandin E-1 (PGE-1) is best known. It protects against heart attacks and strokes by preventing blood platelets from clumping together, slows down cholesterol production, and improves circulation. This wonder substance also inhibits inflammation and is helpful in arthritic conditions, operates as a diuretic, makes insulin work more effectively, improves nerve function, and may even prevent the development of cancer cells. When it comes to the "aphrodisiac factor," PGE-1 aids erections by relaxing muscles in the blood vessel walls, allowing the blood to flow into the genitals.

Series 2 are the "bad" prostaglandins, and they too are made from linoleic acid. They promote the formation of blood clots, cause water retention, high blood pressure, and inflammation. Series 3 are closer to series 1 in that they also have anti-sticking effects on blood platelets, but they are made from linolenic acid, which they convert to something called eicosapentaenoic acid (EPA). EPA is also found in high quantities in fish oils, hence the reputation that fish oils have gained in recent years as possible preventers of heart attacks. You may have heard of these series

3/EPA substances referred to as omega-3 fatty acids. Salmon and sardines are excellent natural sources, and the best source of these essential fatty acids are flax seed, soy, and walnut oils.

In order for your body to produce these critically important prostaglandins from the fatty acids in your diet, you also need to have adequate supplies of vitamin C, vitamins B-3 and B-6, zinc, and magnesium.

You can now begin to see the interplay between these nutrient substances and how subtly diet can affect your sex drive and performance.

Mucopolysaccharides

Mucopolysaccharides are probably less well known to most of us than vitamins, minerals, or even fatty acids. They are natural substances made of proteins and sugars that together with collagen form the glue that holds together all our body tissues and give strength and elasticity to tissues and membranes. Among their other functions are regulating the flow of nutrients, controlling inflammation, and protecting against infection. Most important, they boost the production of seminal fluid and increase potency and sex drive. Oysters and mussels are good providers of mucopolysaccharides.

Glandulars

The use of glandular supplements for healing and rejuvenation dates back to Homer, who prescribed lion's-bone marrow for the warrior Achilles. Homer was working on the same principle as our mothers when they urged us to eat liver for our blood. And, of course, the centuries-old custom of eating animal testicles for sexual potency is a form of glandular therapy. The contemporary version of glandular remedies involves using specific hormone treatments for specific diseases. But this is powerful medicine, and unless hormones are administered in correct and carefully monitored doses they can have the side effect of shutting off the body's own glandular functioning. Sometimes, though, this is the desired effect. Birth control pills work in exactly this way, as do thyroid hormones administered for goiters or thyroiditis.

Apart from the prescribed hormones mentioned above, there are glandular supplements available over-the-counter. Those supplied to physicians tend to be of a higher quality than those on sale at the health food store, so consult your doctor before purchasing any at the store. There is some controversy about whether or not they are effective, but radioisotope tracing has shown that material ingested for a specific gland will end up in the gland toward which it is directed. Generally, these glandular supplements will support the gland's function by supplying nutrients. Glandular extracts contain not only small amounts of hormones, but also vitamins, enzymes, polypeptides, essential fatty acids, and prostaglandins.

Some companies produce glandular extracts from which the specific hormone has been removed, such as thyroxine-free thyroid extract. The best preparation of glandulars is in freeze-dried form because all of the enzymes, fats, and polypeptides remain intact. When buying glandulars, check to make sure that the company lists the source of their product and buy only those taken from animals that have not been fed synthetic hormones or antibiotics.

You can take adrenal-gland extract for stress, chronic illness, asthma, and allergies. Thymus extract is excellent for infections such as chronic viruses. Thyroid extract is helpful for a sluggish thyroid, or as an addition to prescribed thyroid hormones when taken for hypthyroidism. Ovarian glandulars are good for women who suffer from amenorrhea, ovarian cysts, PMS, or menopausal symptoms. Prostate glandulars, in turn, might help men with prostate disorders such as prostatitis. An extract of progesterone and DHEA (dihydroepiandrosterone) is available suspended in vitamin E oil. These preparations—all from the Mexican yam root—are excellent for PMS, menopause, and other problems associated with aging.

Homeopathic preparations containing glandular extracts are

another effective and gentle way of stimulating glandular functioning. Many homeopathic combination remedies contain glandulars when they are indicated for conditions with endocrine imbalances. I have found a specific benefit in using homeopathic thymus extract for chronic infections, especially in children, and homeopathically prepared ovarian extract for ovulatory disturbances and menopause.

Whether you are a vegetarian or a carnivore, the sensualist's diet is a balanced one. Fresh foods are best, organic if possible. Meats should be from healthy sources, without hormones or antibiotics. A light meal with pleasurable tastes can be a delicious prelude or afterlude to lovemaking.

5

DRUGS AND LIBIDO

Formerly, when religion was strong and science weak,
men mistook magic for medicine;
now when science is strong and religion weak,
men mistake medicine for magic.
—THOMAS SZASZ

The human brain is wired to respond to certain drugs with feelings of extraordinary pleasure—no wonder our primitive ancestors learned to use them to beef up their sex lives. Unfortunately, humanity has a poor track record in choosing which drugs to take and which to leave alone. A good example is cantharides, known colloquially as Spanish fly.

Cantharides is not an aphrodisiac, despite having had a reputation as such since the days of ancient Rome.

Extracted from the iridescent green and gold "blister beetle" found in Spain and other Mediterranean countries, Spanish fly is an irritant and an inflammatory agent. Even tiny doses can cause burning of the mouth and throat, abdominal pain, kidney damage, and extreme irritation of the urogenital tract. Presumably it is this last effect that put this noxious poison into the annals of aphrodisiacs. Genital burning, accompanied by swooning and screaming, was once regarded as a proof of passion. In a leap of faith, ignorant people presumed that if the substance produced the symptoms of lust, it would also produce the lust. Today, medicine classifies Spanish fly as a blistering agent and a Class

One poison so deadly that a mere one ten-thousandth of an ounce, taken orally, can induce kidney failure.

Unfortunately, Spanish fly has not been entirely relegated to the junkyard of erotic mythology, and ads for products claiming to contain it can still be found in many "adult" magazines. The small print calls the ingredients "pseudo" Spanish fly or something similar, and the products generally contain useless, if harmless, ingredients. True Spanish fly is illegal except in some highly specific medical instances but is available in big-city slums and cities such as Tijuana and Bangkok.

Other dangerous substances that should also be struck from the pharmacopeia of aphrodisiacs include nux vomica, better known as strychnine; ergot, made from a fungus that grows on grains and causes the uterine muscles to contract; capsicum, which derives from tropical pepper plants and is used as a gastric stimulant; and sanguinaria, a topical ointment most commonly used for removing warts.

Most of these substances have lost their folkloric reputations as aphrodisiacs, but in the quest for the erotic Garden of Eden a whole new mythology has grown up around other drugs, both social and pharmacologic. Some people continue to seek out dangerous illicit drugs for the purpose of sexual thrills while others refuse to take necessary medications because they adversely affect their sex drive or ability to reach orgasm.

The issue of drugs and sexuality is indeed a fascinating and complex tangle of factors.

Drugs that influence sexuality function in a number of ways, usually by altering the chemistry of the brain. When evaluating a drug that impinges on a patient's sexuality, doctors first look at which phase is affected—desire, arousal (erection), orgasm, or ejaculation. This is essential when it comes to diagnosing side effects. For example, many drugs block the effects of acelycholine, the neurotransmitter that controls vaginal secretions and dilates blood vessels during arousal. The system that responds to this neurotransmitter is called the cholinergic system, and the drugs that block it are known as anticholinergics. The common side effects caused by this class of drugs are dry mouth, dry vaginal secretions, and difficulty with urination, which can make having sex a problem. Certain antidepressants interfere with desire, arousal, and orgasm/ejaculation by blocking the cholinergic system. Antipsychotic drugs also act in this way. Antihistamines (Benadryl, Atarax, and Periactin) have anticholinergic effects that reduce desire and hinder erection.

Many drugs used to treat nausea, stomach cramps, and urinary spasms also block the cholinergic system. Atropine-containing medications (Lomotil, Urised, Pro-Banthine, Scopalamine, Donnatal, Ditropan) may interfere with erection but not arousal or orgasm. And so on . . .

On the other hand, some antidepressants enhance sexual functioning by cutting off the body's reabsorption of "sexy" dopaminergic neurotransmitters, allowing them to continue their work of inducing arousal and excitement. Some drugs influence sexuality by exerting a push-pull effect on the central nervous system. Generally speaking, these substances do not inhibit arousal— sometimes they encourage it—but they do suppress the orgasm. Many recreational drugs fall into this category, like alcohol, which, as Shakespeare put it, "provokes the desire but takes away the performance."

There are drugs that influence sexuality by changing hormone response, particularly those that decrease testosterone levels. These include chemotherapeutic agents, some birth control pills, certain antipsychotics, certain drugs for ulcers and gastritis, and steroids.

Some drugs work on sexuality in more ways than one. Alcohol sedates the central nervous system and can lower inhibitions, but too much can interfere with erection and orgasm. Chronic use also decreases testosterone levels in men, probably by suppressing the production of this hormone in the testes, and then good-bye performance!

Here is a closer look at some commonly used drugs.

Therapeutic Drugs

If you have noticed an abrupt drop in desire, do not automatically assume that the cause is an inevitable cooling of passion toward your lover or because of the passage of time. Yes, there will be gradual and subtle shifts in the nature of sexual encounters as time passes, but sudden or dramatic changes are more likely to have specific causes, one of which could be pharmaceutical. When sexual dysfunction—in the form of a sudden drop-off in desire, inability to become aroused, difficulty in attaining orgasm, or pain during sex—coincides with your taking a new medication, bring these symptoms to the attention of your doctor.

Even today, many physicians still hesitate to introduce discussions about sex because of their own timidity and because they know that their patients are equally shy. In my office, patients fill out a questionnaire in which they are asked, "Are you having any problems with sex?" Even if they leave the line blank, as happens often enough, it gives me an opening to diplomatically bring up the topic. Remember: It is self-defeating to suffer in silence when there could be an alternative to the medication that is causing the problem. If your doctor is unable or unwilling to recommend a different medication, consider getting a second opinion. If a drug you are taking is listed in the following sections as causing unwanted sexual side effects but you are not having any, good! You may never have a problem. Also, I have found that the effects differ in men and women.

The information that follows is based on reports in the scientific literature and by pharmaceutical companies. Ask your doctor to explain the sexual ramifications if you are taking any of the following drugs.

Antihypertensives

High blood pressure is a widespread problem in the United States and is a risk factor for developing coronary artery disease and strokes. Drugs that control high blood pressure may act on the neurotransmitter norepinephrine, either by curbing its release, depleting its stores, or blocking its receptors, all of which can repress erection and ejaculation.

Unfortunately, these sexual dysfunctions were necessary side effects of the earliest blood pressure medications. Centrally acting sympathetic blockers such as Methyl-Dopa, Reserpine, Clonidine, and Guanfacine (Tenex) potentially block all phases of sexual function including desire, arousal (erection), and orgasm/ejaculation (except Tenex, which does not block orgasm). Beta blockers are notorious for affecting sexual function. Propranolol (Inderal) blocks both desire and arousal but not ejaculation, as does Timolol (Blocadren). Normodyne (Labetalol) blocks all three phases. Lopressor and Atenolol are more specific for the heart and are the least of the offenders in this class, with only mild effects on erections. Diuretics also affect sexual performance with Furosemide (Lasix) affecting erection, Spironolactone (Aldactone) affecting both desire and erection, and Hydrocholothiazide affecting all three phases.

Newer drugs have far fewer inhibiting effects on sexuality and fewer side effects all around. Calcium channel blockers (Nifedipine, Diltiazem, and Verapamil) have less sedative side effects and are reported to affect erection only. Angiotensin-converting enzyme inhibitors (Captopril, Enalapril) now used as first-line drugs for hypertension are said to affect erection only. Lisinopril is reported to affect both desire and erection. Neither affect orgasm or ejaculation. Unfortunately, they all can cause an annoying cough.

Another class of antihypertensives called alpha-adrenergic blockers—marketed as Prazosin and Terazosin—can interfere with the blood flow into the smooth muscle of the blood vessels in the penis and in the vaginal wall, but reports of impotence and loss of orgasm are rare among those taking these medications. Initially used in a secondary role to control blood pressure, the comparative safety of these drugs has been established and they are now being used as first-line therapy. They are also now used to treat the symptoms of an enlarged prostate gland.

Those with high blood pressure have few, if any, symptoms, which is why the disease is called the silent killer. Consequently, some patients have a tendency to be cavalier and simply stop their medication when they experience side effects, especially in sexual responsiveness. This is dangerous and unnecessary. There are many drugs available now, so talk it over with your doctor.

Cholesterol-Lowering Medications

Clofibrate (Atromid-S) is used to lower cholesterol levels. Unfortunately, this drug also interferes with the testicles' ability to produce testosterone; depressed libido and impotence are common side effects that resolve when the drug is discontinued. Other cholesterol-lowering drugs that do not interfere with sexual functioning are available; if you take Clofibrate and have sexual problems, ask your doctor about products such as Mevacor.

Antidepressants

One of the first symptoms of depression is sexual indifference. Men and women who go to their doctors with complaints about their sex lives are often clinically depressed, yet until recently the antidepressants they were prescribed exacerbated sexual problems.

Antidepressants work by increasing the amount of neurotransmitters available to the brain cells, either by slowing down the breakdown of neurotransmitters or by preventing these chemicals from being reabsorbed. Recent research has shown that antidepressants have a combined effect: Not only is the reabsorption or "re-uptake" of the neurotransmitter affected, but the chemical receptors change their sensitivity. This is one reason antidepressants take several weeks to show clinical effects. Many of the MAO inhibitors and tricyclics cause sexual side effects.

The first antidepressants inhibited monoaminoxidase, preventing this valuable enzyme from breaking down norepinephrine, serotonin, and dopamine, thus allowing more of these neurotransmitters to produce their effects. The earliest types of these MAO transmitters also caused episodes of high blood pressure when the user ingested food containing tyramine (cheese, wine, beer, salami, chocolate among others). Parnate and Nardil are two MAO inhibitors that specifically cause loss of erection and orgasm. One of my female patients had such severe anorgasmia on Nardil that she decided to change antidepressants. Prozac, now widely prescribed for depression, is classified as a MAO inhibitor but is more "selective"; it affects serotonin only and doesn't have the same dietary restrictions. Prozac, unfortunately, reportedly causes sexual dysfunction among 8.5 percent of users. Some doctors believe the figure is higher; many women report a decrease in orgasmic intensity or difficulty in attaining orgasm at all.

Tricyclics and tetracyclics work by blocking the "re-uptake," or reabsorption, of neurotransmitters. These include Elavil, Norpramin, Tofranil, Asendin, Anafranil, Sinequan, Ludiomil, Pamelor, and Vivactyl. These drugs have many anticholinergic side effects, including dry mouth, constipation, difficulty in urinating, and loss of sexual desire, erection, orgasm, and/or ejaculation. A newer addition to this class is Zoloft (sertraline HCl). Compared to these other drugs, Zoloft causes many fewer side effects. But in a clinical study of the drug, 10 percent of those who took it had difficulty with ejaculation; in 3 percent the problem became persistent. When compared with Elavil, the percentage of impotence and decreased libido in Zoloft users was the same at 2 percent.

In an effort to find a way of counteracting the sexually negative side effects of antidepressants, a study was conducted on men having difficulty reaching orgasms while on Prozac. The researchers used Periactin, an antihistamine with antiserotonergic and anticholinergic side effects. Periactin was given at a dose of 2 to 6 mg two hours before making love. While the Periactin did help the men attain orgasm, it also negated the antidepressant effects. Some therapists have found using a continuous daily dosage of 2 mg three times daily to be more effective.

If you are experiencing unpleasant sexual side effects with any antidepressants, be sure to discuss this with your doctor. You may be able to switch to Wellbutrin or Trazodone, or try Periactin, or Bethanecol, a drug with cholinergic effects.

Trazodone (Desyrel) may increase libido. However, there have been reports of priapism in both men and women. Be sure to discuss this with your doctor.

Antianxiety Medications

Anxiety for many people in today's world is an everyday occurrence. Not surprisingly, drugs to reduce the symptoms of anxiety are commonly prescribed in this country. Some experts believe that panic disorders are not "all in your head" and that genetic factors may contribute to an imbalance of brain neurotransmitters such as norepinephrine and serotonin.

Initially Valium (diazepam) was the most commonly used benzodiazepine prescribed for anxiety. Referred to as "Mother's Little Helper" in the 1960s, Valium was found in medicine cabinets throughout the country. When the seriously addictive properties of Valium became clear, other drugs were developed for this purpose. Unfortunately, other related benzodiazepines such as Xanax (alprazolam), Ativan (lorazepam), Tranxene (clorazepate), and Librium (chlordiazepoxide) are very effective but also cause dependence. Since all of these drugs act to depress the central nervous system, naturally they can decrease libido, delay ejaculation, and possibly even inhibit orgasm. When using these drugs for a long period of time, they must not be abruptly discontinued. I have had several patients try this unknowingly and have serious withdrawal problems. Slow reduction of the dosage over a period of weeks or even months under the advice of your doctor is recommended.

BuSpar (Buspirone), a newer drug for anxiety, is often used because it does not create dependence and also does not cause drowsiness. It is thought to work by interacting with the dopamine and serotonin systems in the brain, although the exact mechanism is unclear. BuSpar has also been noted to affect sexual function. Both increased and decreased libido, priapism, delayed ejaculation, and impotence are infrequently reported. Atarax and Vistaril (both are hyroxyzine) have an antihistamine effect as well as an antianxiety effect. They may depress sexual desire and arousal as well as cause dry mouth, dry vaginal secretions, and drowsiness.

A group of drugs related to the benzodiazepines are prescribed for sleep disturbance. Restoril (temazepam), Dalmane (flurazepam), and Halcion (triazolam) are the most commonly taken. Restoril and Dalmane have no sexual side effects reported. The controversial drug Halcion has been reported to cause decreased libido. Halcion must be used cautiously for it has been accused of causing psychological disturbances and amnesia when used with alcohol.

All of these drugs can potentially interact with other drugs, including alcohol, with dangerous consequences. If your are taking any of these medications, discuss this with your doctor.

If you are prone to anxiety or sleep disturbance, support your nervous system with the right nutrients. B-vitamin supplements and specific natural remedies (see chapters 4 and 7) may help you reduce your symptoms.

Antipsychotic Drugs

Drugs used for psychotic symptoms have many undesirable side effects, sexual dysfunction included. Predominantly due to interference with the cholinergic system, these drugs can block all phases of the sexual response. Haloperidol (Haldol), Chlorpromazine (Thorazine), and Thioridazine (Mellaril) may cause impotence, anorgasmia, or painful ejaculation. Haldol, Thorazine, and Mellaril block all three phases; Thiothixene (Navane) affects erection and ejaculation; Trifluoperazine (Stelazine) interferes with orgasm/ejaculation. Priapism has been reported with Mellaril and spontaneous ejaculations with Stelazine. Navane has caused all of the above.

Chemotherapy

Most drugs used to combat cancer are either extremely toxic or have antihormonal effects. Depression, agitation, and fatigue, not to mention severe nausea and vomiting, are likely consequences of treatment for this disease. Often chemotherapy or radiation will damage the ovaries, bringing a woman into a premature menopause. Hormone-sensitive cancers—breast, ovarian, uterine, prostate—are usually treated with hormone-blocking agents, particularly antiandrogens, or by the removal of the affected gland. These therapies often result in loss of libido. Women with breast cancer are often treated with Tamoxifen, a drug that induces menopause with its low sex drive, vaginal atrophy, hot flashes, and mood swings. When that occurs, some women can be treated with testosterone, in the form of a cream topically applied directly to the vagina.

Men with prostate cancer are often treated with estrogenic drugs such as Diethylstilbestrol or GnRH Agonists like Lupron, and these can cause testicular atrophy and impotence. But again, there are alternatives. Other drugs found under the names Flutamide and Casodex (which is still experimental) do not have nearly the same effect on the libido or male potency.

GnRH Agonists

These drugs were first used as chemotherapeutic agents for prostate cancer. Today they have wider applications, especially for women suffering from endometriosis, uterine fibroids, and even PMS. These drugs are based on the polypeptide, gonadotropin-releasing hormone secreted by the hypothalamus. Normally this hormone stimulates the secretion of hormones in the pituitary, which causes maturation and release of eggs in women and sperm in men. When used in drug form, these functions are suppressed, causing a menopausal state in women and loss of sex drive. Lupron and Synarel are the drugs in this class now available.

Major side effects of these drugs are reduced sex drive, vaginal dryness, hot flashes, headaches, depression, and, if taken for more than six months, severe bone loss.

Before using GnRH agonists, be sure to ask your doctor about these side effects and the possibility of alternative treatment.

Female Hormones

Prolactin, the hormone that tells a new mother's breasts to produce milk, inhibits testosterone production, so drugs that increase prolactin have the effect of decreasing libido as well as causing breast enlargement in men and breast discharge in women. Antipsychotics in the phenothiazine family—Haldol, Thorazine, Stelazine, Mellaril—fall into this category. Antiemetics (drugs that prevent vomiting), such as Compazine and Phenergan also increase prolactin, as does Tagamet, a drug frequently prescribed for stomach ulcers and gastritis. Spironolactone, taken as a diuretic by either sex or for hirsuitism (excessive hair growth) in women, also may cause breast enlargement in men, irregular periods in women, and a lackluster libido in both.

Progesterone, one of the female sex hormones in birth control pills, also has an antiandrogen-like effect, resulting in low sex drive among women taking it. The birth-control pill can also provide too much or too little estrogen compared to the amount your body would normally produce. Talk to your doctor about finding exactly the right-dose pill for you. After all, the birth control pill is not supposed to work by turning you off sex altogether.

At the other end of the spectrum are fertility drugs: Clomid and Pergonal are two used to stimulate ovulation. Although both affect female hormones and may cause mood changes, neither are associated with any decrease in libido.

Anabolic Steroids

A lean, strong, muscular physique has become an ideal in our civilization, even for those with desk jobs. Our professional athletes compete in an atmosphere of "win or else," so it isn't surprising that men and women who enjoy amateur sports are tempted now and then to seek a little help from the medicine cabinet. This is especially true in the case of anabolic steroids, which are taken by thousands of people in order to build muscles.

Anabolic steroids are specific synthetic hormones that have a testosterone-like activity and masculinizing (androgenic) effects. They alter the body's metabolism. The most common are the 17-methyl-testosterone in oral form or testosterone ester in injectable form. They are used primarily by body builders and athletes to enhance strength and performance. When taken in traditional pharmacologic doses for a limited number of diseases, some side effects will occur. However, the doses used to increase muscle mass are 10 to 40 times that of standard dosage, which understandably results in greatly increased side effects, including liver disease, acne, and mood swings.

The use of anabolic steroids will very likely wreak havoc with your love life. Men can develop testicular atrophy, which eventually means destruction of the libido, loss of the ability to achieve an erection, and sterility. Women can lose body fat to the point at which their periods become irregular or stop. Women also run the risk of developing symptoms usually associated with the menopause, including lack of interest in sex, vaginal dryness, and, in some cases, bone loss. Heavy or extended use can cause masculinizing effects, including decreased breast size, baldness, hirsutism, deepening of the voice, and clitoral enlargement. These symptoms may not be reversible.

The message would seem to be clear: avoid steroids. Nonetheless, too many men and women persist in the chemical search for the body beautiful.

Instead of gambling with your health, read the chapter on herbs. You may find some safe, natural muscle-building alternatives there.

GHB

Until the FDA took it off the market because of its dangerous side effects, GHB—gamma hydroxy butyrate—was sold in health food stores. I mention it here because it is still available in Europe and under the counter in the U.S. GHB is a substance produced in the brain by the metabolism of the neurotransmitter gamma-aminobutyric acid, also known as GABA. GHB is active in the brain by increasing dopamine and affecting the endorphin system of the brain. Before being banned in the U.S., it was used as a sleeping pill and for its steroid-like ability to build muscle. It also stimulates the libido, probably because of its effects on dopamine. A man in his seventies whom I spoke with, suffering from vascular disease, took GHB and noticed a return of his morning erections, which had disappeared for many years following cardiac surgery.

Unfortunately GHB can be dangerous. For example, if taken in conjunction with alcohol, decreased respiration and coma can ensue. Dosage is weight-dependent: Lower doses of 10 mg for every kg of body weight can cause amnesia and muscle weakness; more than 50 mg per kg of body weight can induce coma or seizures. Nausea, vomiting, dizziness, confusion, and drowsiness have been reported. GHB must be taken with potassium to prevent severe headache.

GHB is illegal and emphatically not recommended as a cure for impotence and related problems.

Proscar

Proscar (Finasteride), manufactured by Merck and recently approved by the FDA for treatment of prostatic hypertrophy, is the first oral drug put on the market for this condition. It acts by blocking the conversion of testosterone to dihydrotesterone, a potent hormone that is thought to be responsible for the abnormal growth of the prostate (high levels of dihydrotestosterone may be related to cancers found in the enlarged prostate). Proscar may help prevent prostate cancer, but more research is needed. Proscar also lowers the prostatic specific antigen level, a blood screen used to detect possible prostate cancer, so the PSA should be checked before starting the drug. Proscar does not block testosterone, so it can be taken at little risk to the male libido.

Narcotics

OPIUM

Opium has been used for centuries and is still available in the Middle East and in Asia, although it is not as fashionable a drug in this country. Historically, it has been used to treat diarrhea, headaches, coughs, asthma, epilepsy, and snakebite. Today we use synthetic opiates for diarrhea, coughs, and, of course, for pain relief. All drugs derived from opium, whether natural or synthetic, including morphine, Demerol, Dilaudid, methadone, codeine, and Darvocet-N, are addictive and can have negative effects on all phases of arousal, erection, orgasm, and ejaculation. In small doses opiates cause decreases in sensation, which accounts for the reports of prolonged erections without ejaculation. In large doses, opium causes a hypnotic, dreamlike state in which the addict loses all interest in sex. Long-term abuse of opium seems to result in impotence.

HEROIN

Heroin (diacetylmorphine), which is synthesized from morphine, is also associated with loss of sexual energy, delayed ejaculation, and impotence as long as its use continues. Users report impotence within the first hours after injection, followed by increased desire and erection. This cycle usually ends with episodic premature ejaculations. We do not know the mechanism that causes these dysfunctions except for the fact that opiates such as heroin block the alpha-adrenergic system, which is responsible for the dilation of the blood vessels. This means that blood is shunted away from where it is needed for sexual arousal and satisfaction. Another downer.

CODEINE

Codeine is frequently prescribed as a cough suppressant. Among its known unpleasant side effects is hindering urination and orgasm. One of my patients was being treated for severe bronchitis with antibiotics and cough syrup containing hydrocodone, a synthetic codeine. She became anorgasmic, but the condition reversed itself after she stopped the medication. Another patient had persistent problems emptying her bladder until the drug was stopped. In most cases codeine will not interfere with sex, but you should tell your doctor if you suspect it is doing so.

Methaqualone

The false reputation of this drug (now illegal in the U.S.) as an aphrodisiac merits its inclusion in this book. It was sold under the brand names of Mandrax, Parest, Sopor, and, most widely known, Quaalude ('ludes or wallbangers on the street). Quaalude, that bogus aid to Eros so popular during the Vietnam war era, was released in 1965 and immediately became the stylish drug of abuse. It was eventually pulled from the pharmacists' shelves when its side effects were discovered. Quaalude consists of methaqualone combined with diphenhydramine, an antihistamine, and was marketed as a nonbarbiturate, nonaddictive (!) sleeping pill. The euphoria it induced before knocking out its users was the cause of its cult-like popularity.

Dubbed "heroin for lovers" by the respectable *Washington Post* in 1972, men often dosed reluctant girlfriends with Quaalude in order to make them "more relaxed." Researchers found, however, that Quaalude actually inhibited arousal and affected performance as well. It appeared that Quaalude's effectiveness in the bedroom was owing to its ability to lower inhibitions. The drug is addictive and can be fatal if taken with alcohol.

Miscellaneous Drugs

The following may cause sexual side effects: Diamox, a potent diuretic, is associated with suppressing desire and erection but not orgasm. Antabuse, used to dissuade alcoholics from imbibing by making them ill, may cause loss of erection and orgasm. Norpace, Mexitil, Digoxin, and Cordarone are cardiac medications used to treat congestive heart failure and cardiac arrhythmias. Norpace has caused loss of erection; Cordarone has caused loss of desire; and Digoxin and Mexitil have caused loss of desire and erection without inhibiting orgasm/ejaculation.

Fenfluramine and Masindol are appetite suppressants used to treat obesity, and have amphetamine-like effects. Fenfluramine causes loss of desire and erection; Masindol affects orgasm/ejaculation.

Current reports on the sexual effects of antibiotics show no specific inhibitory problems except for an antifungal drug called Nizoral and an antituberculosis medication called Ethionamide. Both are reported to inhibit erections. Interferon, used to treat hepatitis-C and other viral diseases, may interfere with desire and erections.

The anticonvulsants Dilantin and Mysoline are said to affect desire and erections; Tegretol reportedly affects only erectile problems. Neither interferes with ejaculation or orgasm.

And Now—Some Good News!

The list of drugs with unhappy sexual side effects may have sounded as though the pharmaceutical researchers spend their days inventing ways to keep you from enjoying sex. Nothing could be further from the truth. For example, an important recent discovery came when suffers from Parkinson's disease reported unexpected increases in their libido when being treated with L-Dopa. This gave researchers an indication that dopamine is an important neurotransmitter for mediating sexual arousal, and drugs that provoke the body's production of dopamine or mimic its effects have potential for the future.

Another substance, oxytocin, is also under investigation for its potential aphrodisiacal properties. A neuropeptide that is a precursor of hormones, oxytocin is secreted by the pituitary and is known to stimulate uterine contractions during delivery. Recent findings have indicated that small amounts are also released by both sexes during orgasm, and animal studies relate the intensity of maternal behavior to levels of oxytocin. These facts have led scientists to speculate that this may be the "love hormone."

While a pharmacological aphrodisiac pill or potion may still be years away, there are several classes of drugs already on the market that act as sexual boosters. Not without flaws by any means—like most drugs, these can have unwanted side effects—they nevertheless hold out the most hope that one day, perhaps within your lifetime, medical science will discover the perfect love potion!

SELIGILINE

Marketed under the names Eldepryl and Deprenyl, Seligiline is one of the most promising aphrodisiacal substances available today. Originally prescribed for Parkinson's disease, it proved dramatically effective in improving the quality of life for many people fighting that condition. Also an effective antidepressant, it is now being touted as an anti-aging agent and an aphrodisiac.

In an experiment with mice, Deprenyl appeared to increase their life span by 34 percent. In another study of male rats, aging rodents which were given Deprenyl were mounting females and ejaculating like youngsters. As of yet, no long-term studies have been conducted on humans, but a growing number of healthy people concerned with increasing their life-span and maintaining their sexual vigor are rushing to doctors for prescriptions. Anecdotal reports from Europe, Canada, and the United States seem to bear out claims that the drug does have aphrodisiacal properties.

At the recommended dosage of 5 milligrams taken twice weekly, there are remarkably few side effects, which is not the case with the higher doses used to treat Parkinson's. Nausea, dizziness, dry mouth, confusion, headache, abnormal movements, skin problems, heart palpitations, high or low blood pressure, agitation, and mood changes are all possible consequences, but in fifteen years of use for this purpose, there have been no reported deaths attributed to the drug.

BUPROPION

The generic name of the antidepressant Wellbutrin, Bupropion has been found to heighten libido and general sexual performance. In a test conducted before the drug hit the market a few years ago, 63 percent of subjects who were classified as sexually dysfunctional reported heightened libidos on Wellbutrin.

Although the drug shows promise in studies, Bupropion cannot be labeled a panacea for sexual difficulties for everyone. Because it is cleared from the body by the liver and kidneys, it should be used with caution by anyone who has problems with those organs. It is also not for people with a history of seizures or who at any time have suffered from eating disorders such as anorexia and bulimia, because there is a small risk that the drug may induce seizures in them. As of the present time, Bupropion is not being prescribed as a remedy for sexual problems. However, it is worth being aware of since there is such a close connection between depression and sexual doldrums, and Bupropion is one of the very few antidepressants that enhances rather than blocks libido.

ANDROGENS

Androgens are substances that induce masculinizing qualities. Numerous studies conducted on men and women show that the relationship between male sex hormones and sexual arousal is very clear. The equation is simple: When testosterone is low, libido is listless; when testosterone is replaced, the sex drive returns.

Postmenopausal women and some elderly men can experience testosterone deficiencies, and the remedy of choice is supplementation of the hormone by way of tablets or injection. In terms of strengthened libido, the results are dramatic. Women may have to watch for side effects including an enlarged clitoris, increased hair growth, acne, and irregular periods. Additionally, both sexes could also suffer side effects ranging from water retention to jaundice, even cancer of the liver, and, in men, cancer of the prostate.

Women have a choice: They can get their testosterone in a cream applied to the vagina. The benefit here is that the small amounts used go directly into the vaginal tissue instead of passing through the digestive tract and liver. Estra-Test, a drug recently marketed for menopausal women, has also proven successful in replacing testosterone and estrogen in women who suffer from a depressed libido. Estra-Test comes in different strengths. It can be taken in small doses two to three times a week to prevent side effects. Your doctor is the best person to determine if you are a good candidate. The use of DHEA may be a way to supplement and support testosterone levels as we age.

VASOPRESSIN

Vasopressin (Diapid) is an antidiuretic hormone that regulates electrolytes, urine volume, and blood pressure in high doses. Recently, Vasopressin has been shown to increase the ability to incorporate new information in the brain and is now thought of as the "brain hormone." Vasopressin research with animals has shown that it facilitates memory retention, reverses amnesia, and protects against memory loss caused by chemical or physical injury. Since the initial animal research, Vasopressin has been studied in healthy volunteers and showed measurable increases in learning ability and memory. One of the side effects reported by Durk Pearson and Sandy Shaw in their book *Life Extension* is prolonged orgasm. Drug companies also report an increase in potency, though to date little hard information is available.

YOCON

Yocon is a preparation made from yohimbine hydrochloride, containing 5.4 milligrams of compressed yohimbe, a powerful West African herb. This pharmacological version is recommended for impotent men, but doctors are finding that it is successful in only about one-third of cases. Its side effects include nausea, dizziness, irritability, tremors, and elevated blood pressure; it should not be used by the elderly or people with gastric or duodenal ulcers.

Social Drugs

In every known culture human beings have managed to find some substance to smoke, swallow, or sniff in an effort to alter consciousness. The attempts to expand the mind, to experience life a little more fully, to get closer to God, have been as rigorous a pursuit as the quest to find the perfect aphrodisiac. That the two coincide is hardly surprising.

Today, people usually reach for a recreational drug when they want to perk up their love lives. However, tobacco and alcohol are the only two legal recreational drugs in the U.S. As a result, many medical researchers cynically attribute the aphrodisiacal qualities of the remaining—illegal—drugs to the fact that those who use them tend to be more sexually adventurous than the norm. To this add the fact that illegal drugs are usually taken in an intimate setting that is designed to heighten arousal. The skeptical researchers are partially correct, but they do not tell the entire story, for the erotic effects of recreational drugs also depend heavily on physiology.

TOBACCO

Tobacco is the most widely used addictive substance in the world. It is indigenous to North America, and in Native American cultures tobacco is sacred, used as an offering and in pipe ceremonies mixed with herbs. Only after tobacco was introduced into Europe in the 1500s did it become widely popular as an "everyday" narcotic.

From the time it was first exported, tobacco has been the subject of debate as to its effect on the libido. At one time, Turkey deemed smoking a death-penalty offense; the Sultan believed that it was making his subjects infertile. And at various times through the ages, Catholic priests have been encouraged to smoke to dampen incipient ardor. On the other hand, colonists in Virginia believed that tobacco must be an aphrodisiac because they equated the male natives' smoking with their propensity for having more than one woman.

The active ingredient in tobacco is nicotine, a highly addictive substance. Research has shown that the chances a first-time cigarette smoker will become hooked on nicotine are nine out of ten. Nicotine is rapidly absorbed from the lungs into the bloodstream after inhalation: The body extracts about 0.2 milligrams from each cigarette smoked, which impacts on both the sympathetic and parasympathetic nervous systems.

This is why smoking leads to the apparently paradoxical results of being both relaxing and stimulating. Nicotine mimics the neurotransmitter acetylcholine and causes the release of epinephrine from the adrenal glands. The result is a slackening of the skeletal muscles, which causes the initial sensation of relaxation. But then the nicotine has an overall stimulating effect by increasing the heart rate and blood pressure. Finally, nicotine constricts the blood vessels, and the resulting decrease in circulation impairs blood flow to the genital area for a decline in sexual performance. Long-term tobacco use, whether it is in the form of cigarettes, cigars, pipes, or for chewing, damages your health by increasing your risk for heart disease and cancer. Tobacco smoking accelerates the process of atherosclerosis, or hardening of the arteries, one of the causes of physiological impotence. If you want to have a healthy sex life into your later years, don't smoke!

The same can be said if you want to have healthy babies. Scientific studies of nicotine and male fertility are not totally conclusive, although there is some consensus that heavy smoking reduces sperm motility. In women, however, the effects on the reproductive system have been substantiated. Nicotine inhibits the release of some hormones, and higher incidences of infertility are reported among women who smoke. Female smokers generally go through menopause earlier than those who have never smoked. Cigarette smoking also affects the cervix, with increased rates of cervical dysplasia and cervical cancer among smokers. Smoking during pregnancy also can result in stunted growth of the fetus. More good reasons not to smoke.

ALCOHOL

Alcohol has a much longer history than tobacco. In literature and philosophy, its reputation as an aphrodisiac has gotten mixed reviews. Aristotle and Plutarch shrewdly discerned that heavy drinkers were not great lovers. Other writers have damned alcohol as the root of all sexual sins, particularly wanton fornication and adultery. A Greek poet came closest to the truth when he wrote, "The best measure of wine is neither much nor very little . . . 'tis most suited for the bridal chamber and love. And if it breathe too fiercely, it puts Love to flight. And plunges men in a sleep."

This observation is right on the mark: Research has shown that alcohol's aphrodisiacal properties are dose related. A little alcohol can release inhibitions, make you relaxed and euphoric, but larger amounts cause depression, loss of coordination, agitation, and a decrease in sexual performance. Chronic use is even worse, triggering hormonal changes that hinder sexual responsiveness.

Alcohol is absorbed primarily from the intestine, and the body takes about an hour to metabolize one ounce. A drink taken with a meal will take a little longer, for food slows the absorption of alcohol into the bloodstream. When you consume more than an ounce in an hour, alcohol accumulates in your blood, fat, and organs because your liver, which breaks down 95 percent of alcohol, cannot metabolize it as fast as you can drink it. After three drinks, it's more difficult for you to become aroused, and with even higher blood-alcohol levels (100 milligrams or more), excitement and ejaculation can be obstructed. The suppressive effect of alcohol is thought to be due to impairment of spinal reflexes, causing decreased sensation and nerve response. Studies also show that alcohol lowers serum testosterone even in the short term. Chronic alcohol users have lower libidos than the occasional drinker due to permanently decreased testosterone levels that occur as a result of injury to the liver and possibly also malnutrition since many alcoholics stop eating.

Women and alcohol are embroiled in a mythology all of their own. Through the ages, drink has been perceived as a powerful female aphrodisiac. In ancient Rome, "good" women were prohibited from drinking wine because it was thought that it would make them lascivious.

Our own popular culture is rife with clichéd scenarios of Don Juans trying to get a woman into bed by plying her with drink: "Candy is dandy but liquor is quicker." Woman's susceptibility to alcohol has been attributed to generally smaller body weight and higher percentage of body fat, which can increase blood levels of alcohol. In recent years scientists have discovered that women produce smaller amounts than men of a gastric enzyme that helps metabolize alcohol.

So women *do* tend to get drunk more easily. But do they become more aroused? This cliché has also come under scrutiny. Two studies found that when women drank, they reported an increase in the sensations of arousal, but a decrease in physical responsiveness—a result that parallels what we know about how alcohol affects men. Researchers tend to believe that the aphrodisiacal properties of alcohol have as much to do with social mores as anything else: In our society, it is more acceptable to be uninhibited if you've downed a few. A glass of wine or a cocktail may, under the right circumstances, put a woman in a sultry mood. But women should be aware that the more they drink, the less pleasure they are likely to feel.

Alcohol is a danger for women if taken chronically. It can have a toxic effect on the ovaries and abate the hypothalamus-pituitary release of hormones, thus causing infertility. Women alcoholics usually have an earlier menopause compared to the general population. The dangers of heavy drinking while pregnant have been thoroughly documented. Alcohol can compromise the well-being and development of the fetus and increase a woman's risk of miscarrying.

MARIJUANA

Marijuana—pot—known also by its botanical name, *Cannibis sativa*, has for centuries had a remarkable worldwide history as a medicine and an aphrodisiac. Five thousand years ago, Chinese emperor Shen Nung—known as "the wise healer"—made the earliest written record of the therapeutic properties of the hemp plant. The Hindus have used it since 1000 B.C., and marijuana is a common ingredient in aphrodisiac formulae prescribed in Ayurvedic medicine. Ayurveda—the "knowledge of life span" in Sanskrit—is a 5,000-year-old system of mind/body medicine that has recently been winning converts in the West. Marijuana has a place in Tantric practices, too. References to its effect on sexuality is described in the *Arabian Nights*, where it is credited with inducing a state of arousal. In Africa, a popular aphrodisiac is made from marijuana and resins, and smoking *ganja* is an integral part of the Rastafarian religion in Jamaica among people of African descent. The ancient Greeks were divided on the subject. Dioscorides advised using the juice of marijuana seed for treating low libido, but Galen and Pliny wrote that too much juice could bring on impotence.

The drug's more recent history is no less controversial. One hundred years ago marijuana was often prescribed by doctors for women suffering from menstrual problems. In 1852 clinical trials in England confirmed what folk-medicine practitioners had known for years: Marijuana expedited childbirth by strengthening contractions and shortening labor. Anecdotal evidence exists that George Washington and Thoreau used marijuana. As unlikely a source as Louisa May Alcott, author of *Little Women*, once wrote that hashish was an aphrodisiac. Also, when cannibis fell from grace this century, its downfall was due largely to its reputation as lust-inducing. During the "reefer madness" climate of the 1930s, ignorant persons accused marijuana of inciting "deviant" behavior such as premarital, interracial, or homosexual unions. Unfortunately, contemporary official attitudes have not changed that much.

Most contemporary studies conducted among both men and women reveal that they experience an increase in sexual pleasure with marijuana use. One 1977 survey conducted at the Haight-Ashbury Free Medical Clinic in San Francisco reported that marijuana was the drug cited as being the one most often chosen "to make sex better." The active ingredient in marijuana, tetrahydrocannabinol (THC), induces relaxation, euphoria, short-term memory impairment, distortion of time, and heightened sensory perception. With greater doses these effects are enhanced and hallucinations can occur. Some people, however, can experience extreme anxiety or even paranoia on pot. Few studies have been conducted on the physiological mechanisms of marijuana in connection with sexuality. Much of its reputation as an aphrodisiac is attributed by experts to the fact that the user's perception of time slowing down leads, in turn, to a perception of extended lovemaking. Others credit heightened tactile sensitivity for increasing sexual pleasure.

We do have more data on the drug's impact on the endocrine system. Female hormones do not appear to be affected much by marijuana. Male hormones are more susceptible to the drug. A study conducted on mice measured a rapid sustained increase in testosterone when administered low doses of THC. With higher doses there is a rise in testosterone, followed by a decrease to below starting levels. Chronic use also depresses testosterone, although it rebounds to normal levels after the user quits. So, an occasional joint may increase sexual pleasure, but heavy or long-term use will adversely affect the libido.

Unfortunately, marijuana, which many doctors and some lawmakers believe to be the most benign of psychoactive drugs, is not available legally in the United States. Penalties for possession range from a misdemeanor fine in states such as California to felony convictions with brutal twenty-five-year prison terms handed out by judges in Texas. In some countries marijuana is prescribed for illnesses such as glaucoma and asthma. Here, the only medical indication for using the drug is to control nausea and increase the appetite of patients with AIDS or those receiving chemotherapy for cancer. Even in these instances, the federal government has recently cracked down on accepting new patients into the program because it was decided that there are other viable legal alternatives.

COCAINE

Cocaine was labeled an aphrodisiac by the *conquistadores* when they discovered that the natives of what is now Peru seemed to be indecently lusty and also inclined to chew on the mildly stimulating leaves of the coca bush. The far more potent white crystalline powder we know today as cocaine was first extracted from the coca plant in the 1860s. It immediately gained widespread popularity in the U.S. as an ingredient in patent medicines—elixirs that were used primarily as stimulants but also on occasion to enhance desire. Cocaine is a central-nervous-system stimulant, as is crack, the highly concentrated form of cocaine that is smoked. Although cocaine has a street reputation as an aphrodisiac, it could eventually ruin your love life. Cocaine makes its adepts feel sexy or euphoric or both by preventing the body from reabsorbing dopamine, thus helping to build up the neurotransmitter that is largely responsible for desire and excitement. Those who inject, rather than sniff or smoke coke, report spontaneous erections and multiple orgasms. There are chronic users who have learned to prefer the cocaine rush to sexual union, and some long-time addicts have eliminated the body's production of dopamine altogether, thus destroying the sexual drive.

The side effects of cocaine far outweigh its pleasures. Why risk high blood pressure, sexual dysfunction, heart attacks, seizures, and even strokes? Pregnant women and their babies are especially vulnerable. Cocaine has been linked to miscarriages, premature labor, birth defects, and low birth weight. Complications continue after the baby is born. Cocaine or crack babies can be born addicted, and are more at risk for sudden infant death syndrome—crib death. When these babies survive, they often suffer from behavioral difficulties.

Cocaine is more addictive psychologically than physically. Recurrent use will cause depression, anxiety, and even psychosis.

Not the ideal love potion!

AMPHETAMINES

Amphetamines—"speed"—are among the most powerful stimulants known. They exist as respectable prescription drugs but are also available on the street in pill form for thrill-seekers. Familiar trade names are Dexedrine ("dexies"), Benzedrine ("bennies"), and Methedrine. Often used as in the 1950s and 1960s as a stay-awake substance and widely prescribed as a dieting aid up to the early 1980s, amphetamines are now rarely used for these purposes because of their psychologically addictive properties and dangerous side effects.

A version of methamphetamine is cooked up in back-alley amateur laboratories and peddled on the street as "crystal-meth" or "crank." Users often inject this poison to get a euphoric rush and a burst of energy. Amphetamines in low doses can increase desire but may also cause delayed ejaculation and delayed orgasm. High doses completely inhibit orgasm and in the long term will result in reversible impotence. Amphetamines can damage the nervous system and cause extreme mood swings, irritability, and depression.

Also not the ideal love potion.

Hallucinogens

Hallucinogens, or psychedelics, create illusions by distorting sensory perceptions. Dozens of hallucinogenic substances occur in nature and for centuries have been used in religious rituals as a means to attain higher levels of spiritual consciousness. Plants such as the peyote cactus, psilocybin mushrooms, and yage produce visions by altering levels of neurotransmitters. Most hallucinogenic compounds available now are synthetically produced, but they resemble the substances that occur in nature. Mescaline, the active chemical found in the peyote cactus, has been synthesized and was researched by the United States Chemical Warfare group in the 1950s. First synthesized in 1938, lysergic acid diethyamide (LSD) is found naturally in ergot, a fungus that grows on rye and other grains. During the drug revolution of the 1960s, man-made hallucinogenic drugs became widely available on street corners in every American city and were used to such an extent that for the first time researchers had the opportunity to study the drugs' effects on sexuality.

LSD

LSD—"acid"—probably the best-known hallucinogen, is believed to exert its effects because of its structural similarity to serotonin. Although LSD was rumored to create birth defects by altering chromosomes, I believe this danger was exaggerated. The drug can be a valuable tool when used in psychotherapeutic situations and especially in dealing with sexual problems.

In his book *Beyond the Brain*, Stanislav Grof describes the benefits of LSD in producing profound sexual changes in patients undergoing psychotherapy. According to Grof, LSD enables users to reach deep into the subconscious, wherein lie experiences of death and rebirth that reflect levels of the mind that he calls Basic Perinatal Matrices. Within these matrices are the emotional and psychosomatic principles that affect each individual. Grof found that emotional disturbances interfering with sexual functioning are often linked to images of archetypes or animal symbols in the subconscious. With LSD therapy, patients were able to "access" these images in the subconscious and to resolve whatever is inhibiting them sexually.

As an added benefit, patients using LSD experience an expansion in their concept of orgasm. They reported discovering that orgasm is not an all-or-nothing phenomenon, but that there are many degrees of sexual satisfaction and release. Grof reported that those who experienced a freedom from the obsession with issues of self-esteem and control were able to reach greater levels of spirituality in relationship to their sexuality. Since therapeutic use of LSD was made impossible by its classification as a Schedule I drug, Grof has turned to the use of a breathing technique that has a similar "altered state" effect.

LSD continues to be prohibited from study in universities due to its potential for abuse. As an aphrodisiac, acid has its drawbacks. Although it may increase sensations of pleasure and empathy with your partner, there can be difficulties in maintaining erection or reaching orgasm. Some people may experience paranoia, confusion, and disorientation—the fabled, frightening "bad trip"—resulting from tapping into the subconscious, as well as flashbacks long after the actual experience. LSD is powerful medicine and is not recommended for casual use.

MDA

MDA (3,4-methylene-dioxyamphetamine), known on the street as the love drug, although a hallucinogen is in the same chemical class as amphetamines. The military tried MDA in the 1950s as a possible truth serum. Later, researchers explored it as an appetite suppressant. Like LSD, MDA has been used as a psychotherapeutic tool in research settings. In studies conducted among drug-culture casualties at the Haight-Ashbury Free Medical Clinic in the 1970s, MDA was rated highly as a drug to "make sex better." This may be because of the increased sense of intimacy that many people feel under its influence. After taking 128 milligrams, renowned chemist and author Alexander Shulgin said, "the tactile sense is beautiful . . . (but) nothing erotic would be do-able. Intimacy, yes, but no performance." Although it is credited with increasing sensual pleasure and prolonging sexual activity, MDA has been generally reported to decrease the desire for orgasm, with a small group claiming just the reverse—that it causes multiple orgasms. The effects of the drug vary greatly according to the dosage, method of administration, and the individual, with occasional users apparently experiencing more pronounced sexual benefits than regular devotees. MDA is toxic at high doses. One death was reported in 1953 when a psychiatric patient was given a 500-milligram intravenous dose of MDMA, a synthetic version of MDA.

MDMA

MDMA, better known as ecstasy, is currently a fashionable recreational drug, especially on college campuses. MDMA is no longer used in experimental psychotherapy and has been placed in the "most-restricted" category under the Federal Controlled Substances Act because of its potential to damage serotonergic nerves. Even in recreational doses, ecstasy can cause unpleasant side effects, such as teeth clenching and abnormal eye movements. Ecstasy is presumably so popular because it creates a sense of euphoria and well-being, but as an aphrodisiac it falls short of the promise implicit in its name. This clone performs similarly to MDA—generating extended periods of arousal but with an impaired ability to reach orgasm.

PHENCYCLIDINE

PCP is another psychedelic available on the street. "Angel dust" was originally a respectable anesthetic but is no longer used for this purpose because of its hallucinogenic and stimulating side effects, which kick in at doses of about 20 milligrams. At lower doses, up to 10 milligrams, PCP has more pleasing outcomes, such as euphoria and feelings of weightlessness. But—and this is a big but—even at low doses there is a danger of vomiting, depression, disorientation, agitation, panic, and paranoia. "Dusted" individuals are well known to the police as being particularly violent and difficult to control. Sexual enhancement under this drug has more to do with lowered inhibitions than with increased libido.

AMYL NITRITE

Nitrites were used medically starting in the 1800s for patients with angina pectoris, severe chest pain caused by constriction of blood vessels in the heart. They are no longer prescribed for that purpose. Few studies have been conducted, but amyl nitrite is commonly used to enhance sexual pleasure, especially in the gay community. Small glass bottles of the black-market substance are "popped" and inhaled just before orgasm in order to prolong and magnify the feeling.

Nitrites cause dilation of blood vessels and relax the muscles in the genital area, resulting in warmth and increased sensitivity. They also loosen the anal sphincter muscle, perhaps accounting for the drug's popularity among people who practice anal sex. But "pop" too soon and the amyl nitrite can wilt an erection.

Some users also experience unpleasant side effects, such as nausea, dizziness, headache, and light-headedness.

Buyer Beware!

No drug, legal or otherwise, has been the perfect love potion, but you can be sure that plenty of people are going to continue experimenting with drugs in the never-ending search for heaven on earth—the brief paradise of sexual bliss. Though this could change, the possibility of arrest and conviction is not the only risk involved. Because street drugs are illegal, there is no quality control. The substances are not always what they are said to be, and the sellers aren't going to give you any money-back guarantee that their product will produce the desired effects and not something nasty and unexpected. He or she may have diluted the product in such a way that it is useless or dangerous, and you obviously have no legal recourse if you land in the hospital.

If you take the chemical road to heightened sexual pleasure, use plenty of caution and common sense.

6

EXERCISE AND OTHER PLEASURES OF THE FLESH

Sex is first of all a matter of energy. The more energy you have, the more blissful you can be, and the better sex becomes.
—MARGO ANAND

The strength to support the weight of your lover, the endurance to maintain a rhythm that carries you and your partner to the sexual heights, the suppleness that allows you to experiment with different positions—all these help make good sex great.

They are not the exclusive property of athletes. They are the logical and inevitable result of *regular physical exercise,* one of the most efficient, easy, and least-expensive of the aphrodisiacs.

There are two distinct but not mutually exclusive ways to apply exercise to sexuality. The Western approach is to emphasize the physical. Those brawny guys sweating and grunting under barbells in the gym or the nimble women in aerobics classes may not have sex on their conscious minds, but on another level they believe that their workouts will make them more attractive to potential partners. They may be enjoying their workout for the sensual pleasure of movement, the flexing and pumping, the feel of blood coursing through their veins, and the thrill of competition. Those who exercise feel more fit, cheerful, and youthful; they especially appreciate what their increased strength and stamina can do for them in bed.

In the East, the principal goal of exercise is often to achieve more prolonged sex. Lovemaking is commonly regarded as sacred; its purpose is physical bliss but also mental, emotional, and spiritual well-being. And exercise is considered a celebration of the self.

The Eastern approach is becoming more popular in the West. Classes in such ancient disciplines as Hatha and Tantric yoga, tai chi, and Taoist exercises are available in most communities today, and excellent books on Eastern ways to ecstasy are available should you wish to explore the subject. Either the Eastern or the Western approach may suit you better, but a combination of the two is probably the best.

The Western Approach

The evidence that regular exercise makes for better sex is well documented. Linda De Villers, Ph.D., a sex therapist and psychologist in Santa Monica, polled 8,000 women nationwide. She discovered that of those who did some type of aerobic activity on a regular basis, 25 percent felt heightened sexual desire after working out; 40 percent were more easily aroused; 31 percent had sex more often; and 25 percent reached orgasm more quickly. A study conducted by Dr. James White, of the University of California at San Diego, showed similar results: Middle-aged men who worked out consistently were considerably more lusty than their sedentary brothers. They had a greater sex drive, became aroused more often, and had more orgasms. A Harvard study revealed that exercise particularly benefits people past the first bloom of youth: In terms of frequency and enjoyment, over-forty swimmers had the sex lives of men and women in their twenties. Various running, cycling, and swimming organizations report identical findings from their members.

Exercise makes you feel sexy because you are a physical creature: Your body is designed to thrive on movement. Like a machine that has been left idle for months, the sedentary body becomes "rusty" and difficult to crank up. Physical activity keeps every system tuned: The musculoskeletal infrastructure operates smoothly; the endocrine and digestive systems are balanced; even the complexion often takes on a dewy, youthful glow.

Regular exercise also helps control weight. In bygone times, fat was associated with abundance and fertility and consequently was desirable. But unlike eras when a Rubenesque figure was irresistible, this is an age in which people simply do not consider themselves desirable with excess poundage. Not since the ancient Greeks held the athletic physique as a moral ideal has a society made such demands on its members to hone their bodies. If you have no health problems and feel comfortable and confident being on the plump side, that's fine. Many people relish the voluptuous form. But some people don't want to be seen undressed, or be touched, or indulge in erotic play until they reach a socially acceptable weight. For them, intimacy is more appealing when they feel attractive. On the other hand, a weight gain might signal a problem in the relationship. There are men and women who use weight to desexualize themselves and act as a buffer between them and their mates. In dealing with your weight, you will also be forced to deal with any underlying relationship or sexual difficulties.

Sticking to a regular workout program does long-term good by preventing age-related muscle atrophy and bone loss. Researchers once believed that only weight-bearing exercises such as walking or running helped combat osteoporosis, the progressive thinning and weakening of bones. Recent studies show that other forms of exercise—for instance cycling or weight lifting—are just as effective in combating this debilitating condition. The force transmitted to bones when their surrounding muscles are used builds more bone, much as muscles grow strong when used. Healthy muscles and bones keep a body youthful, strong, and sexy throughout life.

Life in the fast lane can be stimulating and fun. But, on the downside, contemporary living is almost always stressful and fatiguing, which often puts a damper on the libido. Regular exercise defuses stress and, because energy begets energy, it counteracts mental and physical tiredness. At the Institute for

Aerobic Research, in Dallas, studies were conducted on people who complained of chronic fatigue. As the participants' cardiovascular fitness increased, their levels of fatigue decreased. However, some people with severe cases of chronic fatigue become worse with physical exercise. More recently this has been thought to be related to an irregular breathing pattern. If you have this problem, check with your physician before beginning any exercise program.

Anxiety and depression are sexual killjoys. A vigorous workout helps banish the blues by triggering the release of beta-endorphins, the body's natural "feel-good" opiates. And the self-confidence that comes with gaining mastery over our own bodies not only engenders robust sensuality, but is also powerfully alluring.

An exercise program that will get you in shape to better please yourself and your partner or partners requires four things: *specific exercises* for men and women that develop the muscles used during sex, *aerobic exercises, resistance training,* and *stretching.*

This might sound like too much to fit into a busy schedule, but don't worry—about four hours a week will do the job. Taking this modest amount of time will very likely pay off in the bedroom.

Kegel Exercises

Kegel exercises are some of the simplest but most effective exercises you can do specifically to increase sexual pleasure. These tone the pubococcygeus (PC) muscles around the genital area. The system was developed in the late 1940s by Los Angeles gynecologist Arnold Kegel, primarily to help older patients suffering from incontinence. As a positive side effect, many of these women reported that they were able to achieve orgasm more easily. That is hardly surprising, since the women were exercising the very muscles that contract during orgasm. Today these exercises are recommended for both sexes to gain greater sexual control and satisfaction. They employ the same principle as a body builder "pumping up" his or her biceps. The better toned the PC muscles, the more they expand and the greater the flow of blood to genitals during lovemaking. A woman can flex these muscles around a man's penis for additional enjoyment, and a man can control his erection by tightening them to increase arousal and delay ejaculation.

The PC muscles form the pelvic floor between the legs. Both sexes can identify them by trying to stop a flow of urine. To achieve the desired effect, women should do this with their legs apart so that they do not clamp their thighs together. You will find that you are drawing upward with your pelvis and will also feel a tightening around your anus. The exercises are simple, based on the above sensation. The beauty of Kegel exercises is that you can perform them almost anywhere: sitting at a desk, in the subway, standing on line, watching television. There's no reason why you cannot do the following set of exercises as often as five times a day. Women can check their progress from time to time by slipping a finger into the vagina to monitor the change in pressure.

Pumps. Squeeze the PC muscle as described above. Hold for three seconds, relax for three seconds, and repeat. Do as many as you can at first, working up to 30 three-second squeezes at a time.

Pulses. Squeeze and relax the PC muscle as fast as possible in a fluttering motion. Start with 10 and work up to 30 at a time.

Bear-Downs. Bear down gently as though trying to have a bowel movement. You may find that you engage your abdominal muscles for this variation. As with clenches, hold and release for three seconds at a time. Work up to a set of 30.

Aerobics

In the last ten years, aerobic exercise has become a worldwide fitness craze. Activities like brisk walking, running, swimming, cycling, jumping rope, cross-country skiing, and aerobic dancing, not to mention gyms full of high-tech exercycles, treadmills, and rowing machines have allowed millions to experience the elation of invigorating physicality. The payoff is a svelte, healthy, vibrant body.

The first big benefit gained from aerobics is weight loss. Aerobic activities, if done with intensity, burn off more calories than any other form of exercise. Aerobics step up the metabolic rate as much as 25 percent, not only during the workout, but for some hours afterward. This means you can lose weight more efficiently than by simply limiting food intake. Furthermore, the weight lost will be all fat and not lean muscle, which is partially what you lose on a low-calorie diet. Exercise actually builds muscle mass, and that's just fine, because muscle tissue is a calorie-burner. As you decrease your percentage of body fat and increase your muscle through exercise, your body becomes slimmer and firmer. Most people do not notice an immediate difference on the scale, since muscle is heavier than fat, but your tape measure and the fit of your clothes will testify to the fact that you are trimming down. Oddly enough, you will find that you are eating less. It is a myth that exercise stimulates appetite. On the contrary, aerobic exercise raises levels of blood sugar, serotonin, and adrenaline, all of which are appetite suppressants; you feel less hungry for as many as six hours after a hard workout.

Aerobics is the only sure way to improve and maintain an optimum level of cardiovascular fitness. Done regularly, it can increase blood volume so that your body transports oxygen better, resulting in increased stamina in every area of physical endeavor, including lovemaking. Lung capacity increases and the heart muscle grows stronger. The ratio of high-density lipoprotein (HDL)—the "good guy" in the cholesterol battle—increases and you are better equipped to ward off heart disease. Combating the atherosclerosis that results from too much "bad" cholesterol has an added sexual bonus for men: Better blood flow means harder erections.

To gain these benefits, it is important to work out to maximum capacity. The best way to gauge if you are doing that is to monitor your pulse. To determine your conditioning pulse rate, subtract your age from 220, then multiply that number first by

70 percent, then by 85 percent. Thus, if you are 30 years old, your working heart rate range is between 133 and 161. (220 minus 30 = 190. Times .70 = 133. Times .85 = 161.) If you are just starting out or are not in peak physical condition, aim for a working heart rate at the low end. Fit people can aim for—but should not exceed—the higher number. To take your heart rate, lightly place your index and middle fingers on the pulse in your neck: count for 15 seconds and multiply by 4. To become aerobically fit, you need to exercise at your target heart rate on a consistent basis. Once a week or less will not better your condition and may even prove harmful since your heart is put under stress each time. Twenty minutes three times a week is a minimum for maintaining good condition, while four or five times weekly will foster weight loss and reflect marked improvement in your overall fitness. Thereafter, if you want to improve your conditioning benefits, lengthen your workout to thirty minutes or more.

It is not advisable, however, to do the same aerobic activity every day. Each time you exercise your muscles they are slightly injured. They need forty-eight hours between heavy workouts to heal so as not to cause more permanent damage. Sore, tired muscles that make you flinch every time you move make your workout regimen self-defeating and are hardly conducive to satisfactory lovemaking. Should you choose to exercise every day, vary your routines so that you use a different set of muscles. Switch between, say, a low-impact aerobic dance class, swimming, and cycling. Find activities that are stimulating and irresistible, and the feeling they engender will carry over to every area of your life, including your sex life.

Aerobic activities, when done with energy and enthusiasm, are strenuous. If you are over thirty-five and have not been exercising regularly, are overweight, smoke, or have back or heart problems, see your doctor before starting a program. Then, when you start, if you feel any stress in your joints or lower back; get pains in your chest, arms, shoulders, or neck; or feel nauseated or dizzy, you are overdoing it. Slow down and work at your own pace. You will be amazed at how quickly your conditioning improves from session to session—and with that overall conditioning, your sexual vigor.

As you get more fit, don't make the mistake of believing that more is better. Aerobics have been said to be addictive. Some people become so obsessed that they reach a state of chronic fatigue or "overtraining," and sustain painful overuse injuries. All of which defeats the object. Furthermore, you don't want to *substitute* exercise for sex.

Women have an additional factor to take into account. Their greater percentage of body fat is believed to be nature's way of enabling them to carry and nourish a baby. When, through aerobics or diet, a woman lowers her body fat to a point where that capability is jeopardized, the delicate interaction been the sex hormones and the brain is thrown off balance, and she may suffer from amenorrhea—the cessation of menstruation. A consistent program of *moderate* exercise, however, is, for many women, the perfect antidote to debilitating periodic pain.

Coming on Strong

For the truly sexually fit body, you need to supplement your aerobic workouts with strength—or resistance—training. One form is isometrics, which involves using the body's own weight as resistance: for example leg lifts, push-ups, chin-ups, and sit-ups. The other method is weight lifting. The idea is to tone and define muscles to give your body a sleek look or build up those parts of your body that are underdeveloped or out of proportion.

For those areas that you want to contour, you should use light weights and two to three sets of about 15 repetitions with a thirty-second break between sets. For body parts you want to build, you would use higher poundage and only 8 to 10 repetitions per set. The exciting thing about using weights is that you can see noticeable results in a short time. Don't, however, be tempted to rush out and buy a set of dumbbells or an expensive home weight machine before you know what you are doing. To avoid the risk of injury, do your initial weight training under competent supervision. Most health clubs and Y's have training equipment and facilities, and a membership is well worth the investment if you are serious about wanting to get in shape. As with aerobics, give your muscles time off to recoup between workouts: Three times a week is sufficient to get results. You can, however, do isometric exercises every day.

The idea that strength is sexy is nothing new—if you're a man. Some women still tend to harbor myths about weight training, the most common being that if they pump iron they will end up looking like a heavyweight body builder. This simply is not biologically possible; the vast majority don't have sufficient quantities of necessary male hormones to build muscle mass. By working with weights, women can achieve lean, well-defined, strong bodies. When it comes to sex, a woman's lack of strength can sentence her to being the weaker half. But a strong woman is a match for a strong man; both will take pleasure in her increased physical prowess.

Stretching

Stretching is an important adjunct to any exercise program. For well-balanced fitness, supplement the cardiovascular endurance and strength with flexibility. Stretching after your other workouts will help prevent "next-day soreness," decrease incidents of pulled muscles and tendons, and promote a greater range of motion and better development in your weight training. Not only that, stretching helps you relax mentally and physically, and it feels good too. Gentle stretching can make you more flexible and youthful. Yoga that involves a lot of stretching is a great way to stay limber.

Don't bounce or stretch until it hurts. Gentle, slow, and sustained stretching releases and lengthens the muscles. Begin by holding the stretch for 5 seconds and build to 30 seconds. At first you'll feel impossibly rigid. But don't hold on to the negative perception that "this is uncomfortable and I'll stand it for just a few more seconds." Your muscles will detect your tension and stiffen. Melt into the stretch and become aware of your muscles being energized. This way they will "let go" because you are giving them a positive message. Stretching is something you can do every day, and you needn't limit it to *après* workout. Imitate cats and dogs—stretch languidly a dozen times a day. Your flexibility will improve dramatically, and you'll be delighted to find how youthful and sensual a supple body feels.

The Eastern Approach

In the ancient cultures of countries such as China, Japan, India and Nepal, the act of love has long been deemed as deserving of scrutiny and practice, and to the Western way of thinking is remarkably uninhibited. Eastern wisdom holds that personal development is incomplete without an understanding of the sexual principles that form the basis of human existence. To that end, Taoist and Tantric masters developed exercises that developed sexual potential and helped attain sexual bliss. Some were designed to return energy to the hypothalamus, pituitary, and pineal glands in the brain to help keep the sex glands functioning and to retard the aging process. These are sometimes called neuroglandular exercises and were designed to help royalty maintain their youth and vitality. Although science has yet to prove that this type of exercise can directly stimulate glands, it is true that sexual activity keeps hormones flowing. Men exposed to provocative pictures have demonstrated measurable increases in testosterone levels, and women who are sexually active after menopause will continue to produce estrogen and maintain vaginal tissues. So if these exercises encourage you to have sex more frequently, they have the indirect effect of increasing hormone production. There are exercises that emphasize breathing as a way of releasing and circulating subtle energies in a precise way. Others strengthen the body for various lovemaking positions. Here are some handpicked exercises that will ignite your sex life if practiced on a daily basis. Some are best done alone, others need a sensitive partner.

The Tao of Loving

Love and sex have always been an important and integral part of the Taoist philosophy—the ancient Chinese firmly believed that men and women who have satisfying love and ecstatic sex lives generate peace and harmony and are generally happy in other areas. Two thousand years ago Chinese physicians wrote treatises on the subject, and many beautiful works of erotic art were produced to instruct women in marital skills prior to their wedding. Sex was something to be enjoyed and savored, and was considered life-sustaining and wholesome. Dutch scholar/diplomat, R. H. van Gulik, in his 1961 book *Sexual Life in Ancient China* commented that "it was probably this mental attitude together with the nearly total lack of repression that caused ancient Chinese sexual life to be, on the whole, a healthy one, remarkably free from the pathological abnormality and aberrations found in so many other great ancient cultures." (Current reports of widespread sexual dysfunction due to extreme modesty may be explained by the culture's relatively recent and dramatic philosophical changes and a resulting movement toward sexual repression.)

The Taoist believes that there is a basic imbalance between men's and women's sexuality. The female *yin* essence, they contend, is sexually stronger than the male *yang* essence. This is because women need the extra strength to bear and nourish babies, and this fortitude is manifested sexually in the fact that a woman can accommodate a man as often and for as long as she wishes. A man, on the other hand, is limited by his ability to maintain an erection. In ancient China, a man's capacity to have frequent and prolonged intercourse was held in far greater esteem than his physical appearance.

Consequently, three principles underlie the Taoist approach to sex. The first is that men must find the correct interval between ejaculations to suit their age and state of health. This is thought to strengthen them so that they are better able to satisfy their partners. That is not to say that they should curtail lovemaking, only the emission of semen. One ancient text recommends that men over fifty not ejaculate more than once a week. The second concept also involves ejaculation and may require a leap of faith for the Western mind. Taoists assert that the wild, uncontrolled ejaculation as found in Henry Miller's novels is not the pinnacle of pleasure for men, but that there are greater and more subtle delights to be experienced from repeatedly *almost* ejaculating, but ultimately holding back. Further, they believe that semen contains vital energy that is lost to the man when he spills his seed. As proof, they point to the fact that some men typically are completely spent after ejaculation and immediately fall asleep, often abandoning their female partners, who are ready for more.

This leads to the third principle, that satisfying the woman is extremely important in achieving yin/yang harmony. According to Taoist teachings, a man's orgasm is one sharp peak, while a woman's rises gradually in nine stages. In the course of those stages, various parts of a woman's body become stimulated, causing observable responses. Taoists claim that Westerners often stop at stage four, which is merely a vaginal spasm. But there is further to go in the pursuit of total ecstasy: In stage five a woman's bones are energized, causing her pelvis to loosen and the woman gently to bite her lover. By stage seven her blood is hot and she tries to touch the man with every part of her body. At stage nine her entire body is enraptured and she surrenders to the "little death," exchanging her yin essence with his yang essence. A man's purpose in delaying or waiving ejaculation is to take his lover to the higher levels.

This does not mean, however, that men must sacrifice their own pleasure on the altar of female bliss. Many Westerners are unaware that men can intentionally have an orgasm without ejaculating. This is possible because orgasm and ejaculation are controlled by two different neurological mechanisms. The emission stage, during which the seminal vesicles and prostate gland release semen in to the urethra, is controlled by the lumbar nerves in the spinal cord. For most men this irrevocably leads to the second stage—expulsion. With rhythmic, wavelike contractions, the pelvic muscles controlled by the sacral nerves discharge semen out of the penis. This expulsion is the orgasm, with its accompanying emotional release. Because these two responses can be separated, men can bypass the first stage and go straight to the orgasmic contractions without having any semen to ejaculate. The Taoists have evolved the following exercise to help men master the techniques of semen retention.

Testicle Breathing. This is a simplified version of a longer and more esoteric regimen that contemporary Taoist master Mantak Chia calls "the dance of the testes." In their book *ESO: How You and Your Lover Can Give Each Other Hours of Extended Sexual Orgasm,* Dr. Alan Brauer and Donna Brauer have a similar exercise labeled "testicle elevations." Testicle breathing directs energizing breath to the genitals and helps tighten and refresh the scrotum. Practicing daily also eventually leads to a man's being able to elevate and lower his testicles at will. Because the testes need to lift a little for ejaculation to take place, if a man is able to lower them voluntarily, he can delay his ejaculation while making love.

> Make sure the room you are working in is comfortably warm as you will be nude from the waist down. You can do this exercise sitting on the edge of a chair with your feet flat on the floor and your genitals hanging freely. Or you can stand in a relaxed position with your feet apart, lower spine straight, and shoulders and neck slightly rounded. Focus your attention on your scrotum. Inhale slowly and deeply through your nose and visualize the breath going down and into your testes, filling them. As you do so, raise the testes. Exhale and lower your testicles. Imagine expelling negativity and accumulated toxins as you breathe out. Repeat this exercise nine times, then take a short rest. Do at least three and up to six more sets of nine. At first you will find that you are engaging all kinds of muscles—anal, abdominal, PC—and probably will not discern much movement. The aim is to be able to visibly make the testes "dance" with as little muscular movement as possible.

The Million-Dollar Point. This technique for men consists of pressing at the time of orgasm the Jen-Mo, an acupuncture point at the base of the scrotum before the anus. This point, referred to as the Energy Gate, is the Number One point on the Conception Meridian.

With sexual arousal, the prostate swells with fluid. At ejaculation it contracts rhythmically, pumping secretions into the urethra. With ejaculation, most of the semen goes out the urethra, and a small amount—perhaps a third—goes into the bladder. When the Jen-Mo is pressed, the fluid released by the prostate is preserved, and the semen is reabsorbed into the bloodstream. According to Dr. Stephen Chang, author of *The Tao of Sexuality*, pressing on this point with ejaculation makes his students feel like a million dollars.

Several of my male friends have been using this technique. Instead of feeling drained or depleted after orgasm, they tell me they feel an extraordinary surge of energy. Sometimes men have prolonged orgasms. The technique is recommended for male athletes who are concerned about losing vital energy before an important event.

To verify that you are doing it right, try this experiment. After having sex with normal ejaculation, urinate into a glass. You may notice that semen is mixed with the urine. The urine will be cloudy at first, then the semen will settle at the bottom of the glass. Do the same test after pressing the million-dollar point. If you are using this method correctly, no semen will be seen.

A word of caution: Do not use this technique if your prostate is infected, as it could spread the infection.

Circulation of Sexual Energy.   Part of the Taoist canon is a belief that potent sexual energy should be cultivated and directed around the body by the nervous system. Mantak Chia calls the channels via which the energy moves the Microcosmic Orbit. Other Taoists call it the Hollow Bamboo. In *The Art of Sexual Ecstasy*, Margo Anand most elegantly describes the same phenomenon as playing the Inner Flute. "Without the inner flute," she says, "the sexual music played on the single instrument of the genitals could not expand so readily into a symphony in which the whole body becomes involved." Circulating the energy requires that you be familiar with two acupuncture channels called the

Functional and the Governor. The Functional, or yin, channel starts at the perineum—the point between the anus and the genitals—and travels up the front center of the body, ending at the tip of your tongue. The Governor or yang channel starts at the same place and travels up the back, across the crown, and to the roof of the mouth. Spend a few minutes in meditation each morning circulating energy in the following manner.

> Sit in a comfortable position—on a chair with spine erect and feet on the floor, or cross-legged—and close your eyes. Touch the tip of your tongue to the roof of your mouth to close the circuit. Starting at your eyes, move energy down the yin channel continuing to the perineum and up the yang channel along the spine. Do not simply visualize the path in your mind's eye, as though you were following an imaginary map. Consciously move energy along the channels. It may be difficult at first, but after a few times you will begin to feel a tingling warmth along the circuit. In fact, the glands are along these paths, and you can intensify the effects of the exercise by working on revitalizing them and balancing your hormone output.

Male Deer Exercise. The deer was a symbol of longevity and sexual potency to the ancient Taoists. In characteristically colorful manner, they named the following exercises after the deer's peculiarity of twitching its rear end. This exercise is thought to be powerfully effective for a number of sexual problems including wet dreams, low sex-hormone levels, impotence, and premature ejaculation. If done immediately before making love, the deer exercise is particularly helpful for premature ejaculation. For maximum effect, do the exercise every morning and every night before retiring.

> You should be naked for this exercise, so make sure the room is comfortably warm. Sit on a chair with your spine erect and feet flat on the floor. Rub the palms of your hands together vigorously to create warmth and generate energy.

Gently grasp your testicles with your right hand and hold them so that you transmit the warmth of your hand to them. Position your left hand on your belly about an inch below your navel. Rub this hand in a circular motion 81 times. Rub your hands again and repeat the sequence with your hands reversed, and rubbing in the opposite direction with your right hand. When you have finished, pull in your anal sphincter, as described in the Tantric Horse Gesture (see page 128). Hold it as long as you are able, relax, and repeat the anal contraction as many times as is comfortable.

Female Deer Exercise.   Every bit as powerful as the male deer exercise, the female version is said to promote the natural production of estrogen and alleviate many of the symptoms of PMS. But perhaps the most startling result of doing this daily over a period of time is the cessation of monthly menstrual flow. (The stimulation of the nipples in this exercise theoretically could increase production of the hormones prolactin and oxytocin, which could stop menstruation.) The Chinese deemed this desirable because they believed that as a man loses his energy through ejaculation, a woman loses hers through menstruation. As soon as she stops doing the exercise daily, her monthly flow will resume.

Sit naked on the floor with your legs crossed so that you are firmly pressing the heel of one foot against your clitoris. If you are not flexible enough for this, or the position is uncomfortable, hold an object such as a baseball in place so that there is a pleasing pressure on your vulva. Warm your hands by rubbing them together briskly. Place your hands on your breasts and rub them slowly in an outward direction. Make at least 36 circles (as many as 360 may stop your period). Once you have accomplished the stoppage, you can maintain by doing 100 circles twice a day. After you have finished your self-determined number of rotations, perform the Kegel "pump" as many times as feels comfortable. You may perform this exercise with a lover. Have him warm his hands and massage your breasts while you press your hands against your clitoris.

This exercise takes a high degree of commitment. The only patient of mine who has tried it was a devotee of transcendental meditation. She was doing it daily, and she reported that her periods did stop. I am not recommending that my readers do this to the point of stopping menstruation, as no studies are available that have confirmed its safety.

Hatha Yoga

The ancient Indian practice of yoga is one of the world's great all-purpose disciplines for achieving health and well-being. Although not a religion, yoga contains pronounced spiritual elements and has been integral to life in the civilized East for over 6,000 years. Yoga is a unique, noncompetitive system that works to perfect the body, compensating for its defects and filling it with glowing health while at the same time striving for spiritual elevation. There are several types of yoga, with varied emphasis on the physical and the spiritual. Hatha Yoga, which concentrates on the body, is the one we are most familiar with in the West.

Yoga consists of a series of postures—asanas—that bring the body into perfect alignment and release latent energies, often sparking highly desirable physical and psychological transformations. Breathing techniques, used in conjunction with the postures, circulate life-giving oxygen throughout the body.

When you first try the difficult poses, it is helpful to visualize the posture and the energy flow. Cleanse your mind of negative thoughts about the exercise that you are engaged in: the thoughts that so often keep you from enjoying the highest and best in life, including sex. Yoga exercises will improve your endurance, pump energy into your vital organs, and make your body more supple. You can try lovemaking positions you never dreamed were possible. Wear loose clothing or none at all and do the postures barefooted. Always warm up first with ten minutes of aerobics, walking, jumping rope, or the salutation to the sun before beginning your yoga postures. This will prepare your muscles.

There are yoga classes available in every large city, and books such as *Sexual Secrets* give instructions for postures that help stimulate the sex glands and other organs that have a bearing on your love life. The Yogic Sex Gestures that follow are specifically designed to enhance your sexual pleasure.

Yogic Sex Gestures. This three-part exercise consisting of the Horse Gesture *(Aswini Mudra)*, the Root Lock *(Mula Bandha)*, and the Thunderbolt Gesture *(Vajroli Mudra)* are Tantric variations on the Kegel exercises. They strengthen the anal sphincter and urethral muscles but, unlike Kegels, concentrate on these muscles separately and also introduce breathing techniques. Men and women who practice these exercises report improved sexual control and increased sensitivity in the genital area.

Lie on your back on the floor with bent knees, your spine pressed into the floor and your feet slightly apart. Start with the Horse Gesture. For this you need to isolate your anal sphincter muscles by sucking in the anus. As you pull up, you will feel a distinct contraction, which means you have engaged the inner sphincter in the rectal canal. Having identified the feeling, you can begin the exercise. Take a deep breath, and as you exhale slowly, engage the anal sphincter. Once you have mastered control of this specific muscle group, follow your Horse Gesture with the Root Lock. Take a shallow breath and lower your chin to your chest to enable you to "lock in" the air. Pull in the anal sphincter as before but now continue tightening the PC muscles across the pelvic floor to the genitals. Relax the muscles, release your chin, and breath out. Breath in and out once, before repeating the root lock. Now you can move on to the Thunderbolt Gesture, which involves only the urethral muscle. As with Kegels, this is the muscle used to stop the flow of urine, but now you are trying to isolate it from the anal sphincter. You can do so by contracting your lower abdominal muscles. Lock in a shallow breath as with the Root Lock, contract the urethral muscle, relax it, release the breath. Do ten each of these three gestures in sequence every day.

Tantra and Conscious Loving

Whereas Hatha Yoga is primarily a physical discipline, Tantric Yoga is a spiritual system that teaches love as a sacrament. Tantric doctrines originated in a series of ancient Hindu books written as a dialogue between Shiva, God of Creation and Destruction, and Shakti, his female consort. One of the tenets of Tantra is the belief that during sexual union, kundalini energy moves up the body from the base of the spine to the higher centers of the third eye and crown via the seven chakras, which are part of the electromagnetic field surrounding the body. In ancient texts, these energy vortexes are often described as rotating wheels of lights that vibrate at various frequencies to emit different colors. They are also depicted as lotus flowers with between four and sixty-four petals.

1. The first chakra in the Tantric system is located at the base of the spine. It is associated with survival and vitality, the color red, the sound *Lum,* and the sex organs.

2. The second chakra is in the abdominal area. It is associated with emotions and creativity, the color orange, the sound *Vum,* and Peyer's patches in the intestines.

3. The third chakra is in the solar plexus. It is associated with inner power, the color yellow, the sound *Rum,* and the adrenal glands, the pancreas, liver, and spleen.

4. The fourth chakra is in the heart center. It is associated with love and self-acceptance, the color green, the sound *Yum,* and the heart and thymus.

5. The fifth chakra is in the throat. It is associated with expression and communication, the color blue, the sound *Hum,* and the thyroid and throat.

6. The sixth chakra, in the center of the forehead at the "third eye," is associated with perception, the color purple, the sound *Om,* and the pituitary gland.

7. The seventh chakra is at the top of the head. It is associated with joy and spirituality, the color indigo, and the pineal gland. It is the opening to cosmic energy.

The word Tantra derives from the Sanskrit *tanoti* (to expand) and *trayati* (to liberate). Since expansion and liberation of sexuality are major goals of aphrodisiacs, Tantric exercises can be a powerful aid in your quest for fulfillment. And you can use these exercises without embracing the entire philosophy.

Riding the Tiger. This exercise was developed by Margo Anand, who conducts sexual ecstasy workshops and authored the book *The Art of Sexual Ecstasy.* You will be bringing sexual awareness, vigor, and healing warmth to the chakras, with a view to stimulating the glands associated with each. The exercise calls on the skills you have learned in the above techniques.

The exercise takes about 30 minutes, so choose a time when you are sure to be free of interruptions. Sit cross-legged in a comfortably warm room. Wear no clothing, or a robe that gives you free access to your body. Rub your hands together vigorously to create warmth, then begin to lovingly stimulate your body. Massage your breasts for about three minutes, then move down to caress your belly and finally your genitals. The aim is to arouse yourself sexually, but not to the point of orgasm. When you feel your body pulsating with energy, inhale and hold the breath as long as you are able. While holding, do Kegel pumps. Be sure to relax the rest of your body. After exhaling, take another deep breath, continue with the pumps, but additionally visualize a ball of golden light spiraling all around your pelvis bringing warmth and power to your sex organs. Repeat this last exercise six times. Now you are going to go through the same procedure at each of the chakra points: breathing, pumping, and feeling the light bathing and electrifying your glands and organs. If at any time you feel your level of arousal waning, warm your hands and massage your body again between chakra points. When you reach the crown chakra, imagine the light bursting out of the top of your head and returning energy to the universe. Then picture it coming back in through the crown and shooting through your body and out of the genitals. Repeat three to six times. After completing all seven chakras, lie prone and breath comfortably for a few minutes.

This is a complicated and involved exercise. Anand recommends some props that may keep you focused. Set a lighted candle in front of you. Gazing at it throughout the practice will help you visualize the golden light. Playing some sensual, rhythmic music will keep your sexual energy up and outside distractions down. Some chakra points may be more difficult to focus on than others. For additional help in freeing up their energy, anoint them with the following plant essences:

One: ylang-ylang
Two: sage
Three: tiger balm
Four: rose
Five: eucalyptus
Six: mint
Seven: lavender or rose

Once you are comfortable with your ability to Ride the Tiger alone, you can try it with a loving partner. In this case, you will arouse one another by each caressing the other's body in turn. When you are both aroused, assume a position where your bodies are in close contact. Anand recommends the man sitting on a chair with the woman on his lap facing him. When the man is fully erect, he asks permission of the woman to enter her. She acquiesces and assists by gently drawing him in with the Kegel pump. Now you ride the tiger together from the first to the seventh chakra, moving from one point to the next by mutual consent. At the end, thank one another and sit quietly together for about ten minutes.

Since the sexual revolution of the 1960s, sexuality in the West has continued to transform and evolve. George Leonard, in *The End of Sex*, describes the transition from the sexual liberation and individual and group promiscuity of those heady days to our more or less forced return to monogamy in the somber era of AIDS and other sexually transmitted diseases. Whatever the complex and obscure causes of the new monogamy, it is within that framework that genuine erotic intimacy can be achieved—a concept promulgated by Eastern cultures for centuries.

Consider a program of Tantric and Taoist exercises. It is possible that they will guide you along the path to a heightened state of sexual awareness and oneness with your lover.

7

HERBAL LOVE TONICS AND PLANT APHRODISIACS

Eat the white shallots sent from Megara
Or garden herbs that aphrodisiac are,
Or eggs, or honey on Hymettus flowing,
Or nuts upon the sharp-leaved pine trees growing.
—OVID

The mandrake is one of history's most famous herbal aphrodisiacs. As a member of the nightshade family, it is known as Satan's apple or the love apple. Its legendary reputation for heightening desire and increasing fertility probably came from the shape of its fleshy, branching taproot, said to resemble the lower half of the human body, but the fact that it quickens heartbeat and induces dizziness and high temperatures when eaten probably helped. A perennial with small, bell-shaped greenish flowers, sweet orange berries, and malodorous clumps of leaves that look like horseradish, it is native to southern Europe and the Mideast. In the Bible it was called *dudaim*. Mandrake *(Mandragora officinarum)* is found in the myths of Greece, Rome, Arabia, India, and China.

During the Middle Ages it was believed that the mandrake grew out of the ground where rapists had been hanged, "conceived" by the semen they ejaculated at the moment of death. According to Roman fable, the plant emitted a shriek when pulled from the ground; the sound caused insanity or death to anyone within earshot. This myth endured for centuries. An early English herbal treatise provided a useful illustration of how to pull a mandrake by

way of a trained dog that was tied to the plant and then called by its
master or mistress from a judicious distance. The mandrake finally
lost its mystique in the 1800s, when growing medical knowledge
undermined its credibility as an aphrodisiac.

The use of herbs to treat afflictions, sexual and otherwise, is as
old as mankind. Principles of phytotherapy—the use of plant
substances for healing—were passed on orally for centuries and
are found throughout ancient writings. Babylonian clay tablets
dating back to 3000 B.C. reflect the use of herbal remedies, and
the earliest recorded aphrodisiacs were herbal preparations.

Unlike the mandrake, which failed the test, many plants with
age-old reputations for healing and enhancing sex have proven
themselves under scientific scrutiny. After a period of initial skepticism, pharmaceutical companies isolated certain active substances from plants, synthesized them, and came up with useful
medications. Thus, sophisticated chemical technologies have
taken us far from the tradition of healing with herbs. However,
while the new, synthesized drugs are often effective, some have
bad side effects or are toxic. This is not to say that all natural
remedies are safe and free from side effects. However, prior to
synthesizing, the plants themselves contained mineral cofactors,
enzymes, and vitamins that increased the efficacy of the active
ingredient and which are lost when the active substance is isolated. After years of studying herbal medicines, I have come to
believe that using live plants often can be more beneficial than a
synthesized laboratory compound.

Phytotherapy has always had a loyal following and today is
gaining even more disciples as people become disenchanted with
many aspects of medical technology and increasingly sensitive to
the environment and nature. These converts are finding a number
of different, and sometimes confusing, approaches to herbal medicine.

Western herbalists classify plants according their chemical con-
stituents and therapeutic properties. The Chinese look more to a
plant's effect on the body's meridians, its impact on energy flow,
and its heating or cooling properties. Practitioners of Ayurvedic
traditions classify the patients rather than the herbs, and after
determining body type and the condition of three operating

principles called *doshas* (more about these later), prescribe appropriate herbal remedies. While the methods of prescription may differ, all three forms of herbal medicine generally employ much the same plants—and all have a great deal to offer in the way of aphrodisia.

Following is a look at the major schools of herbal medicine and how they use herbs as aphrodisiacs. First, however, you need to learn the herbalists' terms for the various forms in which one takes or uses plant substances. Not every form is appropriate for every herb; I will specify which is best. Generally, you should only make as much as you need for immediate use, although tinctures are preseved by their alcohol content and will keep in the refrigerator for a couple of months.

Decoction: an herbal obtained by rapidly boiling or gently simmering the plant in water, usually for twenty to thirty minutes. This method is most often used for barks, seeds, and roots.

Infusion: an herbal obtained by steeping the plant in water. Infusions, sometimes also called teas or tisanes, are generally made from dried leaves or flowers.

Tincture: extract of the plant's active ingredient obtained by infusing the plant in alcohol or a mixture of alcohol and water.

Distillation: extraction of the active ingredients in a liquid by evaporation or condensation of the water content.

Combination Formulas: commercially prepared formulas containing combinations of different herbs. They can come in any of the above forms, or as pills, capsules, and powders.

If you have a serious or chronic illness, speak with your doctor and then seek out a qualified herbal practitioner before embarking on any course of herbal treatment.

Herbal Aphrodisiacs From Around the World

The following herbs can be used in one of two ways: taken daily to boost overall vitality in the long term or more specifically as aphrodisiacs to strengthen sexual organs and ignite passion in preparation for lovemaking. They are readily available in herbal or health food shops and used in the general practice of Western herbalism. There is also a list of mail-order sources for herbs in the back of this book.

YOHIMBE

One of the most popular aphrodisiac herbs available, yohimbe has a reputation for producing electrifying sexual encounters. Derived from the bark of the West African yohimbehe tree *(Pausinystalia yohimbe)*, it has been made into a medicinal tea in Africa and the West Indies for centuries to help with problems of impotence and sexual dysfunction. Its notoriety as a potent aphrodisiac, though, probably stems more from its use in African orgiastic mating rituals that sometimes last for two weeks.

Since the 1930s, yohimbe has been studied, analyzed pharmacologically, and even synthesized chemically. We now know that the way yohimbe works is as an alpha-2-adrenergenic receptor-blocking agent, meaning that the active ingredient dilates small arteries by blocking the release of neurotransmitters that otherwise would cause those arteries to constrict. In practical terms this increases blood flow to the clitoris and penis and further compresses veins to prevent the blood from flowing out. Some users also report mild hallucinogenic and heightened sensory effects much like those experienced on LSD or MDA. Unfortunately, yohimbe has toxic side effects; while it may cause a man to get tremendously erect, the nausea, palpitations, excessive perspiration, tension, and irritability it also provokes are hardly conducive to full enjoyment of his tumescence.

Afrodex, an herbal preparation in pill form containing yohimbe hydrochloride, methyl testosterone, and an extract of nux vomica has been tested against a placebo in a double-blind study and found to be helpful in inducing erections in impotent men. Researchers, however, did not first check the test subjects for testosterone levels, so they don't really know whether the testosterone in the preparation had the desired effect by boosting the male hormone in men who were already deficient. The prescription drug Yocon, discussed in chapter 5, also contains yohimbe.

The best use of yohimbe is as an ingredient in aphrodisiac preparations. You can make a decoction of yohimbe by boiling an ounce of bark in two cups of water for three minutes and then gently simmering for another twenty minutes. It also comes in capsules containing 3 to 6 grams and in tincture form, but I do not recommend daily or prolonged use of it alone because of the side effects. Stay clear of it if you suffer from high blood pressure, heart or liver disease, or if you are taking MAO inhibitors.

GINSENG

Ginseng is perhaps the best known of the so-called aphrodisiac herbs. Animal research concludes that despite its reputation, it does not have a specific effect on the sexual organs. The plant has gained its reputation because of its ability to increase all-around well-being, stamina, and endurance. Ancient Vedic texts from India claim that ginseng "bestows the power of a bull on men both young and old." In Japan and China, ginseng is used ritually to increase longevity and prevent senility. Families often invest once a year in an expensive piece of ginseng root and boil it to produce a drink for the elders.

Ginseng is an adaptogenic herb, meaning it is a nontoxic plant with a nonspecific action that influences a wide range of metabolic factors. The overall result of using an adaptogenic is to normalize or balance a bodily system—including sexual arousal and response—whether it is over- or underactive. Ginseng's properties as an adaptogenic were recognized early, and its botanical name, *Panax*, comes from the same Greek root as the word panacea. Research conducted in Russia and Japan has shown ginseng to be helpful in the treatment of many conditions, including diabetes and immune-system disorders. Recently, some experiments with ginseng saponins (naturally occurring glucosides) called ginsenosides, have been demonstrated to inhibit the growth of cultured liver-tumor cells and under laboratory conditions turned them back into normal cells. This suggests that further research is called for into the ginseng's possible anticarcinogenic potential.

Many people consider ginseng to be a Chinese remedy, although species of the plant grow in Northern lands throughout the world. Different species contain diverse properties in varying strengths. You will get different results from the American, Korean, Chinese, or Siberian ginsengs on the market.

American *(Panax quinquefolius)*, Chinese, and Korean ginsengs (both *Panax ginseng*) have immune-boosting effects, and are stimulants and rejuvenators. Menopausal women may benefit from small amounts of these ginsengs combined in tonic formulas to stoke the fire a little. American ginseng is considered the mildest and is the one most commonly recommended for prolonged use. Chinese and Korean ginsengs should not be taken daily for more than two months at a time and then avoided for at least two months. They should also be taken under the supervision of a doctor knowledgeable about herbal medicine, or a qualified practioner of herbalism.

Siberian ginseng (*Eleutherococcus senticosus*) has different properties from the other three. It is prepared from the outer bark of the root rather than the entire root, and is a tonic specifically for the liver and kidneys. This particular species also seems to have more widespread use in support in the fight against diseases such as immune dysfunction and cancer. Siberian ginseng has no androgenizing side effects and in fact has proven helpful to pregnant women. Russian studies using a 33-percent extract of Siberian ginseng resulted in fewer viral illnesses and a decreased incidence of toxemia during pregnancy. I would recommend doses of 3 to 15 grams daily.

All varieties of ginseng can be expensive, and unfortunately there is no standardization of extracts to use as a guideline of quality. Should you try this plant for its tonic properties and to boost sexual endurance, make sure to obtain it from a reputable supplier; mail-order sources are listed in the back of this book. Ginseng can be bought in root form that can be chewed, or it can be made into a decoction, but it is easier to buy commercial extractions.

SPIKENARD

Spikenard *(Aralia racemosa)* is often called California ginseng, but that is a misnomer as it bears no relationship to any of the ginsengs. The root, eaten as a food by Native Americans, has stimulant properties; I usually recommend a daily dose of between 3 and 9 grams as an energy booster for women. A related species grows in Russia, where it is used as a general stimulant and tonic.

SUMA

Suma *(Pfaffia paniculata)* is similarly known as Brazilian ginseng, though it too is of a different genus. Probably it acquired the nickname because like ginseng it is adaptogenic and can be taken to stimulate the immune system and vitality in general. Suma can be taken as a tonic daily for energy and stamina to fortify hormones and stabilize blood sugar. It has even been reported to help reduce tumors and cancers. Take the powder in capsules, use the tincture, or make as a tea. Doses of at least 9 grams daily are recommended.

MUIRA PUAMA

Popularly known as potentwood, muira puama *(Lyriosma ovata)* is a South American aphrodisiac used in the Amazon and Orinoco basins for centuries to stimulate sensuality, as a sexual enhancer, and as a treatment for impotence and frigidity. Muira puama has not undergone the same pharmacological scrutiny as yohimbe but appears to be milder and without the side effects of its African counterpart. Brazilian natives make a strong decoction of the bark of the wood that they rub into their genitals, and they also drink a fluid extracted from the plant.

You can make a decoction by boiling two tablespoons of powdered muira puama wood for fifteen minutes in one pint of water. Drink one fluid ounce before making love. Alternatively, infuse one ounce of muira puama in two cups of vodka for two weeks, shaking daily. One ounce of this tincture can also be taken in preparation for a sexual encounter.

A number of products available from the manufacturers of combination herbals designed to stimulate sex drive contain muira puama, along with other herbs listed here, including yohimbe. In my clinical experience, I have found Cobra, from PEP Products, and Masculoplex, from Biotherapeutics, to have definite arousing effects.

GUARANA

Like muira puama, guarana *(Paullinia cupana)* is indigenous to Brazil and is included in many commercially available herbal aphrodisiac formulas in the U.S. Natives of South America make a powdered substance from the dry bark of this jungle vine and mix it with water as a pick-me-up. It is remarkable for relieving mental exhaustion, as a remedy for a hangover headache, and as an appetite suppressant (not surprising, as guarana contains three times more caffeine than coffee). Use it with caution. Guarana will give you a lift, though it is not specifically an aphrodisiac.

DAMIANA

Damiana grows in the desert areas of Mexico and Texas, and in Africa. The botanical name of this shrub, *Turnera aphrodisiaca*, tells the story. Chemically, this plant has been found to contain several alkaloids that directly stimulate the nerves and sex organs, increase circulation, and have diuretic and muscle-relaxant properties. Native Mexican women have long drunk an infusion of the herb a couple of hours before retiring to prime themselves for their men. It is also reputed to induce erotic dreams when drunk at bedtime. It is believed that adolescent girls whose menstrual cycles are irregular, and menopausal women, can help balance their hormonal systems with damiana. Men can derive some benefit from it, too, as it is said to help increase the sperm count.

The following recipe for a damiana cordial has been circulating for years and was published in several books, although its actual

origin seems to be unknown. I have personally observed its
amatory effects.

> 1 ounce dried damiana leaves
> 1 pint vodka
> ¾ pint spring water
> ½ to 1 cup of honey

Infuse the damiana in the vodka for five days, then strain
through a coffee filter. Set aside the vodka tincture and put
the leaves to soak in the water for another five days. Strain
as before. Discard the leaves. Heat the water infusion just
enough to dissolve the honey. Add the amount of honey
according to how sweet you wish the cordial to be. Cool,
then combine with the vodka.

Bottled, the cordial will keep for a few months. A harmless
sediment may appear at the bottom of the bottle. Drink one or
two cordial glasses of the tincture before retiring; after about five
days, you will very likely experience some delicious results. Highly
recommended.

SAW PALMETTO

Saw palmetto *(Serenoa serrulata)* is a native North American
plant found along the Atlantic shore from South Carolina to
Florida. The olive-like berries of this palm have a specific syn-
ergy with the prostate and are considered a nutrient and tonic
for the male reproductive organs. Thus, saw palmetto is usually
included in herbal formulas designed for prostatic inflammation
and hypertrophy. Although chiefly a man's remedy, women
recovering from urinary-tract infections may find it useful.
Many herbalists regard saw palmetto berries as safe, mild
aphrodisiacs; ten to twelve can be eaten daily for a cumulative
effect. Their potency is increased when they are combined with
damiana.

VITEX

It may strike you as odd that vitex, also known as chaste berry or *Agnus castus,* is included here, as this plant is famous for lowering the sex drive in priests and nuns. But it also has the ability—when taken in small quantities of 3 to 6 grams daily—to stimulate the pituitary secretion of luteinizing hormone, leading to increased progesterone in women, and is an excellent remedy for women suffering from PMS, irregular periods, anovulatory cycles, and infertility. It can be found as a tincture or in capsules. In Chapter 8 you will read how homeopathic doses of this plant can help treat a flagging libido.

TANG KWEI

Tang kwei is one of the primary tonics used in Chinese medicine for its blood-building and general rejuvenating properties. It strengthens the heart, liver, and spleen, and is high in betacarotene, a vitamin A precursor. I particularly recommend it for menopausal women, especially when alternated with vitex. Because tang kwei can bring on uterine bleeding when used alone, it is best taken as part of a balanced formula. This herb should not be used by people with high blood pressure, and only when clinically indicated during pregnancy. Contrary to popular belief, tang kwei does not contain natural estrogens but seems to stimulate the body's production of estrogens. The dose can vary from 3 to 15 grams a day.

WORMWOOD

Wormwood *(Artemisia absinthium)* is a European perennial herb that for centuries has been used to produce a bitter tonic that helps improve the function of the liver and gallbladder. Besides the "bitters," wormwood contains a volatile oil that is considered a narcotic-analgesic; it falls into the same pharmaceutical group as codeine and can be dangerous in large quantities. Wormwood is one of the most widely mentioned herbs in ancient botanical texts, used variously as an antiparasitic, as a liniment, to ward off disease, and even as a cure for baldness. Wormwood's historical reputation as an aphrodisiac reached its height in the nineteenth century when the drinking of absinthe, a powerful liqueur made from the herb, became popular with all classes of European society but especially among artists. This is understandable; in addition to its potent aphrodisiac qualities, wormwood induces a dreamy state conducive to creativity, probably because it depresses the central medullary part of the brain concerned with anxiety and pain. Some art historians go so far as to believe that it was the artists' perceptions, filtered through a thick veil from indulgence in absinthe, that initiated the Impressionist movement. Drinks such as Chartreuse, Pernod, and Vermouth (which takes its name directly from wormwood) once contained the herb, but in 1915 the French government outlawed it because overindulgence had extremely serious side effects of mental derangement, paralysis, and convulsions. Absinthe is still made illicitly in some French villages and has assumed a mystique that makes it much sought after. Although absinthe is illegal all over the world, wormwood herb is generally available from reputable herbalists. Wormwood is included in formulas to kill parasites and as a digestive stimulant. It can be taken by infusing one teaspoonful of the dried herb in one cup of hot water.

RED CLOVER

A European weed that now flourishes in North America, red clover *(Trifolium pratense)* is highly nutritive and contains vitamins, minerals, substances that thin the blood, and phyto-estrogens (plant-based hormones). Red clover tea is a pleasantly calming tonic and blood cleanser, especially for those who suffer from infections or inflammations. Make it by infusing two teaspoons of dried flowers in a half cup of hot water for ten minutes.

This old country recipe for red clover wine uses the honey-scented flowers that bloom abundantly in summer. The intoxicating drink makes a great accompaniment for a romantic meal.

2 quarts fresh red clover flowers
or 1 pint of dried flowers

4 quarts boiling water
3 lemons
2 oranges
4 pounds sugar
1 ounce active yeast spread on
    a piece of toast

Put flowers in a large bowl and pour boiling water over them, then leave until lukewarm. Slice the lemons and oranges and add to flowers and water along with the sugar the yeast on toast. Store for five days, stirring twice daily. Strain and leave to stand for a further five days. Bottle and cork loosely for 10 days. Secure corks and leave to mature for one month.

VANILLA

The ubiquitous vanilla *(Vanilla planifolia)* that flavors your ice cream or pound cake can have a mildly stimulating effect on motor nerves when used in greater quantities. Indigenous to tropical Central America, vanilla is steeped in myth. The story is that a beautiful goddess, Xanath, visited earth and fell in love with a young warrior. Since she was forbidden to marry a mere mortal, she transformed herself into the vanilla vine bearing beautiful orchids and its fragrant bean. Native Mexicans have long added vanilla to their chocolate drinks to increase that substance's aphrodisiacal properties; the plant's name comes from the Latin word for vagina. Vanilla has been used in Europe for the purpose of aphrodisia since Elizabethan times. The Comtesse du Barry, the mistress of Louis XV of France, is said to have made extensive use of vanilla beans to keep her many lovers always ready to receive her.

The French *parfumeur* Geurlain contends that the aphrodisiacal qualities of vanilla come from its aroma. In his book *Sex, Drugs and Aphrodisiacs,* Adam Gottlieb hypothesizes that since field workers who harvest vanilla pods are prone to skin irritations, the plant may also cause urethral irritation much like a milder, safer version of Spanish fly. But excess amounts of vanilla can also be toxic. Never use more than two whole beans for consumption at any one time in a recipe. You can make your own aphrodisiac vanilla tincture by infusing two split vanilla beans in one pint of brandy for two weeks. If you prefer your aphrodisiacs without alcohol, try this spicy vanilla milk shake.

> 1 cup milk
> 15 whole cloves
> 15 cardamom pods
> 2 cinnamon sticks
> 1 vanilla pod, split
> 1 cup vanilla frozen yogurt
> honey to taste

Place milk, cloves, cardamom, and cinnamon in a saucepan. Scrape in vanilla seeds from pod. Heat milk but do not boil. Remove from heat and allow to cool, then refrigerate until chilled. Strain milk into a blender goblet and discard spices. Add frozen yoghurt and up to one tablespoon of honey to taste. Blend until smooth and frothy.

SARSAPARILLA

Sarsaparilla *(Smilax officinalis)* is a relative of the asparagus. In North America it has been chiefly used as a flavoring agent. The Victorian ice-cream-parlor drink of the same name was made from it, as was rootbeer when that beverage actually contained roots rather than synthetic flavors. But in Central and South America, various strains of sarsaparilla have been used medicinally for centuries as a general tonic, a remedy for impotence, and a cure for sexual diseases. During the 1930s, researchers discovered that the plant contains phytosterols—the raw material of testosterone and progesterone—and a cortisone-like phytohormone that helps fight infection. Some believe these chemicals can be used as safe replacements for anabolic steroids in building muscle. As a sexual booster, try taking one heaping tablespoon of powdered sarsaparilla or 10 to 30 drops of sarsaparilla tincture three times a day.

WILD YAM

Like sarsaparilla, wild yam *(Discorea villosa)* contains hormone precursors to increase production of testosterones and progesterones, which as you know are sex hormones, in both men and women. This native of Mexico yields such a powerful and useful steroid chemical (called diosgenin) that it is converted at laboratories into synthetic sex hormones used in drugs. Extracts of wild yam are particularly helpful for women with PMS and menopausal symptoms. Make a decoction with 3 to 9 grams of wild yam root or use 10 to 30 drops of tincture.

BURDOCK

Burdock *(Arctium lappa)*, a common weed rich in iron, is known throughout the world as a general tonic and for cleansing the blood, liver, and kidneys. Dandelion and burdock wine is an old—and potent—European restorative, and in the Gypsy culture a decoction of burdock is sweetened with wine, also as a tonic. You can make your own decoction with 3 to 5 grams of burdock or take it in tincture form in doses of 10 to 30 drops.

LICORICE

It may surprise you to see this favorite childhood candy listed here, but the sweet root of the licorice *(Glycyrrhiza glabre)* plant has been used worldwide for centuries for medicinal and aphrodisiac purposes. The ancient Egyptians, Chinese, and Indians used it in various forms to increase longevity and to improve erotic arousal and stamina. Licorice contains traces of phytoestrogen sterols similar to those produced by the adrenal glands, and in the 1970s this knowledge led to a craze for licorice in Europe. In Germany, licorice overtook chocolate as a lover's gift; many women reported that the candy made them feel sexually aroused.

The following two recipes are an enjoyable way to try licorice as an aphrodisiac; use them judiciously, as the use of licorice in excess can raise blood pressure and may adversely affect the body's potassium levels.

The ancient Egyptians made a popular stimulating drink called *mai sus* from licorice, and King Tutankhamen was buried with licorice root. This is a modern-day approximation of that drink. You will need a mortar and pestle; a food processor won't work.

> 1 ounce licorice root
> 1 ounce sesame seeds
> 1 ounce fennel seeds
> 1 pint water

Grind the licorice root and seeds together with the pestle. Bring the water to a boil and add the licorice root and seeds. Boil rapidly for five minutes. Reduce heat, cover and simmer gently for twenty minutes. Cool and strain.

Nicholas Culpeper, the seventeenth-century British herbalist who wrote a seminal text on the subject of herbs, offered a recipe for a licorice decoction, which is adapted here.

> ½ pound dried licorice root, chopped
> 3 pints spring water

Put the root in the water and bring to a boil. Boil rapidly until the water is reduced to about one quart, then strain. Half-fill a cup with the decoction, which will be thick and gummy, and fill up with warm water or milk and honey to taste.

OAT STRAW

Oats *(Avena sativa),* found in almost every all-American kitchen in the form of oatmeal, recently gained in popularity when studies said that oat bran helped lower blood cholesterol. But oat tincture has had a place for centuries in the herbal *Materia Medica,* where it was usually recommended for impotence and menstrual problems resulting from nervous exhaustion. In old Europe, oat-straw tincture was also taken by people withdrawing from opium; modern herbalists often prescribe it as a tonic and nerve stimulant for anyone going through drug or alcohol detoxification. Take the tincture in doses of 10 to 20 drops. You can also make a decoction by boiling 1 to 2 ounces of oat straw in 1 pint of water for 20 minutes.

Several products available today add nettles to green oats as a tonic to increase stamina and sex drive. This combination was initially studied at Budapest University, where the males tested showed increased strength, stamina, and sexual vitality along with increased testosterone levels. The Institute for the Advanced Study of Human Sexuality in San Francisco tested forty men and women and found it successful in increasing sexual desire and performance. Two products are available: Exsativa from Scandinavian Products, and Nettles and Oats, from Gero Vita International.

FO-TI-TIENG

Fo-ti-tieng *(Hydrocotyle asiatica minor)* is a perennial marsh herb used extensively in the Orient primarily for longevity. The translation of its Chinese name is "elixir for long life." The herb also has been found to contain chemical properties that make it a good remedy for degenerative diseases, such as tuberculosis and diabetes. But of primary interest here are its aphrodisiacal qualities. Two tablespoons of powdered fo-ti-tieng in a cup of hot water taken daily will have an accumulative effect as a sexual-appetite booster, especially when libido is lagging. Gotu kola *(Hydrocotyle asiatica major),* a geographical variant of the plant, is often more easily obtainable and equally effective. Solomon's seal *(Polygonatum)* is yet another related herb that is native to England and is now found in parts of Europe and North Africa. For a particularly effective stimulant, combine a half ounce each of fo-ti-tieng and gotu kola and simmer the mixture in one pint of water for thirty minutes.

GINKGO

Gingko *(Gingko Biloba)*, a tree native to China and Japan is, in Japan, cultivated and revered in temple gardens. Gingko has been known to aid the flow of blood and oxygen to the brain, thus increasing memory and awareness. This powerful and versatile herb also contains chemicals that prevent damage from free radicals. Additionally, gingko strengthens arterial tone and prevents blood platelets from clumping together. Because it improves circulation, it can help in cases where a man has circulation-related difficulties in getting an erection. However, large doses over a long period of time can result in irritability and headaches, so take no more than 3 grams daily in capsule or tincture form.

ASTRAGALUS

Astragalus *(Astragalus)* is a general strengthening tonic that helps keep the immune system and the lungs healthy. The perennial shrub, which is native to southeast Europe and Iran, also promotes healing and is excellent for these recovering from radiation treatment or chemotherapy. A dosage of 6–15 grams can be taken daily.

BEE POLLEN

Bee pollen—the fine powdery material produced by the anthers of flowering plants and gathered by bees—is technically a food, but I have included it here because it is also a plant substance. A compact package of nutrients, pollen contains B vitamins, vitamin C, trace minerals, unsaturated fatty acids, proteins, antibacterial and immune-boosting properties, and—you guessed it!—substances that stimulate the sex glands and hormone production. No more than a couple of teaspoons of bee pollen granules a day will yield powerful results.

KAVAKAVA

A well-known drink found in Samoa, Tahiti, and Fiji, kavakava is made from the roots of the *Piper methysticum* plant. The plant contains narcotic substances called alpha pyrones, which affect spinal rather than cerebral responses, resulting in relaxation and euphoria while retaining mental alertness. The active substances are not water soluble and are extracted by pounding, masticating, or emulsifying in a blender. After treating the root in any of the preceding ways, simmer four tablespoons of the pulverized root in one pint of water for 10 minutes and take between 3 and 9 grams daily.

KOLA

Kola nuts *(Cola nitida)*, native to West Africa, for a while supplanted cocaine as the basis of Coca-Cola, although they too were eliminated from the soft drink's secret recipe. Kola contains large quantities of caffeine and other substances called theobromine and kolanin; combined, they make a strong central-nervous-system stimulant. The Brazilians still produce a popular beverage from kola, and in Jamaica it is employed as an aphrodisiac.

Two lesser-known aphrodisiacs from South America are matico and quebracho. Matico *(Piper angustifolium)* is an herb from the Amazon Basin that has been used for centuries by the natives as an aphrodisiac and tonic. The bark of quebracho *(Aspidosperma quebracho-blanco)* contains quebrachine, an ingredient chemically equivalent to yohimbe.

Exotic Herbal Aphrodisiacs

These following herbs are included because they have legendary reputations as aphrodisiacs in various parts of the world. You may have heard of them from travelers or read about them. Some of these are considered to be dangerous, or are illegal in the United States.

BETEL NUTS

Betel nuts are a sort of candy made from the nuts of the Asian areca palm combined with a pinch of burnt lime and various spices, all wrapped in the leaf of the betel vine. This nifty little package is held in the cheek, sometimes for hours, where it releases a mild central-nervous-system stimulant called arecoline, yielding a pleasant "high." Overindulgence can be extremely unpleasant, with dizziness, vomiting, and convulsions. Betel nuts are arguably the most widely used mood-altering substance in the world, and throughout Asia entire population groups have the red teeth characteristic of immoderate use.

PSILOCYBIN

Psilocybe mexicana or *Stropharia cubensis* are known colloquially as magic mushrooms. They grow in grasslands, usually in the dung of hooved animals. The mushrooms contain large amounts of psilocybin, a tryptamine hallucinogen. These plants were used by primitive societies in tribal sexual gatherings, what we might call orgies, for their sensory stimulating and aphrodisiacal properties. In his book *Food of the Gods,* Terence McKenna postulates that it was the use of these mushrooms that allowed human consciousness to expand its capacity for the integration of knowledge and was a factor in the birth of religion in early nomadic societies. Although these mushrooms are not toxic, and can be of help with diseases of the liver, they are classified as Schedule One drugs, which means they are illegal in the United States.

CALAMUS

Also known as sweet flag, calamus *(Acorus calamus)* is found all the way from Northern Europe to the Himalayas and in parts of North America. This swamp plant has been used for thousands of years in Chinese medicine; in Ayurvedic medicine it is combined with gotu kola to stimulate sex and promote wisdom. Another popular Indian aphrodisiac called cachunde contains calamus combined with wormwood, ambergris, and musk. The Arabs and Iranians also use calamus to boost the libido, and some Native American tribes chew on it daily as a sexual nerve tonic. Calamus contains two psychoactive ingredients, asarone and beta-asarone, which in large enough doses can cause hallucinations.

EPENA

Epena *(Virola calophylla)* is legendary among explorers of the South American rain forests. Amazonian natives scrape the resin from this tree—a member of the otherwise innocuous nutmeg family—dry it, and combine the resulting powder with ashes from a wood fire. They inhale the mixture like snuff, giving themselves an instantaneous "high" with a sex kick. Alas, this extremely potent MAO inhibitor is not without unpleasant side effects. At the least it can cause uncontrollable sneezing and at worst damage to nasal mucous membranes.

IBOGA

Iboga *(Tabernanthe iboga)* is a shrub found in the tropical forests of Gabon and Zaire. In the Bwiti religion, among the Fang, a tribe in these regions, the root bark of the iboga tree is used ceremonially as a stimulant to give the users the wherewithal to fight lions, to dance, and to copulate all night. Terence McKenna, in *Food of the Gods,* postulates that the active hallucinogenic ingredient, ibogaine, may have a pheromone that helps to keep the tribal marriages together. In the 1867 Paris Exhibition iboga was promoted in the form of an extract to cure everything, including impotence. High doses, however, were reported to cause convulsions, paralysis, and respiratory collapse. Iboga is classified as a Schedule One drug and is therefore not available in the U.S.

JIMSONWEED

"Jimson" is a bastardization of "Jamestown," which is where colonial settlers found the weed growing, although it is known also in Asia and Europe. A fabled aphrodisiac, the plant—its botanical name is *Datura stramonium*—is called by many other names, including Devil's apple, stinkweed, thorn apple, and Gabriel's trumpet. Highly poisonous and extremely narcotic, jimsonweed, when combined with aconite and deadly nightshade, forms a substance that is called "witch's flying ointment" because when rubbed into the skin it causes hallucinations of flying or astral projection. In American Indian culture, the leaves were smoked to produce fanciful dreams, especially in combination with cannabis: This was the notorious herb in Carlos Castaneda's *The Teachings of Don Juan*. Jimsonweed should be used with extreme caution—a dose over two grams can kill you. Ingestion causes anticholinergic symptoms, including dry mouth; dry, hot skin; increased blood pressure and heart rate; urine retention; hallucinations; and confusion. Treatment of acute jimsonweed poisoning is recommended with Physostigmine, a drug that reverses the more serious effects.

YAGE

Yage, sometimes called *ayahuasca*, is a hallucinogenic substance made from the South American jungle vine *Banisteripsis cappi*. Shamans in Brazil take it during religious ceremonies to heighten perception, and it is used in male rites of passage. Yage contains harmine and harmoline, which are some of the most potent MAO inhibitors in nature: Small doses produce states of euphoria and empathy that enhance the sexual experience. In a therapeutic context, yage has a role similar to other hallucinogens but is not recommended for casual consumption.

Herbal Love Potions

Although single-herb recipes can be effective, herbs are often more powerful when taken in combinations, the properties of one reinforcing those of another. Following are recipes for making your own aphrodisiac potions. Included in the ingredients you will see herbs that were not described individually. Alone, they are not regarded as aphrodisiacs, but as part of a recipe they contribute valuable properties. You should have no difficulty in finding the ingredients at health food stores, herbal emporiums, or even some pharmacies. Look under "herbs" in your Yellow Pages or consult the appendix of this book. While fresh plants are likely to have higher medicinal value, dried herbs are more accessible and available year round. Unless otherwise stated, the recipe quantities are given for dried varieties. Should you have the luxury of picking your own fresh herbs, a general guideline is to use three times more fresh than dried. Herbs and other plant substances are generally inexpensive, ranging from 50 cents to two dollars an ounce for dried materials, so it will cost you little to experiment, and the payoff could be well worth the investment and effort.

Preparation of most herbal concoctions is simple, but there are a few general rules you should observe. Never make your aphrodisiac preparations in metal pots or bowls; the minerals that leach from them may react with the plant's active ingredient. Enamel, glass, or earthenware are better bets. Similarly, use only spring or bottled mineral water. Hard water can prevent the release of the plant's active ingredient.

FLIBUSTER ORGASMIC

One night I prepared this punch for a party but told no one what was in it. By the end of the evening, one normally reserved and long-married couple was kissing passionately in a corner. A friend called me the next day and said she'd been "all over" her boyfriend on the way home; she asked what I'd put in the punch.

This recipe calls for herbal tinctures that you will find at a health food store. A tip: You will get more juice out of your oranges if you dip them in hot water before squeezing them. Serves about 20.

> 2 bottles of white rum
> ⅔ liter of dry white wine
> 1 cup Triple Sec
> Juice of 10 oranges
> Juice of 6 lemons

20-ounce can of pineapple chunks, drained
1 cup of sugar
2 vanilla beans, split
2 nutmegs, ground
2 ounces of muira puama tincture, preferably in
    a base of vegetable glycerin and alcohol
1–2 ounces of damiana tincture
2 whole oranges studded with cloves
A handful of fresh or dried rose petals

Place the alcohol, juices, pineapple, sugar, vanilla, nutmeg, muira puama, and damiana in a large punch bowl and stir well until sugar is dissolved. Carefully float the clove-studded oranges in the punch, and immediately before serving sprinkle with rose petals.

The following formulas were developed by Amanda McQuade Crawford, M.N.I.H.N., director of the California School of Herbal Studies in Forestville, California, where she teaches a class on sexuality and herbalism. Amanda's philosophy is that love cannot be forced—but it can be created.

VANILLA ROSE CORDIAL

This cordial makes a wonderful aperitif to be sipped before climbing into bed or while between the sheets. The rose, long a symbol of love and of the heart chakra in Tantra, contributes a soothing quality. It also has medicinal properties, relieving liver congestion and helping regulate menstruation.

1 pound fresh or 4 ounces dry rose petals
2 ounces vanilla extract or 4 vanilla beans
4 ounces vitex
4 ounces damiana
1 liter brandy

Thoroughly mix all ingredients in a large container with a well-fitting lid. Store in a cool, dark place for two weeks,

shaking daily. Strain and bottle. Drink your cordial by stirring one to three tablespoons in a cup of hot coffee or tea,
or in a glass of cold, sparkling mineral water. Alternatively,
you can drink up to a wineglassful at night. In this case you
may wish to sweeten the cordial with a little honey or flavor
with a few drops of essential oil of rose.

RED-TO-ORANGE CHAKRA EXPRESS

Another pre-sex enlivener, this spiced wine should be made with
leaves, seeds, barks, and roots as whole as possible. The herbs and
spices are not strained out but remain in the wine, which you can
store in the refrigerator for as long as three years, replacing herbs
and topping off with additional wine as you use it up. Leave out
the guarana if you do not want the caffeine content.

> 1 ounce allspice
> ¼ ounce whole cloves
> 1 ounce cinnamon sticks
> 2 ounces astragalus
> 1 ounce nutmeg
> 2 ounces root ginger
> 1 ounce fennel seeds
> 1 ounce star anise
> 1 ounce bay leaves
> ¼ guarana (optional)
> 2 bottles good red wine (Beaujolais or Burgundy)

Place all herbs and spices in a large see-through container
that has a tight lid. Cover with wine and refrigerate for two
weeks. Strain off a wineglassful and bring the wine to room
temperature or warm it over a gentle heat before drinking.

AMANDA'S TONIC FOR WOMEN

This standard women's tonic, when taken daily for at least three
months, will act as a vitality booster. The addition of the ginger

brings warmth to the drink, helps soothe nausea, and aids digestion.

>3 ounces vitex
>1 ounce tang kwei
>½ ounce ginger root
>3 ounces chamomile
>2 ounces cramp bark
>1 ounce Siberian ginseng
>40 percent alcohol

Place all herbs in a container with a tight-fitting lid. Cover
with alcohol of your choice—vodka or brandy perhaps—
and set aside for two weeks. Strain and bottle the tincture,
and take ½ teaspoon in a glass of water three times a day.

TONIC FOR MEN

This potent tonic is a man's equivalent of the above recipe. The
yohimbe is optional, so do not be concerned if you cannot easily
obtain some. Take this potion daily for between two and six
weeks, stopping when you feel a definite boost in energy.

>2 ounces prickly ash
>1 ounce orange peel
>2 ounces sarsaparilla
>1 ounce cinnamon sticks
>1 ounce licorice root
>1 ounce thyme
>2 ounces saw palmetto berries
>1 ounce valerian
>1 ounce ginseng
>¼ ounce yohimbe (optional)
>40 percent alcohol
>Honey or barley malt to taste

Place all herbs in a container with a tight-fitting lid. Cover
with alcohol of your choice—again, vodka and brandy are

good choices—and set aside in a dark place for two weeks.
Strain out herbs and spices but reserve the ginseng. Add
honey or barley malt to taste to the tincture. Bottle, and
replace the ginseng, which will remain in the liquid until all
the tonic is used. Take one tablespoon daily.

ROSEMARY GLADSTAR'S ELIXIR

This spicy, cherry potion is courtesy of herbalist Rosemary Glad-
star, of Vermont. It is an ambitious undertaking, and it takes a
little effort to gather all these herbs, but the resulting high-voltage
aphrodisiac is well worth the trouble. Take one tablespoon daily
for two weeks or until you begin to feel results, then switch to
one teaspoonful for two weeks. Give yourself a break for at least
a couple of months before trying the same regimen again. The
elixir will keep in a well-corked bottle.

2 ounces sassafras
1 ounce red clover
2 ounces ginger
1 ounce orange peel
1 ounce sarsaparilla
2 ounces cinnamon
2 ounces spikenard
¼ ounce wormwood
1 ounce juniper
1 ounce wild yam
2 ounces damiana
2 ounces saw palmetto
2 ounces muira puama
1 ounce lemon grass
1 ounce allspice
1 ounce nutmeg
2 ounces coriander
1 ounce fo-ti-tieng
1 ounce yohimbe
1 ounce suma

2 ounces kola
1 ounce astragalus
2 ounces kavakava
2 ounces barley malt
1 ounce vanilla
2 ounces burdock
40 percent alcohol
black cherry concentrate

Place all herbs and spices in a container with a tight-fitting lid. Cover with alcohol of your choice and set aside in a cool, dark place for two weeks. Strain and add black cherry concentrate to taste.

Should you have neither the time nor the inclination to become a home-based herbalist, you will find commercial herbal combination aphrodisiacs on sale in health food stores, usually in the form of teas or elixirs. Among other products containing combinations of the above herbs that are available at health food stores (also see resources section) are Love Tea, from Indian Herb Products; Michael's Manpower and Womanpower, Lady PEP, Cobra, and Prime Time, from PEP Products. (Any products containing yohimbe should be used in moderation since long-term use may cause side effects.)

The Chinese Tradition of Herbal Aphrodisiacs

The science of aphrodisia has been an integral part of Chinese medicine for centuries, with physicians including instructions on increasing sexual energy through the use of herbal soups detailed in the earliest Taoist writings.

Most Chinese see the world—and sexual relationships specifically—as being a balance of *yin* (female, receptive, yielding, passive, nourishing, related to the earth) and *yang* (male assertive, active, aggressive, related to heaven) energies. In the Chinese system of medicine, the body's organs integrate to keep the mind and body in this state of balance. Of primary importance to sexual energy is kidney, or jing, essence, which helps generate sperm and ova, balances hormonal systems, and provides energy to cells. To the Chinese the equation is simple: Healthy kidneys equal healthy sex. Many sexual ailments can be diagnosed as a deficiency in jing essence, or since jing essence contains both yin and yang, an imbalance of these energies in the kidneys. One other organ, the liver, also is taken into account because it governs the muscles (including the uterus) and tendons (the Chinese consider the penis the "original tendon"). So two other conditions are looked at as possible sources of sexual problems in Chinese herbalism: liver/kidney yin deficiency and liver qi (energy) stagnation.

Chinese diagnosis is usually made through an evaluation of the symptoms, the condition of the tongue, and the quality of the pulse. This is a rather complex system of diagnosis, and while you may be able to identify your problem from the information given here, if you have a medical condition, you would be wise to seek advice from a doctor who is familiar with herbs, or a physician trained in Oriental medicine. That way you can address any precautions that you need to take from the outset. The person behind the counter at a Chinese herb store generally won't sell you anything harmful, but use your common sense. Remember: Herbs combined with prescription or recreational drugs can produce disagreeable side effects. Find out before you experiment.

These herbal formulas often have a number as well as a name and are available in most large urban areas from Chinese herbalists, doctors of Oriental medicine, and acupuncturists. (Acupuncture is an excellent adjunct to herbal therapy for balancing these energies.) Chinese herbal aphrodisiacs come in several forms from different sources. Pills, powders, and tablets generally are exported from mainland China, the biggest supplier, and China also produces the highest quality of raw or unprocessed herbs. Japan tends to send us drinks and extractions. Taiwan exports concentrated herbs that are expensive but of high quality. When taking any of these tonics on a regular basis, stop when you have an acute illness such as cold or flu. During this time it is best to take specific medicinal herbs.

KIDNEY/JING ESSENCE DEFICIENCY

Low kidney/jing essence can be genetic or can be caused by poor nutrition, overwork, stress, chronic illness, or exposure to extreme cold, which can be damaging to the kidneys. According to Roger Hirsh, O.M.D., L.Ac., a Los Angeles doctor of Oriental medicine and acupuncturist, jing is like one's initial capital investment in sexual health: Aging is a gradual depletion of jing essence that occurs just from modern daily living. The general symptoms of this condition are:

- low sex drive
- inability to maintain an erection
- infertility or low sperm count, especially after having had an STD
- habitual miscarriages
- chronic fatigue
- premature graying or loss of hair
- degenerative bone disorders or weak knees not due to injury
- hearing loss or ringing in the ears
- a red, leathery, and peeling tongue
- a floating and empty pulse

Some specific herbal formulas to treat these conditions include Tai Pang Tang Yi Wan, a general nutritive tonic for both men and women that is especially recommended for low sex drive due to surgery or trauma. Ren Shen Lu Rong Wan is a kidney tonic containing ginseng, tang kwei, and astragalus among other herbs, and is helpful for impotence, premature ejaculation, menstrual problems, and poor circulation. It helps restore women's strength after childbirth. The formula comes as pills that can be chewed or crushed and taken in hot water. One of the most popular combinations for this condition comes in three different forms: Golden Book Tea, Golden Deficient Kidney Qi Pills, and Jin Kui Shen Qi Wan.

KIDNEY YIN DEFICIENCY

Kidney yin deficiency can also be caused by overwork, and in some cases by prolonged periods of excessive sexual activity, especially as a teenager. It can be brought about by taking too much kidney yang tonic. The sexual addict—a person with prodigious desires and an inability to be satisfied—is believed to suffer a certain kind of kidney yin deficiency called "empty fire rising." The more common symptoms are:

- inability to maintain an erection
- premature ejaculation
- erotic dreams and nocturnal emissions
- light or no periods, or dysfunctional uterine bleeding
- severe menstrual cramps
- menopausal symptoms such as hot flashes
- insomnia
- excessive sweating and a sensation of elevated body temperature
- headaches
- blurred vision
- low-back pain
- constipation
- red or red-rimmed tongue with slight furring
- thready, rapid pulse

The classic Chinese formula for increasing kidney yin is called Liu Wei Huang Wan. This herbal mix is especially helpful for people with high blood pressure or diabetes and can be taken for long periods of time with no side effects. Quiet Contemplation Kidney Yin Tonic is a slight variation on the above with an additional six herbs to further nourish kidney yin. This product and another—Da Bu Yin Wan—are both excellent for menopausal women experiencing hot flashes.

KIDNEY YANG DEFICIENCY

There is no particular "cause" of yang deficiency, as kidney yang is an exterior manifestation of kidney yin. In most cases kidney-yang-deficient people will possess at least three of these signs:

- low sex drive
- difficulty in reaching orgasm
- apathy
- frequent urination at night
- low back pain
- cold extremities and poor circulation
- feeling cold, or fear of cold
- painful heels
- dripping of urine or clear prostatic fluid after a bowel movement in men
- pale, swollen, wet tongue
- thready pulse

For symptoms of deficient-kidney yang try Golden Deficient Kidney Qi or a variation of the same formula called Dynamic Warrior, which has been developed specifically to combat twentieth-century syndromes. Kang Wei Ling is an excellent yang tonic to increase sex drive in men: I prescribed it for an older patient who had a new young lover, and he improved his ability to hold an erection and had more frequent intercourse. The enchantingly named Hindu Magic Pills were first prepared by Buddhist monks at the beginning of the Tang dynasty (A.D. 600–906) and increase libido in kidney-yang deficient people when taken an hour before bedtime.

LIVER/KIDNEY YIN DEFICIENCY

The liver stores blood, nourishes the uterus, and influences menstruation. Additionally, in men the liver meridian pathway encircles the penis, and hindrances in the flow of energy through this meridian can manifest in erection and ejaculation difficulties. You may be suffering from liver/kidney-yin deficiency if you have more than five of the following symptoms:

- low sex drive
- light or no periods
- night sweats
- emotional or angry outbursts
- dizziness
- headaches
- dry eyes and throat
- blurry vision or loss of visual acuity
- red, peeled, or cracked tongue
- thready pulse

Tang Kwei and Salvia, a potion based on three patent medicines, was developed by Timothy Ray, O.M.D., L.Ac., and is a good choice for women suffering from PMS, fibrocystic breast disease, menopausal symptoms, anxiety, irritability, and depression. For depletion of sexual energy, men and women alike can try Shou Wu Chih, containing tang kwei and several other herbs.

LIVER QI STAGNATION

According to Oriental medicine, the liver controls emotions and the nervous system. If you have great creative drive and sexual energy, chances are your liver is healthy. But all too often today the liver is congested or stagnant, resulting from unhappy working conditions; frustrating family problems; poor diet with excess coffee, sugar, and alcohol; or years of taking birth control pills. Women are particularly prone to this condition, and the following signs are a tipoff:

- premenstrual syndrome
- irregular periods
- irritability
- depression
- breast tenderness and cysts

• headaches
• bowstring pulse

Shue Gan Wan—often appropriately called Soothe Liver Pill—is excellent for relieving the symptoms of PMS when taken for one to two weeks before the onset of menstruation. Hsiah Yao Wan—Free and Relaxed Tea—is recommended.

If you don't fall into any of these categories, you can safely take kidney-essence tonics to maintain your sexual vitality. Then, when you are looking to light a sexual fire for a special night of lovemaking, try one of the supertonic formulas developed by Timothy Ray. Lady Passion speaks for itself: In women who are already healthy it has potent aphrodisiacal effects, and for those who are feeling a bit jaded it should act as a tonic. Red Rooster is a male equivalent, and you can both take Honeymooner's Tea as a reviver next day. A new product from Lifephase called Love Life I combines Chinese herbs and vitamins and minerals as a vitalizer for sexual potency in both men and women. It is made to be taken synergistically with Love Life II, a homeopathic combination to enhance sexual potency and restore low libidos.

Ayurvedic Herbs and Sexuality

The system of Ayurvedic medicine may date back as far as 4000 B.C. Originating in India, it was spread by way of Hindu and Buddhist cultures throughout the East and influenced the medicine of Indonesia, China, Japan, Ceylon, and Tibet. With today's trend toward integrated global medicine, this holistic approach is being adapted in Western culture. Deepak Chopra, M.D., a widely respected endocrinologist, has described in his book *Quantum Healing* how these theories merge with those of modern physics. Included in this Vedic science are herbal medicine, dietetics, body work, surgery, psychology, and spirituality.

These medical disciplines are brought to bear on three operating principles called *doshas,* or biological humors. Each humor is present in the body, but every individual will have a predominance of one in their constitutional nature, both physically and mentally.

Vata, the air humor, is dry, cold, and light. Vata-type people are said to be thin, small, and feel chilly. They have dry skin and hair, tend toward diseases of the nervous and immune systems and arthritis. Their minds are quick and changeable and they easily experience feelings of fear and anxiety.

Pitta corresponds with fire, and is hot, moist, and light. Pitta people generally have medium frames and musculature, are intolerant of heat, and suffer from infections and inflammatory diseases. They are more passionate than vatas but can also be more angry and quarrelsome.

Kapha, the water humor, is cold, moist, and heavy. They are the fattiest and can lean toward obesity. They have oily hair and skin and a propensity toward diseases of the respiratory tract, excess mucous, and edema. Of the three types, kaphas are temperamentally the most steady, calm, and sentimental.

Another important aspect in considering the Ayurvedic approach to aphrodisia is the concept of *ojas,* the essential energy of the body, the "vigor" of the reproductive and immune systems. We are born with a certain amount of ojas, which is depleted by such factors as overwork, stress, anxiety, poor diet, inadequate sleep, use of drugs, and too much sex. (If this is beginning to sound familiar, it's because ojas could be considered the Ayruvedic version of jing essence in the Chinese system.) When we have a deficiency of ojas, we are prone to disease. When ojas is completely depleted or destroyed, we die.

The science of Ayurveda sees rejuvenation—the replenishment of ojas—and sexuality in the same context, as a reflection of inner vitality. The reproductive tissue is considered the source of creation in the body. Specific herbs called *vijakarasana*—vija means stallion—promote this vitality and invigorate the body by rejuvenating the sexual organs. These herbs are either tonics that nurture and direct sexual energy toward regeneration or are stimulants that excite sexual activity through irritation of the sex organs. Often they increase kapha or pitta, depending on your constitution.

Other herbs are known as *rasayana*. These help prevent disease and promote positive health. In other words they enhance natural immunity. As part of that process they promote ojas and increase youthfulness and sexual vitality.

Vijakaranas and *rasayanas* include some of the herbs you are now familiar with: Solomon's seal, saw palmetto, tang kwei, wild yam, licorice, ginseng, and fo-ti-tieng, as well as spices such as saffron and cloves, and flowers like roses and hibiscus. In addition, there are a number of herbs specific to India that are listed below.

AMLA

Amla, or amlaki, is believed to increase ojas and is one of the strongest rejuvenative herbs in Ayurvedic medicine. It contains large amounts of vitamin C, which remains stable in the herb even when heated. Amla is the primary ingredient used in one of the most renowned Ayurvedic herbal formulas, called *Chayavanprasha*.

Chayavan was a great sage. According to legend, the emperor's daughter was playing blindfolded in the forest when she stumbled on the famous man. Not realizing he was a stranger, she ran her fingers through his hair and decorated him with garlands of flowers. At that moment her father came upon the scene and requested that the sage marry his daughter, as it was customary that a woman touch only one man in her lifetime. Since it had been some years since the aged sage had been with a woman, he asked for some time to prepare. He created chayavanprasha and lived on it for two months, during which time he regained youthfulness and sexual vitality.

Beside amla, chayavanprasha contains between thirty and fifty other herbs depending upon where it is prepared, and is full of iron, calcium, silica, sodium, potassium, phosphates, plant sterols, and vitamin C. A published study has shown its effectiveness in treating debilitating diseases such as tuberculosis.

This formula comes in the form of a jelly and is found in most markets throughout India. One-half teaspoonful stirred into warm water each morning is said to bestow love and longevity to all who take it.

ASHWAGANDA

Also known as winter cherry, ashwaganda *(Withania somnifera)* is one of the most widely used rejuvenative tonic herbs in India. An adaptogenic, ashwaganda has been studied scientifically and shown to contain numerous nutrients, including plant sterols. Since it is anabolic, this herb provides an excellent, safe alternative to steroids for increasing muscle mass. Ashwaganda means "that which has the smell of a horse," indicating the sexual power of the horse. Since ashwaganda is nontoxic, it is safe to take over long periods of time to increase vitality; it can be used by men, women, and even children. The root is usually used in powdered form and prepared by boiling in milk for 10 to 20 minutes.

BALA

Bala is a member of the mallow family. It has cooling and sweetening properties. Although many species of mallow are used in Ayurvedic medicine, bala is specifically mentioned here for its tonic and rejuvenative qualities and its ability to soothe inflammatory conditions of the nervous system. Bala also has a healing effect on the urinary tract, particularly the prostate. It is recommended when there is prostatic enlargement, impotence, or inflammations in the genitourinary tract, such as cystitis or prostatitis.

GOKSHURA

Known in the United States as goat's head, puncture vine or caltrop, gokshura *(Tribulus terrestris)* is used as a kidney tonic in Ayurveda. Not only does it strengthen, rejuvenate, and calm that organ, it also has diuretic properties without any side effects known to other diuretics. Women can take gokshura to increase lactation when their milk supply is low due to emotional upset.

KAPIKACCU

This rejuvenative herb can be used by both men and women. For men kapikaccu can help relieve sterility, enlarged prostate, and impotence; for women it is a nutritive during pregnancy as well as menopause.

LOTUS

The lotus, India's most sacred plant, symbolizes spiritual unfolding, and, being linked with Lakshimi, the goddess of prosperity, also represents material abundance. Both the seeds and the root are employed in herbal aphrodisiacal preparations, and they can be combined with basmati rice. Further, lotus seeds are considered to have an affinity for the heart and are used in powdered form as a heart tonic. The root is said to stop bleeding, especially abnormal uterine bleeding or that associated with miscarriages. It is also recommended for diarrhea and hemorrhoids.

PIPPALI

Pippali *(Piper longum)* is an Indian long pepper related to black pepper and used as a stimulant to the reproductive, digestive, and respiratory systems. As an aphrodisiac it warms and energizes, but because it increases heat, it is not recommended for people with excess pitta. Pippali is especially good for the lungs when there is a buildup of mucous due to colds and bronchitis.

SHATAVARI

A member of the asparagus family, shatavari *(Asparagus racemosus)* is regarded as one of the finest tonics for women. In Sanscrit shatavari means "who possesses a hundred husbands." This root nourishes and increases fertility and is also excellent for menopausal women or those who have had a hysterectomy. Shatavari is said to foster deep feelings of love and compassion.

As in Western and Chinese herbal disciplines, Ayurvedic herbs often exert a stronger action when taken in combinations. The following three tonics were devised by David Frawley, O.M.D., director of the American Institute for Ayurvedic Studies in Santa Fe, and are modern versions of ancient formulas. Some of these ingredients will be available from herbalists, some even in Indian markets. You can also consult an Ayurvedic doctor or order your herbs by mail from sources listed in the appendix.

WOMAN'S TONIC OR SHATAVARI COMPOUND

This can be taken for all "female complaints": menstruation, menopause, infertility, anemia, breast disease.

> 3 parts shatavari
> 2 parts comfrey root
> 1 part cyprus
> 1 part red raspberry leaves
> 1 part saffron

Mix all ingredients together and use 1 to 4 grams mixed in warm milk, warm water, or ginger tea three times daily before meals.

ASHWANGANDA ENERGY TONIC

A safe, long-term tonic for all three doshas, this formula is particularly good for boosting sex drive and for people suffering from arthritis, diabetes, and weak immune functioning.

> 4 parts ashwaganda
> 2 parts shatavari
> 2 parts pueraria
> 1 part pippali

Mix all ingredients and take 2 to 5 grams in warm milk or water three times daily with meals.

SEXUAL VITALITY FORMULA

For men with prostate problems. It can also be taken as an aphrodisiac and rejuvenative.

Equal parts of:
gokshura
asteracantha longifolia
kapikaccu
ashwaganda
shatavari

Mix all the ingredients together and take 1 to 4 grams morning and evening.

There is an abundance of plant species on this earth to nurture and pleasure us; it has been said that the cures for all human ailments can be found growing in the Amazon basin alone. This abundance of plant aphrodisiacs is another reason to prohibit the use of animals that are headed for extinction. The handful of herbs listed here merely scratches the surface of the plants that ultimately may be found, but they are ancient, tried-and-true, and deserve an honored place in any list of aphrodisiacs.

8

HEALING APHRODISIA: HOMEOPATHY AND FLOWER ESSENCES

*The lily is an herb with a white flower. And though
the leaves of the flower be white; yet within shineth the
likeness of gold.*
—BARTHOLOMAEUS ANGLICUS

Sex that transports you to another world—sex the way it is supposed to be—depends on a balance of physical, mental, and emotional factors. When the man is battered by stress, or the woman is seething with premenstrual irritability, they won't enjoy uniting no matter how much they love each other. Prostate problems, depression, and lack of physical sensation are among the many factors that impair lovemaking. It is therefore important to choose a therapy that addresses the specific obstacle to contentment.

Homeopathy, which is believed by many to be an effective way to balance body and psyche, could be the answer. This alternative medical procedure has been used to treat sexual problems with both organic and psychological bases. It has been used for specific male and female complaints such as impotence and vaginal dryness, and for general complaints such as sexual indifference.

Homeopathy employs the natural healing energy of the body in order to return it to a state of healthy equilibrium. The form practiced today was developed in the late eighteenth century by a German physician named Samuel Hahnemann, who used the phrase from Hippocrates: *similia similibus curantur*—like cures like.

With homeopathy, a condition is treated by administering minute doses of substances that would cause similar symptoms when given in large doses to a healthy person. Hahnemann became intrigued by the concept when he discovered that if a well individual took quinine (the accepted remedy for malaria), that person would get symptoms very like those experienced by a malaria sufferer. He concluded that by using minute doses of natural substances, the body more effectively resisted that disease.

Hahnemann and subsequent practitioners of homeopathy cataloged hundreds of natural substances as remedies. Researchers administered them to healthy volunteers, then noted meticulously what symptoms the substances produced. This process is known as proving. After a number of such human trials, a clear picture of the symptoms emerges and the substance is assessed for usefulness against conditions with a similar set of symptoms. This law of similars was documented as long ago as 400 B.C. by Hippocrates—the "father of medicine"— and later by Paracelsus, a renowned Renaissance doctor and alchemist.

Anyone who has had a vaccination has experienced the homeopathic principle in action. When being vaccinated against a viral disease, the patient is given an injection of the offending virus in a minute quantity that causes a mild reaction, followed by immunity. The same principle applies to allergy shots. Injections of allergens such as pollen, horsehair, or cat dander generally will produce mild local reactions to the shot, eventually resulting in immunity to the substances that formerly made life snifflingly miserable.

Homeopathy takes the principle one step further. Hahnemann believed that "miasms" were the root of all chronic disease and also contributed to some acute problems. He believed that miasmic traits deep within the body "in vibrational patterns" contributed to genetically inherited diseases. According to Hahnemann, miasms such as tuberculosis or syphilis could lie dormant in the cells for many years, only expressing themselves when the body becomes imbalanced. After years of carefully documented clinical research, he came to believe that the body contains a vital force that promotes healing. He and his disciples studied thousands of plant extracts, minerals, and other natural substances to determine their effects, not only on the body and miasms, but also on the emotions. Homeopathic doctors treat the patient, not the disease.

Homeopathy is enjoying a cautious revival in a culture accustomed to allopathic doctors who use drugs or surgery to treat disease. An allopathic doctor might prescribe a medicine that will constipate for a patient suffering from diarrhea, whereas the homeopathic doctor will use minute doses of a medicine that will cause diarrhea in large doses. The relationship between the two disciplines has often been stormy, with homeopathy generally finding more acceptance in Europe and India than in the United States from both the medical profession and the general public. Many European heads of state and members of royal families have been public champions of homeopathy. Most recently, Jacques Benveniste, a French scientist and immunologist and member of the French Medical Research Council, has been a respected if controversial advocate for the cause, with his paper published in *Nature*. Even the *Lancet* has published a paper discussing the use and effectiveness of homeopathic medicines. And in 1991, the esteemed *British Medical Journal* published a groundbreaking survey of clinical research verifying the value of homeopathic medicine.

The United States is beginning to catch up in terms of respect for homeopathy. A course in homeopathic medicine is offered at the University of Arizona Medical School, and the application and integration of homeopathy is being studied in a Complementary Medicine Program at Laing-the University of Maryland. Traditional and homeopathic medical disciplines can easily work in tandem. Some people prefer the natural approach to avoid the side effects that often accompany pharmaceutical drugs.

How to Use Homeopathy
for Aphrodisia

Among the hundreds of natural substances in the homeopathic pharmacopeia are many that help overcome sexual problems. Should you decide to pursue the homeopathic route to better sex, first speak with your medical doctor, then work with a trained homeopath to ensure that you are using the best dilution of a given remedy for your particular goal. Homeopathic remedies are available without prescription at many pharmacies, however, and while you may not get optimal results from self-medicating, these remedies will do you no harm.

They are prepared through a process known as potentization, which involves diluting the substance many times with water. With each dilution the water is shaken vigorously. This is called succession. Recent research has shown that the water when combined with kinetic energy during succession creates an electromagnetic imprint that is carried in the water. This may explain why the more dilute remedies are more powerful. Acute health problems are generally treated with the lower dilutions or low potencies. Chronic ailments tend to be treated with the more dilute preparations, called high potencies.

Homeopathic remedies come in the form of tablets, liquids, topicals, and injectables. The tablets have a milk sugar base, and the liquids are in at least 20 percent alcohol to retard spoilage. Injectables are in sterile saline, and the topicals are a cream or gel. The liquid potions are taken under the tongue. Tablets are allowed to dissolve in the same way so the remedy is absorbed by the plexus of blood vessels in that area and transmitted into the bloodstream in a mater of seconds. For the purposes of this book, the liquid or the tablets are most appropriate. Injectables are for the use of physicians only.

Take homeopathic remedies at least 10 to 15 minutes before meals or at least an hour after eating. Avoid lozenges or chest rubs with camphor, eucalyptus, or menthol bases immediately after taking a remedy, and limit intake of caffeine, nicotine, and mint, as these may have a counteractive effect on many substances.

Samuel Hahnemann also exhorted his patients to swear off "debauchery, masturbation and reading obscene books." His attitude was consistent with the puritanical mores of his time, but contemporary homeopaths are not as rigid and, of course, will prescribe remedies for sexual purposes.

Unlike allopathic remedies, which are general cures for specific diseases, homeopathy is an individualized form of medicine. Because homeopathy is intended to promote corporeal and psychological harmony, the personality is considered along with the physical symptoms, and each remedy is categorized for a personality type as well as for a specific condition. Following are some of the remedies most often recommended for certain character traits and specific sexual problems. Used in conjunction with any necessary medical and psychological treatment, they can prove helpful.

AGNUS CASTUS

The typical personality who responds well to agnus castus (derived from the chaste tree) suffers bouts of depression and melancholy overlaid by a sense of foreboding. Agnus castus can be a powerful remedy for reproductive-system problems. In homeopathic doses it is used to treat impotency or frigidity, particularly among the elderly. Men who can benefit most are those who have lost their sexual appetite and vitality. According to homeopaths, these men say their sex organs are "cold" and they get no erections at all, as opposed to the man who has nocturnal erections but doesn't become tumescent during lovemaking. Agnus castus–type women are said to have a distaste for making love, coupled with light menstruation and even sterility.

DAMIANA

Early herbalists were well acquainted with the aphrodisiacal qualities of damiana *(Turnera aphrodisica)*, a plant that is indigenous to tropical parts of North and Central America and the West

Indies. In homeopathic preparations, damiana is used specifically for enhancing sensuality, especially when there is a loss of sensation. It is said to be effective in cases of impotence due to nervousness and anxiety. Young girls whose menstrual cycles are irregular may help balance their systems with damiana.

IGNATIA

The erratic and moody ignatia personality typically is given to irritability, sighing, crying, and hysteria. Made from Saint Ignatius beans native to the Philippines, ignatia is the remedy of choice for those people whose sexual urge and functioning have been affected by emotional trauma, disappointment, or grief, all of which can create psychological barriers to intimacy. Shock often causes people to become cautious and erect a barbed-wire fence around their emotions. Ignatia can help considerably with the opening-up process as well as the revival of sexual interest after mourning. It is especially effective when the grief also has physical manifestations such as loss of menses.

LYCOPODIUM

Lycopodium comes from the spores of club moss, the delicate green plant that grows on tree trunks deep in the forest. The lycopodium personality is a paradox, fearing both solitude and intimacy. Oversensitivity, eruptions of anger, and a proclivity for bursting into tears are also common characteristics.

A patient of mine, Patrick, complained to his doctor of an inability to maintain an erection. He was particularly perplexed because before his marriage he'd had an active sex life with many different women. But now he found it difficult to sustain sexual passion for his wife and was becoming increasingly distant from her. In conversation it came out he feared the responsibility demanded by a structured relationship. This is another telltale characteristic of the lycopodium personality, so I prescribed lycopodium. Patrick reported that it helped; it also bolstered his overall self-confidence.

Lycopodium is also recommended for men with enlarged prostates and those who have difficulty initiating urination. It is a good remedy for impotence, especially when the desire is there but the flesh simply does not respond, and the penis remains small, "cold," and flaccid. Women with tenderness in the ovaries, vaginal dryness resulting in painful intercourse, and heavy periods may also gain some relief with lycopodium. Both sexes with this personality type can have problems with their livers and digestive systems, and should watch for symptoms such as flatulence, constipation, and hemorrhoids.

MEDORRHINUM

You may be surprised to learn that medorrhinum is a homeopathic remedy prepared from gonorrhea bacteria. The personality for whom medorrhinum can be beneficial tends to be anxious and fearful, and can entertain thoughts of suicide. Compulsive by nature, these people often use drugs or alcohol to excess and can have active sex lives characterized by multiple partners, casual sex, and frequent masturbation.

Medorrhinum can have a profound effect on sexuality, especially when the patient has had gonorrhea in the past. Not used as a cure for the disease, medorrhinum is effective rather on the residual effects of the bacteria in the body. It exerts its action on the nervous system, mucous membranes, skin, and joints. The complaints that could be helped by this remedy are burning sensations in the hands and feet, lower-back pain, and hot and cold flashes.

My patient Neal was a healthy man in his forties who had recurring symptoms of burning in the urethra. He'd previously had gonorrhea, which causes this condition, but he had been treated with antibiotics, and tests revealed he currently did not have chlamydia, the other usual suspect for this condition. After I put him on medorrhinum, Neal's symptoms quickly cleared up.

Women may benefit from medorrhinum if they have intense itching of the vulva, heavy periods with severe cramping, pain in the ovaries, or an irritating vaginal discharge. The remedy is also helpful in cases of chronic pelvic disorders.

PHOSPHOROUS

The word comes from Greek mythology, where Phosphor (the Light-Bringer) was the morning star. We know it as an element, a white solid that ignites spontaneously at room temperature. The phosphorous personality is always in love, full of passion, and tends to be the life of the party. But this bright spark is also impressionable, easily confused, and tends to lack perspective. Like the element that rapidly dissolves into smoke, the phosphorous person easily burns out. As a homeopathic remedy, phosphorous has been used for years for balancing the heart, circulation, liver, lungs, and nervous system, and for regulating an excessive sexual urge.

SELENIUM

Selenium is a mineral functioning in the body as an antioxidant. It is particularly important for ailments involving the immune system and for problems associated with aging. When used homeopathically, selenium can be efficacious to the sexual organs, especially in men when there is increased sexual desire with loss of erections.

Symptoms that will respond well to selenium are a tendency toward exhaustion, memory loss, insomnia, and melancholia. Men with prostatic enlargement or who are prone to premature ejaculation may benefit from homeopathic doses of selenium. One cautionary note: Overdosing the selenium supplements can actually cause some of the symptoms mentioned above.

SEPIA

Made from the ink of cuttlefish, sepia is primarily a woman's remedy, specifically associated with dark-haired, dark-eyed women with sallow complexions. It is often prescribed for those unhappy with their lot and feeling overburdened by a job and taking care of the home and children. The sepia personality can be moody and despondent as a result of her amorous concerns, angry around the time of her period, and pessimistic or indifferent toward her family.

Sepia can be effective in relieving vaginal bleeding, fibroids, premenstrual syndrome, uterine prolapse, low sexual energy, and, oddly enough, a craving for chocolate. Sepia is an excellent remedy for women suffering with PMS or menopausal symptoms, especially when depression is a major problem. Almost every homeopath has a "sepia story" involving a woman in tears complaining of postchildbirth sexual indifference. The woman who can benefit from sepia therapy will frequently complain of a "bearing down" sensation in the lower abdomen or of pressure in the genitals. Men suffering from low sexual energy or intellectual fatigue may also find sepia helpful.

STAPHYSAGRIA

Also known as stavesacre, this plant is a member of the Ranunculaceae family, which grows in the Mediterranean basin. The person responding to staphysagria can be, at one extreme, oversensitive and easily excited, and at the other extreme may show sudden outbursts of violent passion. Transsexuals and persons prone to sexual practices such as crossdressing usually fall into this category, too. It can be a wonderful remedy when repressed anger or shame—such as that experienced by most incest victims—is undermining the ability to have healthy sexual alliances.

My patient was abused as a child and was having serious difficulty with her relationships. She was embarrassed to even talk about sex and was repressed to the point at which even masturbation was unthinkable. Traditional psychotherapy along with homeopathic doses of staphysagria helped her to overcome those feelings and freed her from crippling guilt.

Staphysagria acts on the urogenital tract, the skin, and the nervous system. Women with recurring urinary infections, especially "honeymoon cystitis," and men who experience burning that is relieved with passing urine may find some relief from this remedy. In doses other than homeopathic, staphysagria is poisonous.

YOHIMBE

Yohimbe is a centuries-old curative for impotence that comes from the inner bark of the yohimbeye tree, a native of tropical West Africa. Used homeopathically, it can improve sexual function, prolong erections, and increase sensation in the sex organs. In conjunction with medical treatment, it can be a useful remedy for impotence that has an organic cause, such as diabetes or atherosclerosis. Try it if you have problems with circulation and loss of sensation in the genital area.

Homeopathic remedies rarely have the side effects common to allopathic drugs, and, since most contain such small amounts of the original substance, you are unlikely to have an allergic reaction. Some homeopathic compounds have immediate results; others can take months to bring about a change in the condition. But when change does occur, it is often more profound than any produced by allopathic medication.

If the foregoing list does not include a homeopathic treatment that suits you, a combination formula may be the answer. Two excellent products from BHI, out of Albuquerque, are BHI Feminine, for hormonal imbalances in women, and BHI Masculine, for men with prostate problems. BHI Mulimen, a newer product in their line, is recommended for PMS and menopause, especially when depression, anxiety, and sleep disturbance is predominant. Love Life II, a homeopathic combination from Lifephase, is designed to boost and restore sexual energy. All of these products contain several of the individual remedies mentioned above. See the resources section for further information.

Homeopathy is, in its broad definition, an alternative method of healing, but in the context of this book it has an especially interesting offshoot: flower essences, a natural form of aphrodisiac.

Bach Flower Essences

In the early part of this century, Edward Bach, a British pathologist and bacteriologist, became disenchanted with the bad side effects of the drugs he was prescribing in his traditional practice. He turned to homeopathy and during the course of experimentation reached the conclusion that disease is caused by disharmony between the spiritual and mental aspects of the human being. Bach searched for a system of healing that addressed what he believed to be the source of disease: negative emotions that cause an imbalance in the body, mind, and spirit.

Bach was a "sensitive." When he came into contact with certain flowers, he was able to intuit the emotional state that could be helped by each flower. After noticing animals lapping the dew that formed on petals, he ascertained that this water, which had been exposed to sunlight, had a unique quality, and resolved to find a process that would create the same effect. Instead of drying or cooking the flowers, as was done in traditional herbal medicine, Bach covered fresh petals with distilled water and put them to soak in sunlight. This flower essence was then preserved in brandy and administered to patients. Bach considered flower essences a form of "vibrational" medicine. Unlike drugs and herbal medicines, they essentially act on the body's energy field rather than its chemistry.

Bach started out with twelve primary essences, using them on patients who had a variety of physical and psychological problems. Since his time, further exploration has expanded the number of flowers believed to affect emotional states; more than 500 essences are now in use. Doctors in England have continued Bach's work, and the Bach Healing Center in Berkshire has accumulated hundreds of reports on the success of their methods.

How, then, can flower remedies help make your love life more rich and fulfilling?

Flowers are perhaps nature's most radiant form of beauty. Their petals, smoother than the most perfect human skin, and their dazzling colors have always been a method of communicating the feelings of love, carnal desire, friendship, and sympathy.

But herbalists and aromatherapists have gone much further, and have discovered that flowers can cure certain ailments as well as stir the passions.

Sexual intimacy is the most direct and personal expression of who you are. If you bring to the act of love fear and disappointment stemming from previous unhappy relationships, or are tense and anxious, you can hardly expect to achieve the openness and vulnerability necessary for your contentment and that of your partner.

Bach's followers, and many others, believe that these problems not only interfere with intimacy, but also cause sexual indifference, impotency, and frigidity. Flower remedies can be a pleasant, nontoxic way to balance the emotions, raise spiritual awareness, and clear the way to achieving higher states of consciousness. All of these can help the sex life.

The essences I discuss are most successfully used for healing purposes in combination with psychotherapy. I recommend that anyone using them be seeing a therapist, since the essences can accelerate the rise of buried emotions.

The use of flower essences can be easily combined with homeopathic or conventional medicines. I often prescribe three to four essences together. The essences listed below are a few that are more specific for issues regarding sexuality, but there are others that may help you. Check the bibliography for books pertaining to flower essences or contact the organizations in the resources section for a flower-essence therapist.

AGRIMONY

This is prescribed for people who flaunt a devil-may-care attitude, the apparently perpetual optimists who deny that anything is wrong with them, while hiding emotional pain. Afraid to be alone, the agrimony type may be prone to insomnia or alcohol and drug abuse.

ASPEN

Aspen is said to be helpful for the phobic individual, someone who is apprehensive and full of foreboding for no real reason.

CLEMATIS

Clematis is for people who are inattentive and dreamy. These individuals may feel disconnected from their bodies and have difficulty becoming "grounded." Clematis can assist them to be more fully present in the moment.

CRAB APPLE

A possible remedy for those who suffer from feelings of shame or uncleanliness, have a poor self-image, or see themselves as unattractive, crab apple is also suitable for use in any detoxification process.

ELM

Elm is believed to be useful for those who suffer from self-doubt: the person who is capable and efficient yet easily overwhelmed by responsibility and obsessed by his or her own need for perfectionism. It can also ameliorate sexual "performance anxiety."

HOLLY

Jealousy and resentment often destroy relationships. Holly can encourage the individual who feels needy and insecure to open his or her heart to unconditional loving.

HONEYSUCKLE

If you tend to dwell too much on the past, try honeysuckle. It can help people who can't face the present and who cling to old emotions. Incest victims can benefit, as honeysuckle often releases painful feelings associated with that trauma.

MIMULUS

Like aspen, mimulus fights generalized fear, but also specific anxieties of a known origin such as fear of darkness, aging, illness, social situations, success and failure, and sexual inadequacy. It is beneficial in overcoming shyness.

OLIVE

Exhausted? Olive can help with the fatigue experienced after emotional or physical illness. It increases strength and stamina and can have a rejuvenating effect.

RESCUE REMEDY

Composed of five flower essences, Rescue Remedy is the most popular and widely used of all the Bach remedies. It contains star of Bethlehem, rock rose, impatiens, cherry plum, and clematis. Rescue Remedy is indicated when there has been trauma or shock. I have found it especially useful in emergency situations.

STAR OF BETHLEHEM

This remedy can be applied following physical or emotional trauma when the victim cannot be consoled. This also means in "delayed-action" cases when the trauma manifests itself months or years later in the form of illness or dysfunction. Rape is a typical case in point. A woman may experience sexual difficulties or fertility problems years after the incident took place.

Flower Essence Society Remedies

Following the Bach principle, the Flower Essence Society was organized by Richard Katz and Patricia Kaminski in the 1970s. Located in Nevada City, California, the society has expanded Bach's repertoire to include many local garden and wild flowers;

it is the hub of a worldwide network of practitioners who exchange information based on empirical studies. The society also trains and certifies people in the discipline. The cases described in this section were documented through the society.

According to Patricia Kamenski, a practicing flower essence therapist and researcher, there are two aspects to consider when seeking to heal sexual problems with flower essences. The first is the physical. Sexuality is an expression of vitality, and unless you have a vibrant, glad-to-be-alive outlook, you are unlikely to be brimming with sexual energy. The following three essences may help.

FUCHSIA

This tropical shrub with its lovely pendulous magenta flowers also imparts energy to the lower parts of the body. Repressions often can be liberated with fuchsia, allowing the user to blossom sexually and enjoy the delicious release of orgasm.

NASTURTIUM

This fiery-orange, earthy-looking flower brings life force into the body's lower chakras. It should be the essence of choice for people who tend to "live in their heads": scientists, students, and accountants, for example. Anyone who has forgotten about his or her body because of intellectual overwork could benefit from nasturtium. It is also tasty in salads.

PINK MONKEYFLOWER

Fear of vulnerability, of exposing the emotions, is a sadly common condition that pink monkeyflower can alleviate. Try this if you have allowed yourself to be used sexually; it may help resolve feelings of ugliness or bodily shame. It can enable you to be more willing to open your heart, and is especially good for men who mask their fears by displaying a macho front.

SCARLET MONKEYFLOWER

A botanical relative of sticky monkeyflower, this might be useful when sexuality is being sabotaged by underlying feelings of anger. Anger and sexuality are both seen as "red energy" in the human aura, and this flower helps to ensure that the energy is not destructive.

SELF-HEAL

Bringing life force to bear on the personality, self-heal could be the catalyst that makes you aware of all the ways in which you have been denying yourself the joyful experience of being alive. It can awaken inner powers of healing, self-confidence, and self-acceptance. Overweight people might try this remedy.

The second way in which flower essences are said to bolster sexuality is by acting on the emotions. Patricia Kaminski says that the soul, which she defines as the sheath of personality that is worn around the body, must be engaged sexually or it may be damaged. The following essences may help specifically emotional problems that have a bearing on sexuality.

STICKY MONKEYFLOWER

This essence—never mind the funny name—is prescribed for balancing sexual energy that is either out of control or repressed, and for integrating love and sexuality. It may aid in dealing with the fear of intimacy, in experiencing erotic warmth, and in releasing emotional blocks stemming from painful, unresolved past relationships. The person who has bottled up a fear, which then manifests itself in symptoms such as cysts, growths, or organ and sexual dysfunction, is a good candidate for sticky monkeyflower.

Mitchell is the type of patient who was helped by this flower remedy. He was raped by an uncle when a child. As an adult, he was afraid to urinate when others were near him, had some physical complaints, and was confused about his sexual orienta-

tion. This essence, together with counseling, helped him to process his emotional trauma and to discover sexuality as a form of
warmth and intimacy. Sticky monkeyflower can also help people
who for one reason or another have detached their sexuality from
human love and intimacy.

Three other flower essences can be used in combination with
any of the monkeyflowers. Mimulus is useful when you feel
fearful, black-eyed susan helps access feelings or events you may
have blocked and to tap into the unconscious, and bleeding heart
is recommended for helping to break off unhealthy attachments
or when there is a compulsion to behave inappropriately combined with an inability to establish intimacy. For example, if a man
or woman is blatantly flirting socially or having an affair in an
attempt to gain the attention of his or her mate.

BASIL

This warm, spicy herb is sacred in India. It was said to be found
growing around Christ's tomb, and some Greek Orthodox
priests use it to prepare holy water. Basil essence is used to treat
the type of personality that is split between the polarities of sex
and spirit.

Patricia Kaminski tells of a man who was hooked on pornography but was also a deeply spiritual person who practiced meditation daily. Because the man's obsession was traceable to his
mother's excessive interest in pornography, Kaminski treated him
successfully with basil combined with mariposa lily. This combination can be used to treat the Madonna/whore complex, in
which a man has a cold, puritanical relationship with his wife
while taking a mistress for his sexual expression.

BORAGE

This star-shaped Mediterranean plant has long had a place in the
herbalists' pharmacopeia. The Celtic word *borrach*, from which
"borage" comes, means courage. In medieval times competitors
in jousting tournaments drank borage tea to get up their courage,

and the flowers were floated in the stirrup cups given to Crusaders on their departure. As a flower essence, it is recommended for overcoming depression and discouragement and inspiring feelings of contentment and merriment.

EASTER LILY

This remedy, pure as its name suggests, has properties similar to sticky monkeyflower and is particularly effective when there is a sense of contamination—a feeling that sex is dirty—after a case of sexual abuse. It can also help people who are habitually drawn to unhealthy sexual relationships. Women who are good candidates for easter lily tend to have physical problems related to the reproductive system.

HIBISCUS

The dried petals of the hibiscus flower are frequently used in herbal teas, imparting a mild, refreshing flavor and bright-red color. Hibiscus-flower essence brings a female-like warmth to the sexual organs and is used specifically to encourage orgasm. Hibiscus can be used by women, and men too, to restore female softness, warmth, and relaxation to sexuality. The remedy proved effective in the following two cases. Marisa, after a period of intense spirituality, found that her sex life had dwindled almost to nothing—she had been seeking enlightenment, not celibacy! With hibiscus she was able to integrate her spirituality with her sexuality to the point that she now has a warm, fulfilling intimate life and is putting this healing vitality to work on opening her chakras and experiencing full body orgasm.

Sandy's situation was quite different. Although she was otherwise happily married, she was resigned to being anorgasmic. After starting on hibiscus essence, she began to perceive a shift in her relationship with her sexuality. Lovemaking became more enjoyable, and to her surprise she even began to initiate sexual contact after being largely passive. At last report she still had not had an orgasm, but was delighted by her new, more positive attitude toward lovemaking and by her greater intimacy with her mate.

LOTUS

This lovely flower grows on water and is a native of Asia and Egypt, where it was a symbol of spiritual enlightenment and was used in ceremonies and rituals. Ancient texts describe the chakras as lotus flowers radiating petals of brilliant light. The flower essence can be used to increase receptivity, enhance awareness, and create a mind/spirit balance to enable healing to take place. Lotus essence boosts the effectiveness of other remedies and can be used for longevity and tissue regeneration.

MARIPOSA LILY

Suggested for people feeling alienated or in need of nurturing, mariposa is also helpful in healing wounds from the past, particularly those relating to mother/child bonding. Victims of sexual trauma might try this one, too.

POMEGRANATE

The ancients saw the pomegranate fruit as a symbol of fertility. Pomegranate-flower essence is primarily a remedy for women, useful for balancing female organs when there are physical problems such as PMS, ovarian cysts, endometriosis, or infertility. The emotional issue that pomegranate addresses is the anguish women feel when forced to choose between using their creativity for the home and child or for career.

Pamela was a prime candidate for pomegranate therapy. A successful businesswoman who had given up a baby for adoption and also had had an abortion and a miscarriage, she was reminded of these events by each menstrual period. Every month she suffered from migraine headaches and severe PMS, primarily because of the guilt and unresolved feelings she had about being female. First pomegranate, then a combination of pomegranate and fuchsia essences, brought remarkable results. Pomegranate is also recommended for the late-thirties woman who is feeling regrets over not having had a family. This remedy can be equally effective for the reverse scenario: the woman who has played the traditional female role and now, at menopause, is having trouble making the transition into an exciting new stage of life.

How to Use Flower Essences

Whether you are buying essences for yourself or for someone else, keep in mind the relationship between the physical problem you want to treat and the emotional state of the patient. Remember that flower essences should be used judiciously, as they could stir up deeply repressed emotions; you might want to have your loved ones around you for support if this occurs. But don't worry about harming anyone—Dr. Bach was adamant in his contention that flower-essence remedies are benign and cannot produce unpleasant reactions.

Patricia Kaminski believes that flower essences are best used in conjunction with other therapies and can be integrated with medical treatment. Many practitioners of body work disciplines and some psychologists are using flower essences to increase the effectiveness of their therapies. Anne Brawley of Path to the Heart Fragrances adds flower essences and gem elixirs (essences made by placing gems in water and exposing them to sunlight) to essential oils.

You can buy all of the above-mentioned elixirs at health food stores, homeopathy pharmacies, or from the mail-order sources listed in the back of this book. You will need a small, clean, brown glass bottle, usually referred to as a treatment bottle, and some water. Never use tap water. Spring water is most desirable because it is believed to retain the life force. If you have only distilled water available, place the water in the bottle along with a piece of quartz and set it in the sun for a few days. Shake the water every day, as it needs light and movement in order to re-energize.

Put a couple of drops of the flower essence into the brown bottle and add about one to two ounces of your prepared water. This mixture is your tincture. Take it by placing a couple of drops on your tongue or add it to a glass of water or fruit juice. For the most powerful effects, Kaminski suggests taking your essences first thing in the morning or late at night. But essences also can be taken as frequently as every few minutes or every few hours as needed. Make your own flower cocktails by mixing two or more together.

Homeopathy Meets Modern Medicine

Hahnemann, Bach, and many others before them worked on the premise that the mind and body are interconnected, and that thoughts and emotions can affect wellness. As long ago as A.D. 200, the Greek physician Galen observed that melancholy women were struck with cancer more frequently than sanguine women. Today, modern science is beginning to catch up. Recent acknowledgment of the link between the mental and physical states has created a new medical discipline—psychoneuroimmunology (PNI)—which has been sanctioned by the National Institutes of Health. PNI derives its name from the complicated interplay between the mind (psycho), the brain (neuro), and the immune system (immunology). The assumption is far from new, but more and more evidence is accumulating that a person's state of mind strongly affects his or her physical health. Experiments continue to confirm the fact that patients who can reduce their level of stress and maintain a positive self-image will produce more of the immune system's helpful T-cells than do patients who are negative and despondent and who give up easily. Given this knowledge, the assumption that natural substances can be used to help achieve a healthy balance of mind and body no longer seems to be unorthodox or far-out.

Although they may have instinctively known these principles, the founders of alternative medicines did not have technology to back them up. Nevertheless their thinking was not so far removed from that of contemporary science. Substitute Hahnemann's "miasms" for "oncogenes," or "vital life force" for "immune system," and you can see the connection.

By opening your mind to the possible merits in these disciplines, you also open the door to a treasure trove of aphrodisiacal resources.

9

MEN AND APHRODISIA

*The truly sensuous takes time and a feeling for
the deliberate undulating rhythms of the body and of nature.*
—GEORGE LEONARD

Unless specifically stated otherwise, the aphrodisiacs mentioned in this book can be used by both men and women. Nevertheless, each sex has specific physical and emotional concerns that require individual attention if sexual wholeness is to be achieved.

This chapter is addressed to men. Nonetheless, I would urge women readers to study it, just as I would urge men to read the next chapter: "Women and Aphrodisia."

For Men
(and the Women Who Love Them)

During the feminist movement of the 1960s and '70s, women's health care underwent a revolution. Books like the fabled *Our Bodies, Ourselves* taught women bodily self-awareness, how to conduct examinations of their sexual parts, and information on preventive care. Similarly, Dr. Lonnie Barbach's seminal text, *For Yourself: Fulfillment of Female Sexuality,* gave women insight into their own sexuality and orgasmic response. No similar movement took place in men's health, although there is a slow trend in this direction at the present time, and some men are taking note.

My experience is that men have been less likely to take charge of their own health care. Many also tend to procrastinate about seeking professional help of any kind. James Green, author of *The Male Herbal,* believes that in our civilization men have been taught to avoid any display of vulnerability, that they are still bound by a learned macho attitude that says, "Show your enemy your weakness and be destroyed." Because of these fears, many men do not see their doctors as regularly or as soon as they should and are reluctant to discuss their medical, sexual, or emotional concerns. For instance, prostate problems are extremely common, but how many American males could name the causes of prostatitis or the symptoms of prostate cancer? Many men will experience temporary impotence during their lifetime, yet only a small percentage will ever seek help.

To men who are reluctant to go to a doctor, I suggest they consider a woman physician. When I started my practice I didn't expect many male patients, and my assumption proved correct. In my first year a new male patient came into the office and was shocked to discover that Dr. Watson was a woman. After waiting over an hour for another doctor, he reluctantly agreed to see me. I examined him, including his genitals, and he later admitted that he felt more comfortable with me than with his previous male doctor. Since then I have treated men for a full range of problems, including sexual ones. I have seen men cry in my office after discovering that they have given sexually transmitted diseases to the women they love. I doubt that they would have revealed such feelings—a healing and cathartic act in itself—to a male doctor. Perhaps the burgeoning "men's movement" spearheaded by people like author and teacher Robert Bly will help men approach individual self-care in a similar spirit of adventure and exploration.

What Makes a Man?

Shortly after fertilization, a human embryo develops an undifferentiated gonad that can become either testes or ovaries. If the one-in-about-300-million spermatozoa that fertilized the woman's egg at the time of conception contained a Y chromosome, that embryo will develop into a boy. By the twelfth week of pregnancy, the fetal testicle will begin to produce testosterone which, along with its more powerful metabolic derivative dihydrotestosterone, will shape the development of the genitalia into that of a male. At about the twenty-fourth week, the testicle will go dormant and stop producing testosterone until puberty.

Around the ages of thirteen or fourteen, the boy's testicles again become active, stimulated by the hypothalamus and pituitary glands. These cerebral glands produce pulses of Gonadotrophin Releasing Hormone, Luteinizing Hormone, and Follicle Stimulating Hormone just as occurs in females. But the organs these substances target respond differently. Men produce many times more testosterone and much smaller amounts of estrogen than women from both the adrenal glands and gonads.

As levels of testosterone soar, the boy becomes a man. The glands in the skin increase, the voice deepens, body hair grows, the bones lengthen, the penis enlarges, and the scrotal skin develops folds. High levels of testosterone are thought to be responsible for the violence exhibited by many teenaged boys, not to mention a dramatic surge in libido with its accompanying nocturnal erections and wet dreams. Pulses of hormones also cause the maturation of sperm and the secretion of fluid from the prostate.

From puberty to the end of his life, it is the right of every free man to enjoy a richly satisfying sex life. Sexual functioning is one of the man's last activities to deteriorate with age. Men do not even experience the cessation of fertility that women do. Baby girls are born with all the eggs they will release during their lifetime, but men retain the ability to manufacture sperm well into their elder years. Some men will experience varying levels of testosterone, and the ability to sustain an erection may change with time. But others in their eighties produce levels of male hormones comparable to what they produced in their twenties. Why that should be is not entirely clear, but I would guess that good nutrition and overall health, normal vascular and neurological systems, and, most important, a positive outlook, all play a role.

The frequency that men have sex is as varied as men themselves. Some men have sex daily well into their older years.
Others, due to diverse interests or changes in relationships, may
have sex less frequently than in their "prime." Although some
men may experience a slowing of their arousal and orgasm with
aging, studies show that their enjoyment isn't diminished. After
all, in the Eastern tradition, longer foreplay and a slower rise to
orgasm can be just as fun.

Troubleshooting

Most men at some stage of life will experience health difficulties
that can impair their ability to have a satisfying sex life. No
aphrodisiac can rescue your love life if you suffer an organic
problem or live with pain; taking care of your health is the single
most important aspect of aphrodisia.

Following are some common physical conditions that might
affect a man's sex life.

THE PROSTATE

One of the most common sources of problems for men is the
prostate, a glandular and muscular organ that sits below the
bladder, next to the rectum. The prostate surrounds the urethra—the tube through which urine flows from the bladder.
Because of its position, an enlarged or inflamed prostate can cut
off the flow of urine. A man who has a weak or interrupted
urinary stream, difficulty in initiating urination, increased frequency or urgency to urinate, who awakens more than once at
night to urinate, finds blood in his urine, or experiences pain
when he urinates or ejaculates, might have a prostate problem.

On arousal, the prostate secretes a liquid that mixes with and
lubricates the semen to aid its emission upon ejaculation. During
orgasm, muscular contractions squeeze the fluid into the urethra.
The prostate is responsive to the secretion of testosterone, and
loss or diminishment of this male hormone will cause the gland

to atrophy. Low levels of testosterone may be caused by genetic factors, low thyroid function, excess prolactin, medications, steroids, alcoholism, viral infections such as the mumps, or atrophy from unknown causes.

A doctor can examine the prostate by way of a digital rectal examination and a prostatic-specific antigen (PSA) blood test. All men over forty should have their prostate checked yearly since prostate cancer in its beginning stages is without symptoms, and early detection means a better chance of cure. The doctor checks for the consistency of the gland, for enlargement, and for lumps. He or she may also check the prostatic fluid by massaging the prostate and taking a sample of the fluid that is released into the urethra. Most family practitioners are trained in treating uncomplicated prostate conditions; a urologist specializes in treating diseases of the prostate and other genitourinary problems. Below are some of the disorders to which the prostate is prone.

Prostatitis.   Prostatitis is a condition in which the gland becomes inflamed and irritated, causing symptoms such as urinary burning and frequency, blood in the urine or ejaculate, and discomfort during ejaculation. Sometimes these specific complaints are accompanied by systemic symptoms like chills, fever, body aches, and lower-back pain.

Often caused by bacteria, many doctors initially prescribe antibiotics, although in this instance a culture of the urine and/or semen that would confirm the presence and type of bacteria is ideal. I have often seen the symptoms persist after a course of antibiotics, and in these cases I strongly recommend limiting intake of caffeine, alcohol, and spicy foods since they are irritants. Some clinicians believe that sedentary life-style is another contributing factor to prostatitis, as sitting for long periods of time allows blood to build up in the pelvic area. Because men with prostate problems often strain to urinate, hemorrhoids can occur. The Chinese call this state of affairs "stagnation." Exercise will help improve circulation, and will help with another major factor in prostatitis: stress. I have found that many men push their worries into their prostate.

Benign Prostatic Hypertrophy.   BPH is a condition in which the prostate enlarges and blocks the urethra, making urination difficult. This condition plagues men as young as forty, and the percentages rise with age. It is predicted that by the age of sixty, 50 percent of males will have symptoms of an enlarged prostate and that at the age of ninety nearly 100 percent of males will suffer from BPH. In the early stages BPH can have very mild symptoms, however one of my patients had only nausea and vomiting. His prostate had so blocked his bladder that he developed temporary kidney failure, which resolved once a catheter was inserted to open the urethra.

Symptoms of an enlarged prostate are similar to those seen with prostatitis and include the following: waking at night more than once to urinate, frequent urination, painful urination, difficulty in initiating urination, hestitancy, slowing of the stream of urine, straining to urinate, dribbling of urine after voiding, feeling that the bladder has not completely emptied, and retention of urine. If you experience any of these symptoms, be sure to see your doctor immediately for an examination of the prostate and a PSA blood test, since early diagnosis and treatment can save you from the need for surgery.

The causes of an enlarged prostate are multifactorial, although the most common theory is that the prostate enlarges due to an accumulation of the stronger androgen dihydrotestosterone (DHT) in the prostate tissue. Therapy with Proscar (see below) is aimed at helping with this. There hasn't been any research to support a relationship between BPH and sexual activity. Diet may play a role, since a study in Japan showed that there was an increase in BPH with higher consumption of milk and fewer green and yellow vegetables. This supports the theory that a diet high in saturated fats and cholesterol and lower in fiber may be a contributing factor. More research in this area will be needed.

Treatment of an enlarged prostate was limited to waitful watching and surgery until recently. Now there are medications that can be used even for the early stages of enlargement of the prostate and may even be found to prevent prostate cancer. Once the condition is diagnosed and the occurrence of prostate cancer is eliminated, there are several stages of treatment options. Proscar was one of the first drugs developed to help with this problem. It acts by blocking the enzyme that converts testosterone into DHT. Some men, however, may develop impotence, decreased libido, and ejaculatory problems, and the size of the prostate may be reduced by only 20 to 30 percent, which may not be enough to relieve symptoms.

Another therapy used either alone or in combination with Proscar is with a class of drugs called alpha-adrenergic blockers, which relax the smooth muscle of the prostate. These drugs were initially developed to treat high blood pressure and are now being used to aid the symptoms of BPH. Prazosin (Minipres) and Terazosin (Hytrin) are available and several others are being researched. Although they may cause low blood pressure as a side effect, they rarely interfere with sexual performance (7 percent with Terazosin will have erectile dysfunction).

With advances in technology, even the surgical options have changed in the treatment of BPH. Traditional transurethral prostatectomy (TURP) until recently was the most common surgical procedure used for BPH, but it can have long-term complications such as impotence, retrograde ejaculation, incontinence, and urethral strictures (scar tissue that narrows the urethra). Laser excision is now preferred over the TURP since it can be done as an outpatient, there is virtually no blood loss, and there is less risk of retrograde ejaculation after the procedure. The drawback with the laser procedure is that it may need to be repeated. Other procedures are also being researched to help reduce the need for TURP or open prostatectomy such as balloon dilatation, the use of stents, a tube placed surgically to keep the urethra open, and hyperthermia. We will be seeing more studies on these therapies in the coming years that will help improve the quality of life and the sexual vitality in men in their older years.

Nutritional supplementation with the amino acids glycine, alanine, and glutamic acid may help in the early stages of BPH. A product available from Biotech called Pros-Tech-plus combines these amino acids with saw palmetto, zinc, and manganese. A pharmacist colleague has found it very helpful in relieving the symptoms of an enlarged prostate in addition to using supplementation with essential fatty acids.

Prostate Cancer. Each year more than 120,000 new cases of prostate cancer are diagnosed in the United States, and more than 30,000 of those men will die per year. Some reports state that up to one man in ten will develop prostate cancer in his lifetime and the risk may be even higher in blacks, although the cause is unknown. Prostate cancer is the most common cancer in men and is now the second-leading cause of male cancer deaths. Lung cancer is the first.

The symptoms of prostate cancer are similar to those of BPH; in the past, prostate cancer was often discovered when part of the prostate was surgically removed. Recent advances in the diagnosis of prostate cancer have made it easier to detect in the early stages. Another important development is the ultrasound, which can detect abnormalities in the prostate gland.

Prostate cancer is treated with drugs, radiation, or surgery. Surgery for prostate cancer may cause sexual dysfunction. A fairly new procedure in which the pelvic nerves are dissected can preserve potency. The results are unpredictable but about two thirds of the men undergoing this surgery will have success. Drugs such as Lupron, a GnRH Agonist, is the most commonly used pharmacological treatment. It will inhibit testosterone and interfere with sexual function. Other drugs being studied, such as Flutamide and an experimental one, Casodex, will not totally inhibit testosterone and therefore do not always affect potency, but they may not be as effective in slowing the growth of the tumor.

Since prostate cancer may cause the loss of sexual functioning early, detection is the key to a longer, healthier life. Your best protection is a yearly digital exam and a PSA blood test. The earlier prostate cancer is detected, the better the chance of a complete cure. Now with many treatments available to treat prostate cancer in its early stages, perhaps we may see a lower rate of men with metastatic disease and complications due to surgery. See your doctor for that yearly exam and PSA test. It may save your life.

PREMATURE EJACULATION

Premature ejaculation—ejaculation prior to or immediately upon penetration—usually has no physiological basis. In many men it is caused by being exceptionally sensitive and may occur among those who are not circumcised. Mostly, though, it is related to overexcitement or performance anxiety.

Premature ejaculation is usually resolved with specific exercises and, most important, good communication between sexual partners. The most common methods recommended by sex therapists are the "squeeze" and "start/stop" techniques, which they report help in some 85 percent of cases. Both exercises involve the partner's stimulating the man's penis until he almost reaches ejaculation. Then she either squeezes the glans of the penis, or simply stops, until he is able to control the urge to ejaculate. In their book on the orgasm, Dr. Alan and Donna J. Brauer recommend a technique called the scrotal pull. When a man ejaculates, his testicles draw up against his body, so if his partner makes a loose clamp with her thumb and fingers above the testicles on the scrotum and *gently* pulls the testicles down and away from his body, he can rein in the desire to ejaculate. Deep breathing and relaxation techniques may also help.

In Chinese medicine, premature ejaculation is looked upon as either a congenital kidney deficiency or a deficiency of kidney yin due to an unhealthy life-style and fatigue. You may want to read the section on Chinese herbs in chapter 7 and try some of the specific formulas recommended for strengthening kidney chi and kidney yin.

SEXUAL DYSFUNCTION

Many men at some point in their lives will be unable to sustain an erection; this is perfectly normal and should be expected. Every person cannot be perfectly primed for sex at every moment. When someone is not, the aphrodisiacs in this book can help and inspire. But when sexual dysfunction is chronic it is time to look for a physiological—that is, organic—explanation. Twenty million American men reportedly suffer from chronic impotence; in 85 percent of the cases in which the condition persists more than a year, there is an organic reason for the problem.

As mentioned, in order for an erection to take place, neurotransmitters from the autonomic nervous system cause blood to flow into the penis, flood the arteries, and compress the veins so that the blood cannot flow out. Anything that interferes with this procedure will prevent the penis from growing hard, and compromised blood flow is the most common physiological reason for a man's being unable to get an erection. Any number of conditions can restrict flow of blood, but by far the one most often diagnosed is atheriosclerosis, in which the arteries are blocked, or "hardened" by cholesterol plaque. Hypertension often goes hand-in-glove with vascular disease, causing further damage to blood vessels. Diabetes can also cause the vascular, as well as neurologic, damage that makes erections difficult.

Apart from blood-flow problems there are some other important factors contributing to erectile dysfuntion. Erection, orgasm, and ejaculation occur under the neurologic stimulus of different mechanisms. Anything that interferes with those processes will prevent these. Alcoholism, prostate disease, diabetes and hormonal imbalances—particularly those of testosterone, estrogen, and prolactin—can also cause or contribute to dysfuntion.

Finding Out What's Wrong . . .

If you are having difficulties during lovemaking, determine whether or not you have nighttime erections. Healthy males have between two and five nocturnal erections, each lasting about twenty minutes, that occur during periods of REM sleep.* When nocturnal erections do occur, but you have difficulties in having intercourse, chances are the problem has a psychological or emotional basis, and I would advise that you seek professional counseling.

Here is how to find out whether or not you get erect when asleep. Stick a perforated strip of postage stamps snugly around your flaccid penis when you go to bed; if the strip is broken apart in the morning, you likely had an erection. No nocturnal erec-

---

*Any of about five periods in a night's sleep, each period lasting about ten minutes, during which dreams occur and the body undergoes marked changes.

tions generally signifies a physical problem, although the postage-stamp test is not entirely foolproof, as partial erections may still occur with some organic conditions. In any case you should see your doctor for a proper evaluation.

Your doctor can perform sophisticated tests to measure your erections and thereby confirm normal vascular and neurological functioning. One such test is the Penile Biothesiometry, a method of evaluating the sensory nerves of the penis by measuring vibratory sensation with a hand-held electromagnetic device. This technique can help diagnose damaged nerves due to diabetes or alcoholism.

Adequate blood supply to the penis can also be tested, in this instance with a procedure called the Penile Brachial index. Simply put, the doctor takes the blood pressure of the penis with a pediatric blood-pressure cuff or by ultrasound and compares its systolic pressure (the top number when your blood pressure is taken) to that of the brachial artery that conducts blood to the arms. Another technique used to determine vascular problems is a trial injection with Papavarine or prostaglandin E-1 using a doppler ultrasound to measure the blood flow. Both relax the smooth muscles of the penile blood vessels, allowing blood to flow in and an erection to occur. When Papavarine or Prostaglandin E-1 don't work, there is most likely a blood-supply problem due to atherosclerosis or venous leakage. Your doctor may recommend further tests—such as an angiogram—to evaluate the arteries, and take blood to check levels of cholesterol, triglycerides, and serum lipoproteins.

When you see your doctor for sexual dysfunction, he or she will also conduct other blood tests to measure hormone levels and to check various substances to make sure the thyroid and pituitary glands are functioning properly. A glucose tolerance test that helps detect diabetes is another important key. Loss of erection is one of the first signs that tip off a doctor to Type II adult-onset diabetes.

. . . And Making It Right

Medical science has made great strides in dealing with almost all organic and psychogenic causes of sexual dysfunction. Do not suffer in silence and frustration when a remedy for your particular medical condition is probably available. There are a number of therapeutic treatments for impotence caused by blocked arteries. One of the most commonly used for penile arterial disease is a drug called Trental, originally developed for patients who experience pain and difficulty in walking due to poor circulation, has been used with unpredictable success. Herbs such as gingko, suma, ginseng, and formulas for kidney deficiency may also be helpful.

Surgery is another way to deal with arterial blockage. Several techniques are available. Angioplasty, in which a small balloon is inserted into the vessel, then inflated to open the artery and break up plaque, is perhaps the most successful. Arterial grafts are another possibility. A procedure called the Virag Arterial Revascularization technique can be employed to augment blood flow to the penis, but it has only about a 50-percent success rate.

A lesser-known and somewhat controversial process is chelation, involving a series of intravenous treatments with a substance called EDTA that removes the calcium plaque from the walls of blood vessels. Medical opinion is divided on whether or not the process is effective, but a study recently conducted in Brazil showed that men who underwent chelation had significant increases in blood flow to their legs. Another study is under way in this country, conducted by the Veterans Administration. If you are interested in more information regarding chelation, contact the American College for the Advancement of Medicine, listed at the back of the book.

Sexual dysfunction caused by hormonal deficiencies is usually treated with supplementation of the hormone. But if your levels of hormones are normal, augmentation won't help. In other words, testosterone supplements only increase libido and erectile function when you start out with an insufficient natural supply. Further, testosterone taken when you don't need it can result in an enlarged prostate and may stimulate and occult prostate cancer. This does not happen when you supplement with testosterone to correct a deficiency, although side effects can include increased hair growth and abnormal liver function.

Also, there is an important relationship in the pituitary gland between dopamine and the female hormone, prolactin. If dopamine levels decrease as a result of, say, drug use, there is a corresponding increase in prolactin, and elevated levels of prolactin are associated with sexual dysfunction since they in turn inhibit the production of testosterone. Sometimes the pituitary will form tumors that are benign but secrete excess prolactin. Bromocriptine (Parlodel) is a medication with dopamine-like effects that can be used to treat the condition, although if the tumors are large they may need to be removed surgically.

If an underactive thyroid is the root of low libido, simply correcting the hypothyroidism may bring levels of the hormone up to par. But sometimes supplementation with testosterone may be necessary. Go back and reread chapter 7; many of the herbs listed are natural testosterone boosters, such as damiana, wild yam root, sarsaparilla root, licorice root, ginseng, and ashwanganda.

One of the most important new developments in treating sexual dysfunction is the use of injectable medicines to induce erections. Pharmacological programs are available around the world in which men are taught to inject medications into the plexus of blood vessels called the corporus cavernosum in the penis. Initially, drugs such as Papavarine and Phentolamine were used, but now prostaglandin E-1 is the more common choice. All of these substances increase the blood flow into the penis by relaxing the smooth muscles in the blood vessels. Some side effects associated with these injections include local pain, prolonged erections, the formation of scar tissue, and hypotension. Recently, the discovery that the neuropeptide vasoactive intestinal peptide (VIP) is released in men during arousal has led to the use of it to induce erections. Injections of VIP along with Phentolamine are still experimental, but they appear to have fewer side effects as compared with Papavarine and prostaglandins.

Recurrent injections with Papavarine may precipitate a condition similar to Peyronie's disease. The penis becomes erect, but due to the growth of fibrous bands in the outer lining, the erection is bent and penetration is sometimes difficult. Although these fibrous strictures can be removed with surgery, you may need to switch to another form of treatment. Prostaglandin injections have fewer problems with this type of scar formation. Mild burning is the most common effect.

There are two other nonsurgical and noninvasive devices available to augment erections. A vacuum suction device causes engorgement with a vacuum effect, then entraps the blood in the penis with a constriction ring around the base of the shaft. However, it has been known to constrict normal blood flow, and other side effects include bruising, loss of sensation, and difficulty in reaching orgasm. You can get this device only on prescription. Synergist is a soft transparent silicone sheath that attaches to the outside of the penis and helps with penetration. But it, too, tends to decrease sensitivity as well as being quite difficult to apply and irritating to your partner's vagina.

Penile implants have been used since 1973. Other than in the above case, they are most successful when impotence is due to neurologically related causes such as spinal-cord injuries, diabetes, multiple sclerosis, or nerve damage due to surgery. There are basically three types of prostheses in common usage: semi-rigid silicone rods, self-contained inflatables; and multiple component inflatables in which a small pump is implanted in the scrotum and when activated moves fluid into the penile rods from a reservoir in the abdomen.

If you are considering an implant, research the subject carefully. Once a surgical procedure has been completed, changes are difficult to make. Do not have overly high expectations of what an implant can do. Bear in mind that the penis is flaccid when the rods of the prosthesis are inserted, so the most they can achieve is to make the penis rigid enough to penetrate a vagina. Implants do not bolster arousal, although some may increase the length or girth of the organ.

Additionally, there are a number of potential problems attached to the procedure. Implantation with a prosthesis may damage or destroy any erectile capability that you have already. Complications can arise as a result of the surgery, including the formation of scar tissue or blood clots, swelling, and, with wound infections, a higher risk for diabetic patients. There have also been instances of the device eroding through the skin. Mechanical breakdown is a possibility with the inflatable types.

Staying Healthy

To keep your urinary tract healthy, drink plenty of liquids; filtered water is best. Don't hold urine when have to go, as this will reduce the elastic tone of your bladder; eat a diet low in cholesterol and saturated fats; and exercise regularly to reduce stress, lower cholesterol levels, and improve circulation. Nutritionally, vitamin A, vitamin E, zinc, and linoleic acid are important: check chapter 4 for sources and recommended dosages.

Herbal Support

There are a number of herbs that are particularly helpful for the prostate and male urinary system. Pygeum (*Pygeum Africanum* or *Prunus Africana*) is a large evergreen tree that grows on the high plateaus of southern Africa and has been chronicled in herbal texts since the eighteenth century. It has recently come under scientific scrutiny, proving in research to be useful for chronic inflammation of the prostate and for BPH. Pygeum contains beta-sitosterol, which is thought to have an inhibitory effect on certain prostaglandins with the overall effect of reducing vascular congestion and the size of the prostate. It also has pentacyclic triterpenoids, which serve to reduce swelling and inflammation. As if that weren't enough, pygeum also contains linear alcohols, which lower cholesterol levels within the gland itself. Pygeum has been classified as a Guaranteed Potency Herb, meaning that the dosage can be standardized and is safe and effective. Clinical research has shown that pygeum is useful for benign prostatic conditions in daily doses of 75 to 200 milligrams. No specific studies have been done on pygeum's effect on prostate cancer.

Since the prostate is also a muscle, herbs that have muscle-relaxing properties can help with BPH. I recommend drinking infusions of valerian, cramp bark, or scullcap on a daily basis until the condition improves.

Oregon grape root is a good remedy if you have an infection in the prostate or bladder. Other herbs to try are uva-ursi or horsetail, and echinacea and goldenseal for their antibacterial and cleansing properties.

Herbs mentioned in the general herbal chapter that are particularly useful for men are saw palmetto, for nourishing the prostate and genitourinary system; suma and Siberian ginseng, to balance hormone production; damiana, as a prostate tonic and nutrient for the adrenals and sex organs; and wild yam for building hormones.

The Emotional Connection

Even when the root cause of impotence is physical, the situation is so emotionally charged that there are bound to be some psychological aspects involved. Then, although about 80 to 90 percent of impotence cases are physical in origin, there are, of course, instances in which men will have difficulties after emotional stress due to factors such as job loss, death of spouse, or financial or family problems.

Anxiety is a big contributor to erectile dysfunction, and performance anxiety is one of the major causes of psychologically induced impotence. A man's sexual response is an expression of his maleness, and when he cannot complete the sex act, his self-esteem is affected much as a woman's confidence is shaken when she proves to be infertile or feels herself undesirable. Performance anxiety can create a vicious circle. When we are anxious, the body puts out large amounts of epinephrine, which causes vasoconstriction. In order to have an erection, a man needs to be relaxed so that the blood will flow freely into the arteries; constriction of blood vessels due to stress works against this.

Depression can also play a central role in impotence. This creates something of a double-bind situation since most antidepressant drugs are associated with impotence. If you are going on medication for depression, read over the section on antidepressants in chapter 5 and be sure to discuss the various alternatives with your doctor.

Anxiety and depression can be both the cause and effect of impotence. Even after a man has resolved a physical source of the problem, he may experience lingering psychological effects. When a man becomes impotent he can lose self-confidence in other areas of his life, including his social life and his work. Any therapy should therefore be aimed at treating both the body and the psyche.

In the 1970s Masters and Johnson radically changed methods of treating sexual problems, and today's sex therapists have learned to focus on the situational, relational, and psychological causes of impotence. They try to relieve performance anxiety and low self-esteem by encouraging open communication between bedmates and correcting misconceptions of both partners concerning sex. To eliminate the I've-got-to-perform-at-any-cost pressure from the act of love, therapists de-emphasize intercourse and encourage sensual stimulation. Most therapists start couples off with relaxation exercises.

The Sexually Whole Man

A sexually whole man must be in touch with his own vulnerability and must recognize feelings that tend to block intimacy; to be close to a woman he must first develop trust and intimacy with himself. This usually means some soul-searching and/or the help of a therapist.

Within the last three decades, expansion of the male consciousness has been a welcome and beneficial offshoot of the women's revolution. Men are continuing to band together in a self-driven movement whose purpose is liberation from their own male stereotypes of emotional invulnerability.

In his TV interview with Bill Moyers a couple of years ago, Robert Bly said something that helped me to understand this changing male perspective. He said that when he was asked to express feelings, they were so deeply buried that he didn't know that they existed.

James Green, in his book *The Male Herbal,* punningly writes that the number-one killer of men is broken hearts. Heart disease is the primary killer of American males, so his metaphor is apt: The inability to express emotions or show vulnerability contributes to stress—a leading cause of heart disease.

When we connect with our inner selves, all facets of our nature can be expressed. To the extent that men can do that, they will earn the sexual intimacy they want and deserve.

10

WOMEN AND APHRODISIA

Look upon a woman as a goddess
whose special energy she is,
and honour her in that state.
—Uttara Tantra

Women have a natural advantage over men when it comes to understanding their own bodies. Their biology is more complicated, and menstrual cycles and pregnancy compel them to be more knowledgeable about their physiology. Women are also more apt to seek help for problems, either from one another or from a professional source.

The Times of Her Life

Girls biologically turn into women during puberty, when their hormones activate and they become capable of childbirth. Beginning to menstruate is the most significant occurrence of female puberty. It generally occurs between the ages of ten and fourteen. Menstruation comes as part and parcel of events that happen over a period of several years, including a growth spurt, a widening of the pelvis, an increase in body fat, the development of breasts, the growth of body hair, and changes in skin and hair.

The first few cycles are usually irregular, but after a year or two many women will settle into their own menstrual rhythm. The average cycle is twenty-eight days, but cycles of twenty-one to thirty-five days are perfectly normal. Approximately fourteen days after the first day of menstrual flow, there is a surge of hormones from the pituitary. Luteinizing Hormones and Follicle-Stimulating Hormones initiate the release of an egg from the ovary; the rise in estrogen often makes the woman feel extremely sensual at this time. Because she is now fertile, it is important to the survival of the species that she desire sex at this time. Throughout the remainder of the cycle, approximately another fifteen days, hormone levels continue to rise, causing the uterine lining to swell with nourishment for a potential pregnancy. If fertilization doesn't take place, the egg dissolves, the uterine lining sheds, and the menstrual flow starts.

A TIME TO LOVE

The taboo on having sex when a woman is menstruating dates back at least to the Old Testament, and maybe longer. Opinions on the subject are as diverse as humanity itself. Some American Indian cultures teach that a woman should be alone during her period; it is a holy time, when her energies are strong. Jewish custom dictates that a man and a woman should not come together for at least twelve days from the start of her menstrual period. In Tantra, a woman's energy is regarded as very powerful during menstruation, and as long as a man is powerful enough to receive this energy during sex without being weakened by it, he may derive great benefit.

Modern Western society takes a more secular view. Many women prefer to avoid lovemaking at this time because they find it messy or uncomfortable. Some of my patients, however, report relief from cramps by having intercourse while menstruating. The most potentially important information in this regard is a study showing that the risk of endometriosis increases with sex during menstruation, presumably because the tissue from inside the uterus can be pushed up into the abdomen.

If many women don't feel much like making love during their

period, as already mentioned, they often are sexually desirous when they are ovulating and therefore fertile. Fear of an unwanted pregnancy can be a powerful inhibitor of joyful sex, and one of the best aphrodisiacs a woman can use is a reliable method of birth control. There are more choices available today than ever before, although none are without drawbacks. Here is a quick update on the current situation.

The Pill. The Pill, although it offers a high degree of protection and allows for wonderful spontaneity, suppresses a woman's regular hormonal cycle and may affect her sex drive. The Pill replaces the production of estrogen by the ovaries by keeping levels of the hormone constant, thus suppressing ovulation so that a woman cannot become pregnant. Early versions of the Pill contained much higher doses of estrogen and progesterone than the recent ones. There were always a number of side effects associated with the Pill, but these have been minimized with the advent of the low-dose versions. Depending on the type of pill and dose of hormones it contains, you can experience either an increase, a decrease, or no changes in your libido.

Libido is largely related to the amount of testosterone in the blood. The Pill can alter the level in a number of ways. Since it suppresses overall production of hormones, the ovaries may not manufacture as much testosterone. The Pill also causes an increase in the quantity of a sex-hormone-binding globulin in the blood that binds free testosterone, making it inactive. Estrogen and progesterone have a direct effect on the limbic system of the brain; excess or deficiency can dampen the libido. Talk to your doctor if you find your sex drive declining after going on the Pill. Switching to one with lower doses of female hormones or with a more androgenic effect may be the answer. If you are already on pills that act like androgens, you may find that your sex drive is greatly heightened.

A common problem with the Pill is vaginal dryness, which can occur if the estrogen dose is too low for you. In this case, switch to a higher-dose pill. If you do not wish to do that, use one of the excellent vaginal lubricators on the market such as Astroglide, K-Y Jelly, and REPLENS.

For years, women have been concerned about the Pill's possible link to cancer. Although a number of studies have been conducted, there is no evidence that it increases the risk. In fact, many doctors believe the Pill protects against ovarian cancer.

Implants. Another contraceptive that works along the same lines as the Pill, Norplant, has been used in Europe for ten years; it was recently approved for use in the United States. This progesterone implant is inserted under the skin of the arm and remains effective for four to five years. Norplant's benefit is its long-term effectiveness without the side effects of estrogen supplements, but it can cause irregular bleeding, breast tenderness, bloating, and depression. Discuss this technique with your doctor to see if you are a candidate for its use.

IUD. The intrauterine device (IUD) acquired a bad name some years ago due to the damage done by the infamous Dalkon Shield. But there are several different IUDs on the market now, one using copper and one releasing progesterone. Any woman thinking about using one should get counseling regarding possible complications, since IUDs can still result in infections and scarring that can interfere with fertility. If you have multiple partners or are considering having another child—IUDs generally aren't inserted if a woman has not given birth—I strongly suggest you look at other birth-control options, although I have had many women in my practice who use an IUD without complications, and, like the Pill, this option allows for spontaneity.

Barrier and other methods such as the diaphragm, cervical cap, and condom have been around for a long time and are excellent choices since they do not involve the use of hormones or systemic drugs. The diaphragm and cap must be fitted by a physician or nurse practitioner, while the now ubiquitous condom can be purchased everywhere from a grocery store to a vending machine. To ensure maximum protection they require the use of spermicidal cream or jelly. And the spermicidal sponges, films, and tablets on the market are most effective when used in conjunction with a condom. A condom also offers you your best available protection against sexually transmitted diseases, including AIDS.

You can turn these methods into aphrodisiacs by incorporating them into your lovemaking. For instance, keep your diaphragm by the bed and insert it as part of foreplay rather than as an interruption of it, and try putting a condom on your partner while continually stimulating him.

SEX AND PREGNANCY

Pregnancy is of course a welcome and exciting outcome of sexual intimacy for many couples. Despite the fact that most women take on a lush and womanly look during pregnancy, many feel heavy and unattractive. Now is a time to boost your sexual feelings by indulging in some of the "external" aphrodisiacs, such as surrounding yourself with delicious perfumes and fabrics, getting swept away by stimulating music, or getting a sensuous back rub from your mate. As long as they wish to, most women can enjoy healthy sex right up until delivery.

There are, however, a number of conditions that make sex during pregnancy dangerous for the baby. If your doctor tells you that premature labor is a possibility, avoid not only intercourse, but also masturbation to orgasm and stimulation of your nipples. Stimulating nipples triggers the release of oxytocin, which initiates uterine contractions. During a normal pregnancy this presents no problem—in fact, stimulation of your nipples near your delivery date can not only help to ripen your cervix but also prepares the nipples for nursing.

Placenta praevia is a potentially dangerous condition in which the placenta sits on the opening of the cervix instead of higher on the uterine wall. Too much sexual activity can cause bleeding to the point of hemorrhage. If you experience any bleeding at all resulting from intercourse when pregnant, see your doctor immediately.

WHEN THE BABY COMES

After the birth of a child, a woman's body undergoes tremendous hormonal changes. For nine months, the human gonadoptropic hormone has been circulating in extremely high volumes to maintain the placenta, then suddenly is gone. Many women experience

this withdrawal as postpartum blues, which can range from teari-
ness to serious depression requiring medical treatment. Some
emotional upheaval is normal at this time, especially when exacerbated by the demands and responsibilities of the new baby and
the resulting sleep deprivation. Refer to the chapters on homeopathy, flower essences, and Chinese herbalism to find remedies
that might help you through this time. But if your depression
reaches a level that affects your ability to care for your baby, see
your doctor.

After childbirth, your doctor will likely recommend you abstain
from intercourse for six weeks so that any stitches can heal, the
cervix will close, and the uterus will return to its normal size.
Theoretically, thereafter you can resume your accustomed sex life,
but if you are nursing that may not be the first thing on your
mind. Breast-feeding stimulates the body's secretion of prolactin,
which in turn stimulates milk production. But prolactin also
suppresses the release of eggs by the ovary, and therefore the
ovaries don't produce any estrogen either. This lack of estrogen
can turn you off from sex, not to mention causing the vagina to
be dry and sex to be painful.

The first few months after the birth of a child can be a fragile
time in your sex life. Your mate may be eager to get on with
postpregnancy fun and games, but your physical condition, exhaustion, lack of time, concern for the baby, and just plain stress
may make that almost impossible. To keep a marriage healthy
over time, it is important for you both to roll with the cycles of
desire, which are a natural part of a monogamous relationship. It
is important not to let anger or resentment build up to where the
last thing you want to do is make love. Dr. Helen Kaplan, who
works primarily with couples on sexual issues, finds that resolving
feelings of anger by communicating and making time for sex the
best solution to increasing waning sexual desire.

Now is a time when you might benefit from the Tantric or
Taoist sex exercises outlined in chapter 6, especially those that
move energy through the body, unlocking repressed feelings.
Allowing yourselves to experience more intimacy by releasing
deep-seated emotions and fears is the key to restoking the fire.

With the addition of children in your life, it is also time to turn planning your love life into an aphrodisiac. Dwelling too much on the heady, carefree, passionate days at the beginning of your love affair could make the present seem a bit lackluster, even somber. However, preparation for a session of lovemaking could very well add some spice. Making a rendezvous for lovemaking, or setting up a weekend away from home well in advance, might not sound as romantic or as arousing as spontaneous intercourse prompted by raw desire, but there can be a lot of delicious fun in looking forward to and planning a special occasion. Also, by planning ahead you greatly reduce the possibility of snafus and annoying interruptions. You can relax and let the moment unfold. Remember—what your relationship may have lost in spontaneity, it has probably gained in erotic closeness and in substance.

MENOPAUSE

Menopause—the change of life—represents many different things to a woman. It is truly a time of passage, when women move away from their function to create life and into a whole new realm of creativity. Although many women view this time as a welcome transition to freedom from the menstrual cycle and the concern over pregnancy, others carry a heavy burden of fear. Will I still be me? Will I loose my sexuality and looks? Will I age gracefully? For women who wished to have children but were unable to, this can be a time to face this loss. These are legitimate worries, since our society has yet to find the way to utilize and value its elders, especially its mature women. Additionally, the American medical establishment has until recently largely ignored the psychological aspects of menopause that can affect a woman's health and well-being.

With the increased longevity in our society, a woman can live a full third of her life after menopause. Now that baby boom women—those who grew up during the feminist movement— are heading into this stage of life, their outspoken voices are expressing concerns and demanding answers.

What actually happens in menopause is quite simple. There is a gradual decrease in the release of mature eggs and hormones from the ovaries. This decrease usually starts between ages forty-five and fifty-five depending on your family history. Cigarette smoking can bring on menopause earlier than the norm. In the five years or so before the onset of menopause, your menstrual cycles will get gradually longer or shorter and often periods can be heavier. Once eggs are no longer released regularly from the ovary, the pituitary will increase its secretion of Luteinizing Hormone and Follicle-Stimulating Hormone. A blood test for levels of these two substances as well as estrogen level can determine that you are, indeed, approaching menopause and can help your doctor guide you through the process.

Estrogen production continues at a lower level after menopause, and now most of it is secreted by the adrenal glands. Diminished estrogen can cause the tissues of the vagina and skin to loose their elasticity, which for many women translates into painful intercourse with burning and occasionally bleeding. This condition is referred to by your gynecologist as vaginal atrophy or atrophic vaginitis. Some research suggests that continued sexual activity after menopause protects against vaginal atrophy.

Lower levels of estrogen also are associated with the loss of calcium from the bones, which become progressively thinner and can fracture easily—osteoporosis. The greatest percentage of bone loss occurs in the first five years after menopause, and osteoporosis causes many deaths in women over sixty because of the medical complications that occur as a result of fractures. Some women are more prone than others to this disease, and if you have more than a couple of the following risk factors, by all means discuss the subject with your doctor:

- surgical removal of the ovaries before age forty
- are of Latin, Asian, or Northern European descent
- have a small skeletal frame
- have a sedentary life-style
- suffer from thyroid or kidney disease or use corticosteroids or anticonvulsants
- eat a low-calcium diet
- smoke cigarettes

• abuse alcohol
• have a family history of osteoporosis

Another significant effect of estrogen loss concerns blood lipids. Estrogen increases the "good" cholesterol (HDL) and decreases the "bad" (LDL). Consequently, estrogen loss deprives women of their natural defense against heart disease and atherosclerosis, and after menopause a woman's risk of having a heart attack equals that of a man's.

HORMONE-REPLACEMENT THERAPY

The biggest issue facing women entering menopause today is whether or not to undergo hormone-replacement therapy. The major drawback to taking hormones is the potentially increased risk for breast and uterine cancer, and although many studies have been done, the results are still confusing. The risk seems to depend on the dosage, the time period during which the hormones are used, and the type of estrogen prescribed. Estrogen is available in the U.S. in many forms, as tablets, creams, and patches. There are advantages to using the topical varieties since they go directly into the bloodstream instead of having to pass through the digestive system and liver, which causes many of the side effects. One of my patients has benefited from a product now available only in Europe: Oestregel. This topical gel can be applied on the skin in variable doses and can thus be tailored to the woman's individual needs. We do know that taking estrogen alone can greatly increase the risk of endometrial cancer unless you have had a hysterectomy. When the estrogen is combined with progesterone, however, the risk is greatly reduced.

For some women there is no choice. If you have breast or endometrial cancer, a history of strokes or pulmonary embolism, liver disease, unexplained vaginal bleeding, or are pregnant, hormone replacement therapy is not for you. Some other medical conditions such as uterine fibroids, hypertension, migraine, gallbladder disease, phlebitis, and seizure disorders may also disqualify you at the discretion of your doctor.

The use of estrogen replacement can also be associated with a number of side effects, including nausea, breast tenderness, cramps, bleeding, gallbladder disease, skin discoloration, hair loss, headaches, weight gain, bloating, candidiasis, depression, and changes in the sex drive. The severity of these depends on the type and amount of estrogen used. Some studies indicate that estrogen therapy will not keep skin supple, nor will it alter or reduce the nervousness and depression often experienced in menopause. I have found in my practice, however, that taking estrogen does help to return a sense of well-being and to alleviate emotional swings.

Many women need to take progesterone along with estrogen to protect the uterine lining. There is a prevailing belief among doctors that in some women the protective effect of the estrogen on blood lipids is reversed with the addition of synthetic progestogens. For this reason you should be sure to have regular checkups if you are on a program of progesterone.

Testosterone replacement will have the most impact in terms of libido and sexuality. As with the other sex hormones, testosterone production is reduced after menopause. While estrogen will keep the vagina supple and lubricated, testosterone is critical for maintaining sexual functioning after menopause. In several studies of postmenopausal women, testosterone replacement combined with estrogen replacement led to an increase in sexual fantasies, sexual interest and arousal, and frequency of intercourse and orgasm, compared with groups that received only estrogen. There are several products available that offer both hormones, but the most widely used is Estra-Test, which comes in two strengths. Studies of this specific drug bear out the general research: There is a major increase in desire and arousal when testosterone is combined with estrogen. An alternative is a 1-percent testosterone cream applied directly to the vagina to help the tissues regain their function. This is especially appropriate for women with breast cancer, where estrogen is not recommended.

Of course testosterone is not without its unwanted side effects. You may experience oily skin, acne, increased hair growth, and changes in blood lipids. But with low doses of testosterone, most of these conditions are minimal, and a drug called Aldactone can resolve the hair-growth problem.

THE NATURAL APPROACH

In my practice I have begun working with menopausal women who want to avoid the use of chemical hormones by taking a nutritional and herbal approach. A diet to minimize the discomfort of menopause should include plenty of green leafy vegetables rich in calcium, vitamins, and minerals; whole grains; and fiber. To help protect bones, I recommend a daily supplement of 1,000 to 1,500 milligrams of calcium with boron. Vitamin E in doses of 1,000 IUs a day may help keep estrogen levels up, as will pantothenic acid by supporting the adrenal glands. Essential fatty acids are also important either as fresh oils, nuts, or supplements. You will find all the information on them in chapter 4.

An interesting study published in the *British Journal of Medicine* reported that a diet rich in soybeans and linoleic acid (found in flaxseed oil) increased the suppleness of the vaginal tissues, presumably because of the phytoestrogens found in these plants. Plant estrogens can be a wonderful resource for the body, and there is no indication of cancer risk with them. Nevertheless, they should be used along with progesterone-rich herbs.

A wonderful product that has become available recently is a cream called Es-gen, made from soybean extract. It can be applied to the skin of the vagina, the abdomen, the face, or the inner forearm. Because it is absorbed through the skin, it does not affect the liver as orally taken hormones sometimes do. I generally recommend that it be used in combination with a progesterone cream called Pro-gest, or dioscorea extract made from Mexican yams.

Ginseng and some Chinese herbal formulas that support the vital organs can reduce the uncomfortable effects of menopause. Look for Bupleurum and Peony, Women's Journey, and Tang Kwei Four. Homeopathic remedies are also useful. Hot flashes can be treated with Lachesis or Sepia. One specific excellent homeopathic formula to try is Klimaktheel, made by a company called Heel in Germany, or BHI Mulimen. In England, doctors are studying the use of homeopathic doses of estrogen and progesterone, which are also available in the United States.

One note of caution. All the clinical studies for osteoporosis protection have been conducted using synthetic hormones. There have been some studies to support the use of a natural progesterone to reduce loss of bone mass associated with menopause. Other than this small study, we have at this time no specific evidence that these natural remedies will help with this condition. I always recommend an osteoporosis bone densitometry test to determine the woman's risk and follow her progress with treatments, especially when we have chosen the alternative therapies.

COMING TO TERMS WITH MENOPAUSE

With the passage of childbearing, there can be a new level of self-awareness for women. One of my friends describes menopause as a death experience that opens a door to a new perception of oneself. The postmenopausal zest described by Margaret Mead is a very real phenomenon that usually occurs in the late fifties. Women can experience a burst of energy associated with a sense of contentment and self-acceptance.

Troubleshooting

Many of the physical challenges women encounter during their lifetime are directly related to the monthly ebb and flow of their hormones, the same hormonal shifts that affect their libido. Here is how to deal with the most common "women's problems."

PREMENSTRUAL SYNDROME

Premenstrual syndrome (PMS) is the end result of the complex biochemical and endocrine changes that occur from ovulation to the onset of menstrual bleeding. Sometimes the symptoms continue until bleeding stops. Modern medicine has been unable to completely explain the causes of PMS. Dr. Guy Abraham has done most of the scientific work and has divided the symptoms of PMS into subgroups that can occur alone or in combinations.

Identifying which category or categories you fall into can help your doctor select further testing and treatment.

PMT-A. Anxiety is the predominant symptom.

PMT-H. You will complain of weight gain, abdominal bloating, fluid retention, and breast tenderness.

PMT-C. You will crave sugar and chocolate. After eating chocolate you may experience a sense of well-being, probably due to stimulation of dopamine by the phenylethylamine found in chocolate. After the sugar, you may feel tired, weak, shaky, or lightheaded from hypoglycemia. You may get headaches or migraine.

PMT-D. You experience depression as the main symptom. You might cry over trivial problems or feel too confused to make decisions.

Although it has required many years for doctors to take these complaints seriously, they can make your life miserable, especially your love life. Unfortunately, some doctors still have a "Don't worry, honey, it's all in your head" attitude toward PMS. If so, get another doctor! The appropriate response is for your doctor to check your blood chemistry, thyroid function, and levels of progesterone and estrogen just before your period.

There is a great deal you can do to turn around the symptoms of PMS. The life-style changes I am suggesting are important for you generally, and not just for a few days or weeks of the month. Make some modifications and you will find yourself feeling healthier and sexier.

Treatment of PMS with nutritional supplements and dietary changes is highly effective. Research has supported the theory that some symptoms may be related to low levels of magnesium and vitamin B-6. I recommend a daily supplement of 500 milligrams of magnesium citrate, and between 100 and 300 milligrams of B-6, which should be taken with a B-complex supplement. Chromium is important to stabilize blood sugar and reduce sugar cravings. If it isn't a component of your multivitamin and mineral supplement, take it in the form of GTF chromium-glucose tolerance factor. Cystic breasts can be helped with a daily dose of at least 400 IUs of vitamin E. Specific essential fatty acids and linoleic and linolenic acids found in flaxseed oil, evening primrose oil, black currant seed oil, or borage oil help when increased production of prostaglandins cause breast inflammation, cramping, and water retention. Dr. Abraham and his colleagues have developed a supplement called Optivite, which is tailor-made for women with PMS and is available from drugstores.

A diet rich in complex carbohydrates, vegetable fiber, and the above-mentioned specific oils, and lower in meat can go a long way toward relieving the symptoms of PMS. I recommend avoiding alcohol, caffeine, and sugary foods since they rob vital nutrients from the body and can make mood swings worse. Meat and sugar both raise levels of tryptophan in the central nervous system, which in turn increases serotonin in the brain. High serotonin levels exacerbate PMS symptoms like nervous tension, drowsiness, difficulty in concentrating, water retention, and decreased sexual arousal. In most cases, a diet heavy in meat and sugar is also high in saturated fats. These can encourage the production of prostaglandins, already mentioned as the cause of breast tenderness, cramping, and fluid retention.

Nutritional supplements and a healthy diet should do the trick for most women, but those with severe symptoms may also need medication. If you have low progesterone, natural progesterone supplements come in pills and in sublingual form to be taken orally, as vaginal suppositories, or as topical creams. Progest, a cream made from wild yam root, is extremely effective and is available over-the-counter. Madison Pharmacy in Wisconsin (see resources at the back of the book) will mail capsules and suppositories of natural progesterone to you after receiving an order from your doctor. Synthetic progesterone such as Provera or Megace does not in my opinion work as well and has adverse side effects.

Some of my patients have been so affected by PMS that they have needed the extra help of an antidepressant, an antianxiety agent, or a diuretic. If your doctor recommends this route for you, bear in mind that many of these drugs may suppress your libido. Read through the relevant section of chapter 5 and discuss the options with your doctor.

Chinese medicine has a different perspective on PMS. Chinese medical practitioners believe that the symptoms of irritability and breast tenderness are caused by stagnant liver chi or excess liver chi, and cramping and fluid retention are due to blood stagnation. Read the section on Chinese herbs, where you will find some tonic formulas that could help. I also often recommend acupuncture to balance the system.

DYSMENORRHEA

Dysmenorrhea is what is commonly called menstrual cramps. For some women they are inconsequential, but for others they can be so debilitating that they end up spending a couple of days a month in bed. Menstrual cramps are caused by constriction of the muscle wall of the uterus, the constriction regulated by smooth muscle that in turn is controlled by prostaglandins. That is why antiprostaglandin drugs such as Ibuprofen (sold over-the-counter as Advil, Nuprin, and Motrin IB), Ponstel, and the newest on the market, Toradol, offer the best relief from painful cramps. These drugs are most effective for severe cramping if taken several days prior to the onset of the menstrual flow, rather than being taken once the pain starts. Discuss the appropriate timing and dose with your doctor.

Another approach I have found helpful is supplementing your diet with calcium, magnesium, and essential oils such as evening primrose or black currant seed oil (see chapter 4 for sources and dosages). The herbs scullcap, raspberry leaf, or cramp bark made into a tea by infusing one teaspoonful of the dried herb in a cup of boiling water for 10 to 15 minutes, or taken in capsule form bought from a health food store, offer relief to many women. And the homeopathic remedies of Mag Phos 6X and Cuprum Metallicum 6X are usually helpful. Spascupreel, a homeopathic combination remedy from the Heel company, combines these two and others for effective relief from menstrual cramps. Gynecoheel and BHI Menstrual is indicated for the overall relief of problems related to the menses.

When cramps are severe and do not respond to anti-inflammatory medications, talk to your doctor about endometriosis as a possible cause.

ENDOMETRIOSIS

Why, in some women, the tissue that makes up the uterine lining should become implanted outside the uterus on the ovaries, the fallopian tubes, the abdominal wall, or the bladder is still not entirely clear. Theoretically, it is caused by retrograde blood flow from inside the uterus, and research has shown that this may occur in many women—although only some develop the condition. Endometriosis may be congenital, especially when menstrual periods have been painful from the outset. And the condition can also indicate immune-system problems, since normally the immune system will dispose of the cells.

This debilitating disease can cause tremendous discomfort, especially during menses, pain during sex, inflammation, and scarring. Some sufferers live on pain medication. It can also interfere with fertility. I have seen endometriosis in women of all ages, from the teens through the forties. Although it may impair one woman's ability to become pregnant, in another it can clear up during pregnancy only to return later.

This disease is almost impossible to diagnose without surgery. Sometimes an ultrasound exam can identify an endometrioma, a cyst filled with endometrial tissue and blood, but more often the lesions of endometriosis are too small and difficult to spot with ultrasound. Some doctors feel that a blood test, CA-125, a tumor marker used to monitor ovarian cancer, can also predict endometriosis, but there is evidence that this blood test can be misleading.

As with PMS, nutritional supplements and diet are the first line of defense. I recommend supplementing daily with a divided dose of 3,000 to 5,000 milligrams of vitamin C with bioflavonoids, 800 IUs of vitamin E, 25,000 IUs of betacarotene, a B complex, and 750 to 1,000 milligrams of magnesium. Try taking two to three tablespoons of flaxseed oil every day—this has a beneficial effect on prostaglandins. Taking natural enzymes in between meals and eliminating candida infections may be helpful.

Conventional medical treatment of endometriosis takes two forms: hormone therapy and surgery. In some cases, simply going on the birth control pill will control the degree of pain. Danazol was often prescribed for this condition. Danazol, however, can result in temporary menopause and masculinizing effects and increased libido. Newer options are Synarel, a nasal spray; and Lupron, a gonadotropin-releasing hormone that also causes menopausal symptoms and can reduce sex drive. Doctors usually restrict Lupron's usage to six months, and it is often recommended as an adjunct to surgery. Laser or cauterization surgery via laparoscopy is often necessary and effective.

There are some alternative options for dealing with endometriosis. Vitex, dong quai, raspberry leaves, and nettle all have been found to be helpful. Homeopathy, too, offers help, and I would suggest consulting a homeopathic specialist for remedies based on your specific constitution. Acupuncture often helps with the pain.

URINARY TRACT INFECTIONS

Infections of the urinary tract are the most common bacterial infections seen in sexually active women. In the past, sexual activity was blamed for the occurrence of infections, but new findings indicate that the main problem is the existence of bacteria in the vagina such as E coli, enterobacter, Proteus mirabilis, and Klebsiella pneumoniae that are normally found in the anal area. Usually, these bacteria would not be a problem, but they are transferred to the bladder when a woman is sexually active. Another factor is the alkalinity of male ejaculate and vaginal secretions that raise the PH balance of the vagina and encourage the growth of bacteria. Diaphragms are another culprit. They prevent the bladder from emptying fully, leaving it ripe for the growth of bacteria.

In cases of a single occurrence of a urinary tract infection, your doctor will prescribe a course of antibiotics after taking a culture to be sure the infection has been dealt with. For chronic infections, medical treatment is aimed at prevention, and you may be advised to take a dose of antibiotics each time you have intercourse. This is a very effective way of controlling recurrent infections but may lead to problems.

Many of my patients are apprehensive about taking antibiotics, a legitimate concern since long-term antibiotic use can cause recurrent yeast infections. To prevent this, during and after a course of antibiotics eat yogurt or take acidophilus lactobacilli: natural, live bacteria found in yogurt or available in pill or powder form from a health food store. They are part of the body's normal flora and help to restore bacterial balance.

It is also important to drink plenty of water—seven or eight glasses a day—or sip herb teas. I recommend parsley or horsetail, but the best-known herb for urinary infections is uva-ursi (bear-berry), which has an antiseptic effect in the urogenitary tract. Uva-ursi can be taken as a tincture in doses of 20 to 40 drops three times daily or in capsules of 3 to 6 grams daily. Cranberry juice is well known and recommended to further acidify urine. The old standby Vermont cure of one tablespoon of honey with one teaspoon of apple cider vinegar in eight ounces of warm or cold water has brought me relief in a pinch. Avoid caffeine and alcohol, as they are bladder irritants, and citrus and carbonated beverages, which further alkalinize urine.

Homeopathic doses of the infamous cantharidis (Spanish fly) can be used for symptoms of urinary tract infections when there is severe burning in the urethra. Staphysagria is another homeopathic remedy especially helpful for "honeymoon cystitis," the urinary tract inflammation often brought on by an increase in sexual activity. Two Chinese patent remedies I have found helpful are Gentiana Purge Liver Pills (Lung Tan Xie Gan Pill) and the Dianthus Formula (Ba Zheng Tang Pill).

VAGINITIS

The causes of vaginitis—infections or inflammation of the vagina—are similar to those of urinary tract infections: pathogenic bacteria from the anal area being introduced into the vagina, the recurrent use of antibiotics, and overalkalinization of the vagina due to diet. In this case, the bacteria can also be transmitted sexually.

If bacterial infections exist, your doctor will probably prescribe antibiotics. Again, the use of acidophilus during and after treatment may prevent a yeast infection. Douching with acidophilus can also be helpful, and some of my patients have had success with betadyne douches in cases of mild bacterial infections. Herbal remedies offer other douching alternatives. Try 5 to 10 drops of tea-tree oil in a liter of water, and if you want you can add a few drops of either goldenseal, echinecea, or myrhh tinctures. Appropriate homeopathic remedies include pulsatilla, sepia, and medorrhinum.

Candida—yeast—vaginitis often occurs after antibiotic use but also can be caused by stress, a high-carbohydrate diet, and diabetes. Often, when an overgrowth of candida is present in the vagina, a similar condition exists in the intestine. This can cause a wide range of symptoms including headaches, fatigue, persistent stomach bloating, joint pains, and other nonspecific symptoms. After performing a series of blood tests to determine the extent of the problem, I have found the best way to help those chronic conditions is a multipronged approach that includes a high-protein/low-carbohydrate diet; reducing your intake of sugar, bread, alcohol, vinegar, and fermented products; taking lactobacilli products; and taking prescription medication such as Nizoral or Diflucan. A product I especially like is Candida Cleanse, by Rainbow Light—an herbal combination available in most health food stores. Other remedies such as capryllic acid and citracidal, a grapefruit-seed extract, can also be helpful.

A woman's sexuality is never static. Whether you are in adolescence, looking at motherhood, or facing menopause, you can maximize your relationship with your sexual self. If you prepare yourself for these transitions physically, emotionally, psychologically, and spiritually, getting in touch with your sexuality will be easier than you think.

11

THE HEALING POWER OF SEX

*Our Creator has given us five senses to help us survive threats
from the external world, and a sixth sense, our healing system,
to help us survive internal threats.*
—BERNIE S. SIEGEL, M.D.

Sexual intimacy after illness can constitute an important part of the recovery process. After surgery, you may be reluctant or afraid, for various reasons, to resume your accustomed sexual activity. Medications may have altered sexual functions, or fear that you have lost the ability to perform due to illness or surgery may inhibit you. You may worry that vigorous sex will cause a relapse. If you suffer from a chronic disease, your libido could become a casualty.

If you already have negative feelings about sex in general or about your partner in particular, illness will provide a good excuse to refrain. But it can be self-defeating, even self-destructive, to shy away from physical love during an illness, for sexual pleasure can become part of the healing process. During these difficult times, reassurance and the ability to communicate with your partner could be the best aphrodisiacs.

When abilities are impaired, remember that sex can be much more than penile penetration. Mutual masturbation, oral sex, sensual massage, loving touch, and some Tantric techniques that require limited motion can express love and sexuality and at the same time improve your health.

Loving someone who is ill is a challenge. You may unconsciously fear you will "catch" the disease, even when the condition is clearly not communicable, such as cancer or heart disease. Then there are real dangers with diseases such as AIDS, where every precaution must be taken. It is important to talk about your apprehensions with someone. If your partner is not in an emotionally stable enough position to handle your worries, find a therapist or doctor with whom to discuss them, for repressed anxiety will be picked up by your sick partner, even if unconsciously.

Every illness has its characteristic concerns and physical restrictions. Here is how to handle some of the most common in our society.

Matters of the Heart

Cardiovascular illness is the number-one killer in the United States. Take that well-publicized statistic, add the mystique that the heart holds for many of us as the body's most vital organ, and it is not surprising that the onset of cardiovascular illness can be a traumatic and frightening event. A number of factors around this disease can affect your sex life.

Some heart medications impair desire and the ability to perform. When they do, many patients opt to take their chances on open-heart surgery in hope of returning to normal and drug-free sexual activity. Calcium channel blockers and angiotensin-converting enzyme inhibitors cause fewer problems than beta-blockers, but it is important to discuss any sexual side effects with your doctor, so she or he can adjust your regimen.

Depression and anxiety—neither conducive to a robust libido—are common responses to heart disease. I have known patients who didn't realize how depleted heart surgery had left them, so they tried to make love as though the operation had never taken place. When this proved impossible, they were deeply disappointed. Other patients can go to the opposite extreme, to the point of taking early retirement and vegetating. If you are a heart patient whose primary interest in life is your profession, or if, say, a regular game of tennis has been your delight, abruptly abandoning these activities can lead to depression. A well-meaning spouse or children can make things worse by coddling you or not allowing you to do anything for yourself. Ask your doctor to set up a program of activities or physical therapy with specific goals. When you have reached them, ask him or her for the next step. Learning to assess how much physical activity you can handle will also help you reaccustom yourself to the physical demands of lovemaking.

Guilt can contribute to depression. A husband might imagine that his heart attack was a "punishment" for playing around on the side. A woman might feel guilty because she quarreled with her mate just prior to the attack. In delicate cases such as these, counseling, preferably involving both partners, could help resolve the issues that led to the affair or the argument. Thus a heart attack could conceivably turn into an agent for positive change in a relationship.

Feelings of anxiety and depression usually run their course and improve with time, but, generally speaking, people who attend rehabilitation programs or seek therapy tend to suffer less severely and improve more rapidly. If your doctor puts you on drugs, remember that most antidepressants and antianxiety agents can adversely affect your sexual functioning. Read the relevant section of chapter 5 for options in medication and discuss them with your physician.

Sex is of vital concern after a heart attack, but in the past, advice was scarce. Many older doctors have received little in the way of sex education to pass on to patients. The rule of thumb was "do what you feel like doing." Specific advice is now more readily available, and most doctors recommend that sexual activity be resumed four weeks after an acute cardiac event. Studies have shown that many patients are able to jump the gun, to the extent of masturbating while still in the hospital.

Many factors can play a part in what you feel like doing.

Sometimes the patient and his or her partner are terrified of sex, fearing it will trigger another heart attack. Wives of heart patients have described how they have jumped out of bed, their hearts pounding, when their husbands have rolled over in the night and groaned—normal sleep activity.

Many men when diagnosed with heart disease fear that intercourse might bring on a heart attack. Although there are legendary tales about men found dead while making love, in reality very few heart attacks occur during sex. In a study of 5,559 cases of sudden death from heart attack, only six occurred because of the stress of making love. Nonetheless, many men are concerned that the increased heart rate that accompanies intercourse will overtax their heart, and a sad 25 percent of men who have had heart attacks never resume sexual activity. Sexual activity, however, is relatively undemanding, approximately equivalent in physical terms to walking up two flights of stairs.

The following suggestions will give you some peace of mind on this subject.

- Do not make love when you are tired. Sometimes mornings are better because you are more rested.
- Do not have vigorous sex if the room temperature is very hot or cold. When it is, try some of the gentle Tantric sex practices by which you can attain high levels of bliss with little activity.
- Wait for two or three hours after eating to have sex so your body can digest the food. After eating, blood is concentrated in the digestive system, and vigorous activity can pull blood into the muscles, resulting in stomach cramping.
- If you have angina, nitroglycerin taken before intercourse can prevent chest pains during sex. Your doctor will make the appropriate recommendations about usage. If chest pain develops during intercourse, better stop. If the pain is associated with irregular heartbeat or shortness of breath that lasts for longer than ten minutes, see your doctor.
- If you are in a rehabilitation program, ask your trainer to

give you some safe guidelines for monitoring your heart rate; that way you will know when you are in a safe zone.
• Have the members of your household become proficient in cardiopulmonary resuscitation (CPR). About 60 percent of heart attack patients who die do so before reaching the hospital. Many of those who survive are kept alive because someone has administered CPR while waiting for the paramedics. Keep a list of emergency numbers close at hand, and know which hospitals are best equipped to handle cardiac patients. The more in control and secure you and your lover feel about dealing with an emergency should one arise, the more you will be able to relax and enjoy a vibrant love life.

A healthy life-style is one of the most important ways to keep your heart strong. It is often easy to bring about change when you become aware that your longstanding bad habits—smoking, excessive drinking, poor diet, lack of exercise, stress—have contributed to your condition. Once you make a conscious decision that you want to enjoy a better life during your remaining years, you will start to live differently and for the better. Be sure to make these changes under a doctor's supervision. As your general health improves, you will almost surely find that your desire and potency increase exponentially.

Along with exercise, a diet low in cholesterol and saturated fats and high in nutritional content is vital. Foods such as oat and rice bran, whole grains, legumes, and fresh fruits and vegetables have plenty of fiber and help lower blood cholesterol levels while providing vitamins and minerals. Garlic can lower blood pressure and boost high-density lipoproteins. Fish oils have been high on the list of heart protectors because they appear to prevent the formation of small blood clots, but research has yielded varying results, and some reports claim that fish oils have no effect at all. Get your fish oils by increasing your dietary intake of cold-water fish such as salmon, mackerel, herring, and sardines, but beware of the salt content that comes along with them. Olive oil is a good addition to your diet, as it is high in monounsaturated fats that lower triglyceride levels and help protect the heart. But it is low in essential fatty acids, which you can get in walnut, soy, and flaxseed oils.

Vitamins E and C, plus chromium, niacin, phosphatidyl, choline, magnesium, and potassium are important supplements for supporting cardiovascular function: see Appendix A for sources and dosages. The addition of Coenzyme Q-10 in doses of 50 to 100 milligrams three times daily has been reported to help with congestive heart failure, and with cardiovascular function overall, due to its antioxidant properties.

There is also an herb that has a special affinity for the heart and blood vessels. Hawthorne berries *(Crataegus)* increase blood flow into the heart muscle and help lower cholesterol levels. You can buy the herb in tincture form. Take 10 to 20 drops three times a day, or in capsules. The capsule dose is 6 to 12 grams daily.

The best way to avoid heart problems is prevention. Have an EKG at the age of forty and every five years thereafter unless you are at high risk and your doctor suggests more frequent checkups. Stop smoking. Smoking causes more deaths from heart disease than from cancer because of its effect on atherosclerosis. For women, the risk of heart disease increases after menopause. If you are postmenopausal, have your cholesterol checked annually, especially if you are not taking hormones.

Cancer

Cancer can occur in many different parts of the body, thereby creating myriad different health problems that can affect libido and sexual functioning. However, there are some problems that are common to all types of cancer and involve emotional aspects of the disease or concern the side effects of the various cancer therapies.

Let's face it: Hearing a diagnosis of cancer is devastating. At a time when you are feeling, at best, emotionally fragile, or at worst traumatized, you are expected to assimilate a great deal of information about treatment options, shuttle back and forth between specialists, and undergo tests—all the while dealing with the well-meaning efforts of family and friends that sometimes make matters worse. It's no wonder that your sex life is likely to get placed on the back burner, which is sad because a warm and loving intimate life and positive emotions may help the immune system.

An increasing number of oncologists now recommend that patients—as well as their families—seek therapy to help them cope with a cancer diagnosis. The American Cancer Society and the YWCA offer nationwide support groups, and your doctor or hospital will undoubtedly be able to refer you to some local organizations. Whether you decide to see a psychiatrist, join a group, or seek an alternative form of therapy, remember: There is nothing gained by trying to deal with this ordeal and its attendant anxieties alone. Talk over your sexual concerns in the company of others who understand and can offer insight and help.

Many cancer patients undergo a drop in self-esteem concerning their physical appearance, which in turn affects how they view themselves as sexual beings. Cancer surgery can result in scars, even the loss of a limb. Other types of treatment, such as chemotherapy and radiation, have cosmetic side effects; fortunately most are temporary. It might seem trivial or vain to worry about your appearance when you are battling a deadly illness, but most cancer patients need to continue living a normal, productive life that includes sex, and looking "sick" can undermine this.

Focus on your positive features. Even completely well people have a tendency to zero in on their perceived flaws rather than their desirable physical characteristics. Look at yourself in the mirror both naked and dressed and find at least three things on which to compliment yourself. Indulge yourself in a new garment or a beauty treatment to play up your good points. Ask your partner to tell you some of the things he or she loves about your body: the way you look, the feel of your skin, or your fragrance. Explain that these positive views will help you feel better about yourself. Remember them when you are feeling insecure.

Minimize the effects of chemotherapy, which, among other things, may cause you to lose your hair. These tips for dealing with the cosmetic problems of cancer treatment come from cancer survivor Diane Noyes, whose book *Beauty and Cancer* can be an invaluable tool.

- Before commencing treatment, have a color photo taken of you with your hair and, if a woman, makeup at your best. Use it as a model and a goal during recovery. Make sure you have a picture that shows your eyebrows clearly so you can duplicate their natural arch with a pencil.
- If you have long hair, have it cut short before starting chemotherapy. It is easier, psychologically and physically, to lose short hair than long.
- When planning to wear a wig, wait until you have lost your hair, otherwise it will fit badly. Find out if your insurance company covers the purchase of a wig to counteract the psychological effects of hair loss. If so, have your doctor write a prescription for a "wig prosthesis."
- Use cosmetics and personal toiletries that don't contain perfume or alcohol. The perfume may make you nauseous, and the alcohol can aggravate dry skin. Also, keep your makeup applicators and toilet articles scrupulously clean to reduce the risk of infection.

As with heart patients, depression is common among cancer sufferers. It is frequently associated with sleep deprivation, changes in eating habits, trouble concentrating, and feelings of worthlessness and hopelessness. Talk to your doctor. He or she should be able to prescribe medication to improve your sleep, appetite, energy, and ability to feel pleasure, all of which will probably in turn rekindle your interest in sex.

St. John's Wort *(Hypericum perforatum)* can be taken as a tincture to ease symptoms of anxiety and nervous tension. It has been found helpful in patients with immune deficiencies such as cancer and AIDS. The combination of nettles and oats is another restorative nutrient for the nervous system.

Once you start thinking about resuming your sex life, good communication is critical. Many people with cancer withdraw into themselves, leaving each partner to cope alone with the fear and pain. Sexual sharing is a wonderful way for a couple to feel close during the stress of an illness, but in order to dispel your anxiety you may need to take it slowly. Self-stimulation is a good way to test the waters. By touching and stroking yourself—to orgasm, if you wish—you can get an idea of if and how your sexual responsiveness has changed and which parts of your body are sensitive. Then invite your partner to join you for a mutual sensual massage, guiding him or her with words and hands. By the time you are ready for intercourse you should have regained much of your confidence and will be ready to experiment with the positions that work best for your particular condition, keeping in mind that you may have to expand your horizons rather than stick to what was once your "normal" routine.

Women can have an additional problem as chemotherapy, radiation, and some surgery can propel them into menopause, with its resulting side effects, such as vaginal dryness and atrophy. Read the section on menopause in chapter 10 and talk to your doctor about the possibility of hormone-replacement therapy. However, that is not recommended for some estrogen-dependent cancers such as breast cancer. In this case you might try the topical testosterone creams, Pro-gest cream, or use vaginal lubricants.

Nutrition is very important when recovering from cancer. Many cancers have been discovered to be related to nutritional deficiencies, but there remains some controversy regarding the value of taking vitamins, which at this time are not regarded as curative. However, I recommend vitamins C, E, and A for their antioxidant effects, and zinc and folic acid to strengthen the blood and immune system. See chapter 4 and appendix A for doses and sources.

Some herbal remedies also boost the immune system, namely astragalus, suma, and ginseng, which you read about in chapter 7. Additionally, you can make a tea from equal parts of red clover and chaparral—which has powerful antioxidant effects—infused in boiling water for 10 to 15 minutes.

Arthritis

Arthritis rarely causes problems with sexual desire and functioning, but the joint pain and inflammation can be debilitating and
hardly conducive to enjoying vigorous sexual activity. The primary goal in treating arthritis is to keep the pain to a tolerable
level with anti-inflammatory or immunosuppressive medications,
and although these are not without side effects, they usually don't
cause sexual dysfunction. If you are an arthritis sufferer having
sexual difficulties, talk to your doctor because they may signify
some other problem.

Exercise is one of the best things you can do for yourself if you
suffer from arthritis. Water aerobics is especially good for keeping
joints flexible and increasing strength. One of my arthritis patients has reported that she and her husband have taken up
ballroom dancing, which apart from bringing a little romance
back into their lives is a wonderful, fun way to get some gentle
exercise. Remember, however, not to exercise with "hot" joints
or when you are tired.

Diets high in meats and saturated fats keep the system more
acid, boosting prostaglandins that increase inflammation. Milk,
citrus fruits, and vegetables in the nightshade family are also
reported to aggravate arthritis. Tomatoes, peppers, eggplants,
potatoes—except for raw potato juice—contain a toxin called
sotanine that interferes with enzymes in the muscles and may
result in pain. If you are unsure whether or not they are bothering
you, eliminate them from your diet, then after a break reintroduce
them. You will have your answer if the pain gets worse when you
eat those foods.

Vitamin C with bioflavonoids in doses of 500 to 1,000 milligrams a day acts as an anti-inflammatory agent. I also recommend
taking cod liver oil in doses of no higher than 13,800 IUs of
vitamin A and 1,380 IUs of vitamin D—you will find these exact
amounts in one tablespoon of Dale Alexander brand. Take it at
night along with calcium and magnesium for relief from arthritis
pain.

Herbs such as alfalfa or yucca root can be helpful. Take a half ounce of each daily in the form of an extract, in capsules, or as a tea. Several of my patients have reported relief from arthritic pain with a Chinese herbal patent medicine called Tung Shueh.

There are also some specific homeopathic remedies that are excellent for arthritis. Try bryonia, cuprum metallicum, apis, or rhus tox made from poison ivy. Talk to your homeopathic pharmacist about some of the combination formulas containing these and other supportive herbs indicated for arthritis. These internal remedies work particularly well when used in combination with topical homeopathics such as Traumeel or Zeel cream, from the Heel company, and Triflora gel by Boericke.

Lung Disease

Healthy lung function is vital to life. If you have ever suffered from lung disease, you know how debilitated you feel when your lungs are not working to capacity. Chronic conditions such as asthma, chronic bronchitis, and emphysema (COPD) can interfere with sexual functioning. With COPD in particular, men tend to experience erection difficulties that are difficult to treat, and some doctors find that as the lung disease worsens, problems with physiological impotence increase. Testosterone levels drop as a result of chronic hypoxia (low oxygen), and the smoking that almost invariably goes along with the disease is implicated in loss of erectile capabilities due to constriction of blood vessels. Sexually, women suffer fewer problems. The main side effect of COPD is vaginal dryness, which can be easily handled with lubricants.

Asthma attacks can be triggered by allergens such as perfumes, feathers, plants, molds, and pets. Some women are even allergic to their partner's sperm. Exercise can also spur an asthma attack, and, as exercise, sexual intercourse is roughly equivalent to walking five blocks or climbing two flights of stairs. Some shortness of breath is to be expected during vigorous sexual activity, and using an inhaler before intercourse as well as making love in a side-by-side position may be helpful.

Medications used in pulmonary diseases have little direct effect on sexual functioning even though they overstimulate the sympathetic nervous system. But they tend to cause nausea, anxiety, and the jitters, which hardly invites relaxed intimacy. Systemic steroids also elicit unwanted side effects that can cause a decline in self-image and therefore indirectly affect sexuality. These include weight gain, fluid retention, hair growth, and acne. Men may also experience a drop in libido. Inhaled steroids, or taking systemic steroids only on alternate days, may decrease some of these side effects.

Controlling stress, which can bring on wheezing episodes, is central to minimizing the symptoms of lung disease. Learn some relaxation techniques such as meditation and Hatha Yoga. Check your local hospitals. You are certain to find one that holds classes to teach specific breathing exercises to pulmonary patients. Keep the temperature of your bedroom cool with an air conditioner that filters the air and think about installing a humidifier. Attacks tend to be exacerbated in close, heated rooms.

Introduce foods high in vitamin C into your diet and be sure to get essential fatty acids, especially in the form of black currant seed oil. In a pinch, a cup of coffee may help with a wheezing attack; it contains substances that exert a similar action as the medications used in bronchodilators.

The Chinese herb ma huang contains small amounts of natural ephedrine that is used in medications to treat asthma episodes. A number of homeopathic remedies are appropriate for sufferers of lung disease. However, it is best to seek the advice of a homeopathic practitioner. See the resources section for how to find one.

Diabetes

Diabetes is one of the most common causes of impotence, with hormonal, vascular, and neurologic factors all coming into play. The endocrine cells that produce hormones do not work as efficiently, and diabetes sufferers also experience an increase in prolactin resulting from their exposure to high levels of glucose.

Often, atherosclerotic vascular disease limits blood flow to the sex organs. And finally, high glucose levels cause damage to nerves, usually starting with loss of vibration sense due to an alteration in the nerves' ability to conduct electric impulses. Further nerve impairment may result over the long term as malnutrition of nervous tissue causes disease in tiny, thin blood vessels that affect sexual sensation and erectile response. As if that weren't enough, many of the other diseases often found in tandem with diabetes—such as hypertension and heart disease—involve the use of medications that affect sexual performance (for further details see chapter 5).

The best way to minimize the sexual repercussions from diabetes is to manage blood-sugar levels. Complications of diabetes are greatly reduced when blood sugar is tightly controlled. What you eat, of course, is the most important factor here. Dietary guidelines have changed in the last few years, with the American Diabetes Association supporting a low-fat/high-fiber regimen, especially with reduced saturated fats and increased carbohydrates. Your doctor will make recommendations. Stick with them. If you are obese, losing weight is your best prescription. The symptoms of diabetes improve dramatically when body fat is reduced. Exercise—particularly moderate aerobic exercise—is another critical element for controlling weight and managing blood sugar. Additionally, regular aerobic exercise will improve circulation and cardiovascular fitness.

People with diabetes also need to be careful when taking nutritional supplements. They should avoid betacarotene, as they are unable to convert it to vitamin A; large amounts of B and C vitamins, as these inactivate insulin; and the amino acid cysteine, as it can break insulin bonds. Chromium, however, is very important to help stabilize blood-sugar levels. You'll find information, and sources of this important mineral in chapter 4. You also need L-carnitine and glutamine, two good fat metabolizers.

Ginseng, astragalus, and dandelion root are excellent for diabetes (see chapter 7 and appendix A). I also recommend bean pod. Make a tea by boiling a handful of bean pods in a half liter of water until the water volume has been reduced by half. Strain, and drink half the tea in the morning and half at night. This herb is perfectly safe for long-term use.

AIDS

AIDS is paradoxical; a disease that kills but is transmitted by sex, the very expression of life and love. The race for a cure is on, and it can't come soon enough; the number of infected people increases daily despite attempts to educate the public with safe-sex information.

One of the most poignant issues regarding those infected with AIDS is how to enjoy the intimacy and love so badly needed by all of us, sick or well. Infection with the virus presents a broad range of issues, with physical, emotional, and spiritual aspects common to people everywhere. Many AIDS victims feel like lepers or outcasts, and fear desertion by their lovers, friends, and families: justified apprehensions in many cases. The perceived need to maintain confidentiality often isolates these people from those who could offer succor. Some people sick with AIDS feel guilt for the pain they have inflicted on their loved ones, and guilt for perhaps infecting others. Thus they suffer loss of self-esteem. Then, of course, there are the terrible physical symptoms and the acknowledgment of almost certain death.

If faced with this disease, the best path is to become your own healer. Educate yourself about treatment options. Clinics in many major cities are engaged in experimental treatments using ozone, intravenous vitamins, and immune-system stimulators, among others. Find a support group that you feel comfortable with; not only will you get the emotional nurturance you need, but these groups are an excellent means of keeping up with the latest treatments.

Two remarkable women have started movements that have given people tools with which to work and fostered a spirit of healing so badly needed. Marianne Williamson has been teaching "A Course in Miracles" in Los Angeles and New York with specific groups for those with AIDS. I recommend her bestselling book, *A Return to Love*. And Louise Hay, a Los Angeles-based author of a number of books, including *You Can Heal Your Life*, *The AIDS Book*, and *Heart Thoughts*, also conducts classes that uplift and motivate toward self-healing. There is evidence that a positive attitude combined with life-style modifications can improve the condition of many AIDS sufferers.

Among the critical life-style changes are the elimination of habits such as smoking and excessive use of alcohol and drugs, as well as sticking to a rigorously healthy diet and a program of nutritional supplementation designed to bolster the immune system. Detailing such a diet is beyond the scope of this book, although you will find some relevant information in the chapters on food, herbs, and homeopathy. Find a qualified nutritionist or a doctor with nutritional orientation for proper guidance.

It is the duty of every person to avoid giving or getting AIDS. Studies have shown that in over 90 percent of cases a person will test positive for the virus within six months of becoming infected. So if you take two tests six months apart and abstain from intercourse in between, your negative tests almost guarantee that you are free from the disease. From then on, unless you are in a monogamous relationship with someone similarly negative, it is imperative to practice safe sex. That means avoiding the exchange of bodily fluids via oral, anal, and vaginal sex. The problem is that we are up against one of the strongest basic human instincts; sexual passion often gets the better of good judgment. Apart from abstinence, condoms are the best protection available at present, but they work only when used correctly every time you have sex. Even these, however, are not 100 percent safe.

For those who already have AIDS, remember that sex can be more than intercourse. There is a fallacy abroad that "sex" is when a couple achieves orgasm during penetration. Now may be a time to learn new ways to give and receive sexual pleasure. You and your partner can help each other reach orgasm through touching and stroking, and sometimes take pleasure simply from cuddling, massaging, and enjoying the pleasures of all of your senses.

Sexually Transmitted Diseases

AIDS tends to take center stage when it comes to media cover-age, and many people may not be aware that rates of infection with other sexually transmitted diseases (STDs) are also on the rise. There is nothing that will put the damper on sexual relation-ships more than the fear, or the reality, that your partner is dangerous to your health, yet many people don't want to discuss their sexual history for fear of losing their partner's interest. I am constantly surprised at the number of men and women who come into my office with a sexually transmitted infection after entering into a relationship with someone new and not taking precautions. On the other hand, I also see couples embarking on a new relationship who come in together to be tested. No test is fool-proof, but I truly believe intimacy is fostered when a couple puts all its cards on the table. Trust can be lost when a person finds out from his or her doctor that a lover transmitted herpes. Some diseases are easily treated, and some you will have for a lifetime, so honesty and responsible, open communication are essential.

Gonorrhea and chlamydia are serious STDs and can lead to sterility in women. Generally they are detected with cultures of the cervix or urethra and are easily treated with antibiotics when caught early. The ancient curse of syphilis is once again on the rise in this country. It, too, is serious although if detected early it can be cured with antibiotics. However, it often goes undetected, and if left untreated for a period of years can damage the internal organs, nerves, and brain. The earliest symptom is a painless sore that appears about two weeks to three months after contact. Possibly more sores, a rash, and low fever appear within two to six months after that. If not detected by then, the syphilis can go latent for many years, wreaking irreparable damage. A blood test can be helpful for diagnosis.

Herpes, one of the most common STDs, is difficult to detect unless the sore can be cultured in its acute stages. Blood tests measuring antibodies can be helpful if the levels are high enough. But most people have some level of antibody present, since just about everyone has been exposed to this virus. Herpes is recurrent and will often come out when you are under stress. Many women have outbreaks just before, during, or just after their periods. If you have herpes it is important to watch for the signs of an infection such as itching or burning at the place of the lesion. I have found that even this is not foolproof, since many people shed the virus without displaying any symptoms. Medical treatment involves the use of a drug called Zovirax, which can be taken to prevent an outbreak and shorten the course of the infection. Other approaches include the addition of the amino acid L-lysine supplements in doses of up to 3,000 milligrams a day, and increasing intake of foods with lysine, including meats and dairy products. You should also avoid foods containing the amino acid arginine, which increases the growth of viruses. It is contained in nuts, seeds, wheat, and chocolate. I recommend the herbs astragalus, suma, and ashwaganda for herpes; see chapter 7 for sources and dosages. There is a Chinese formula called Chuan Xin Lian Kang Yang Pian containing the herb isatis along with the supplementing antioxidant vitamins A, C, and E, and zinc, which may help.

One of the most serious and difficult STDs to detect is human papilloma virus (HPV), the virus that causes warts to grow on the cervix, in the vagina, on the vulva, and in the urethra or the rectum. Infection with this virus is widespread in the United States; over 80 percent of the population carries it without necessarily developing the obvious symptoms. The most frightening aspect of this disease is its association with genital cancers, including cancer of the cervix, vagina, vulva, or penis. Not all strains of the virus are associated with cancer, but some may cause precancerous lesions to appear on the genitals.

It is difficult to determine if this virus is totally gone, since it lives in the cells of the skin and can lie dormant for long periods. Early detection leads to the best chance of remission. I recommend taking vitamins A, C, and E, zinc, and folic-acid supplements as well as the Chinese herbal formula mentioned above for herpes as a way of bolstering the immune system against this and other viruses.

The saddest thing about sexually transmitted diseases is that they so often lower the victim's self-esteem, cause a sense of being "dirty," and undermine loving relationships. Many men and women are understandably afraid of rejection by their partner if they reveal that they have contracted something, so they panic and refuse to discuss the problem openly. I have seen how treatment for HPV, which is unpleasant and can take months, can strain a relationship. On the other hand, I have been heartened to observe how being infected has actually brought a couple together during the trying time of treatment.

Sexuality, especially when joined with emotional intimacy, can help heal, bringing relaxation, release of tension, and—at least for a while—remission from pain. Sex with love can reassure, relieve men and women of their deepest fears and anxieties, free them to be themselves, and, if the Eastern thinkers are right, lead them to a higher plane of consciousness. There are also Western sages who basically agree that loving sexuality is a pathway to the meaning of life.

The great psychoanalyst and child psychologist Bruno Bettelheim noted that Freud was correct in saying that human beings possess a life drive (Eros) and a death drive (Thanatos). Bettleheim wrote: "As long as the life drive, or libido, is in ascendancy—certainly as long as we are sexually active . . . we are going to live. As long as we are in love with somebody, we try to stay alive to be reunited with them. It is as simple as that."

Appendix A

RECOMMENDED NUTRIENT DOSAGES

NUTRIENT	RECOMMENDED DAILY ALLOWANCE	OPTIMAL DOSAGE FOR WOMEN	OPTIMAL DOSAGE FOR MEN
B 1 Thiamine	1.0–1.4 mg	50–200 mg	50–100 mg
B 2 Riboflavin	1.2–1.6 mg	50–200 mg	50–100 mg
B 3 Niacin	13–16 mg	50–500 mg	50–500 mg
B 5 Pantothenic Acid	5–10 mg	50–1000 mg	50–1000 mg
B 6 Pyridoxine	2–2.2 mg	50–500 mg	50–100 mg
B 12	3 mcg	100–200 mcg	100 mcg
Folic Acid	400 mcg	800 mcg	800 mcg
Choline	N/A	500–3000 mg	500–3000 mg
Vitamin C	60 mg	1000–5,000 mg	1000–5,000 mg
Bioflavinoids	no RDA	200–1000 mg	200–1000 mg
Vitamin A	3000–5000 IU	5000–10,000 IU	5000–10,000 IU
Betacarotene	N/A	15,000–25,000 IU	15,000–25,000 IU
Vitamin E	12–15 IU	400–1000 IU	400–800 IU
Calcium	800 mg	500–1500 mg	500–1000 mg
Magnesium	300–350 mg	500–1000 mg	500 mg
Zinc	15 mg	30–50 mg	30–100 mg
Selenium	50 mcg	100–200 mcg	100–200 mcg
Chromium	50 mcg	200–500 mcg	200–500 mcg
Iodine	150 mcg	150 mcg	150 mcg
Manganese	2.5–5 mg	10–15 mg	10 mg
Iron[2]	18 mg	20 mg	N/A
Phenylalanine	N/A	500–1500 mg	500–3000 mg
Arginine[1]	N/A	100–1000 mg	100–6000 mg

[1]Use caution with arginine if you have herpes or other viral infections.

[2]Supplementation with iron is not necessary unless a condition of iron deficiency is established by a medical doctor. Iron deficiency in men is rare compared to women since they do not loose blood with menstruation as women do. Iron deficiency can occur with vegetarian diets or blood loss.

The Recommended Daily Allowance (RDA) is the established dosage recommended to prevent deficiency syndromes and avoid toxic effects. The optimal dosage ranges will vary depending upon your state of health, the environment in which you live, your dietary intake, medications and habits such as nicotine and alcohol. More research into optimum health and longevity is showing that higher dosages of some vitamins may help to prevent diseases such as vitamin C and vitamin E for heart disease and betacarotene for cancer. It is recommended that you seek the advice of a health practitioner before instituting supplementation to your regular diet.

APPENDIX B
RESOURCE LIST

For information regarding the companion video, call 1-800-927-0158. For an extensive catalog including many of the products mentioned in this book, send a check or money order for $5.00 to:

Love Potions, Inc.
530 Wilshire Boulevard
Suite 203
Santa Monica, CA 90401

For referrals to certified sex therapists contact:

American Association of Sex Educators, Counselors, and Therapists
11 Dupont Circle N.W.
Suite 220
Washington, D.C. 20036
202-462-1171

For confidential sexuality books and videos:

The Sexuality Library
1210 Valencia Street
San Francisco, CA 94110
415-550-7399

For vibrators, sexual toys, massage oils, etc., write for a catalog:

Good Vibrations
1210 Valencia Street
San Francisco, CA 94110

The Xandria Collection
Dept. PB0193
P.O. Box 31039
San Francisco, CA 94131

This shop is open only to women. A catalog is also available.

Eve's Garden
119 W. 57th Street
Suite 420
New York, NY 10019
212-575-8651
800-848-3837

This shop has been well known for many years for its sexual paraphernalia for both gays and heterosexuals; catalogs are also available.

The Pleasure Chest
7733 Santa Monica Blvd.
Los Angeles, CA 90046
213-650-1022

For information regarding Taoist teachings contact:

Mantak Chia
The Healing Tao Center
P.O. Box 1194
Huntington, NY 11743

In Los Angeles:

Healing Tao Center
Pacific Palisades
310-451-5415

Dr. Stephen Chang
Tao Academy
2700 Ocean Avenue
San Francisco, CA 94132

For information regarding Tantra classes: *Tantra* magazine has a teachers' directory in the back of each magazine plus a calendar of events for the coming months.

Tantra: The Magazine
P.O. Box 79
Torreon, NM 87061-0079
505-271-3155

Margo Anand
Sky Dancing Tantra
Right Hand Productions
P.O. Box 544
Mill Valley, CA 94942
415-388-0431

Sexual Energy Ecstasy Seminars
Box 5489
Playa Del Rey, CA 90296

Source Retreats Hawaiian Goddess
Carolyn and Charles Muir
P.O. Box 69
Paia, HI 96779
808-572-8364

For a unique Tantra/Taoist approach for gay and bisexual men; courses are also available in New York.

Joseph Kramer
The Body Electric
6527A Telegraph Avenue
Oakland, CA 96409
510-653-1594

For information regarding courses related to herbs and sexuality:

Amanda McQuaide-Crawford,
BA.D.Phyt. MNIMH
California School of Herbal Studies
P.O. Box 39
Forestville, CA 95436
707-887-7457

For information and ordering
herbs:

Penn Herb Company Ltd.
603 North 2nd Street
Philadelphia, PA 19123-3098
800-523-9971

Herb Products Co.
Box 898
North Hollywood, CA 91603
818-877-3104

This company specifically imports
Brazilian herbs including muira
puama, guarana, and suma:

The Natural and Tropical Source
530 E. 8th St. #204
Oakland, CA 94606
510-451-7862

For a catalog specializing in
plants from the Amazon:

Of the Jungle
P.O. Box 1801
Sebastopol, CA 95473

For organic herbal tinctures (they
carry extracts of yohimbe and
pygeum):

Gaia Herbs and Gaia Herbal
Research Institute:
62 Old Littleton Road
Harvard, MA 01451
508-456-3049
800-831-7780

Herb Pharm
Box 116
Williams, OR 97544
503-846-7178
800-348-4372

To find a licensed Oriental
Medical Doctor and
Acupuncturist in your area
contact:

National Commission for the
Certification of Acupuncturists
1424 16th St. N.W. Suite 501
Washington, D.C. 20036
202-232-1404

To order Chinese herbal patent
medicines:

Meta Labs
1247 7th Street
Suite 201
Santa Monica, CA 90401
213-341-7116

China Herbs
Eden Center (7 Corners)
6763 Wilson Blvd.
Falls Church, VA 22044
703-536-3339

Wing Fung Tai Ginseng Inc.
833 N. Broadway
Los Angeles, CA 90012
213-617-0690

China Herbal Medicine Co.
150 E. Broadway
Chinatown,
New York, NY 10002
212-227-2970

Mayway Trading Co.
622 Broadway
San Francisco, CA 94133
415-788-3646

Nuherbs Co.
3820 Penniman Avenue
Oakland, CA 94619
800-233-4307

For Bioray Tonic Formulas:

Bioray, Inc.
625 Pier Ave. #6
Santa Monica, CA 90405
310-396-5472

For information regarding
Ayurvedic Medicine:

American Institute of Vedic
Studies
P.O. Box 8357
Santa Fe, NM 87504-8357
505-983-9385

Cynthia Copple teaches
workshops, massage, and has
retreats in San Francisco. Call
408-479-1667.

Ayurvedic consultations are also
available through the Maharishi
Ayurveda.

Contact the main office in Iowa
for information regarding a
center in your area:

P.O. Box 282
Fairfax, LA 52556
515-472-5866

For Ayurvedic herbs:

Lotus Light
P.O. Box 2
Wilmot, WI 53192
414-862-2395

S.O.L. Products Co.
P.O. Box 6054
Sante Fe, NM 87502-6054

For information about
homeopathy:

Homeopathic Educational
Services
2124 Kittredge St.
Berkeley, CA 94794
415-649-0294 for catalog
800-359-9051 for orders

To find a trained homeopath
contact:

The National Center for
Homeopathy
801 N. Fairfax #306
Alexandria, VA 22314
703-548-7790

or

The International Foundation for
Homeopathy
2366 Eastlake Drive, E.
Seattle, WA 98102
206-324-8230

For information regarding flower
essences, classes, and to find a
flower-essence practitioner in
your area contact:

The Flower Essence Society
P.O. Box 459
Nevada City, CA 95959
916-265-9163
800-548-0075

Transformation Essence
P.O. Box 1582
Sedona, AZ 86336
602-282-4590

Aromatherapy:

For a unique Signature Scent and
resources for aromatherapy,
contact:

The Carrington Lake House
115 Shoreview Ave.
Pacifica, CA 94044
(415) 330-5482

For aromatherapy formulas and
custom-blended fragrance oils:

Path of the Heart Fragrances
P.O. Box 3509
West Sedona, AZ 86340
602-282-9243

Fragrant Endeavors
4410 N. Rancho Drive
Suite 127
Las Vegas, NV 89130
707-253-8695

For the most luscious body
cremes:

Nadina's Scented Cremes
6505 Old Harford Road
Baltimore, MD 21214
800-722-4292
410-426-5468

This pharmacy will mail order
prescriptions of natural
progesterone for the treatment of
PMS and menopause:

Madison Pharmacy
429 Gammon Place
Madison, WI 53719
800-558-7046

Homeopathic sources:

This company has several
products mentioned that are
available to pharmacies and
medical professionals. Contact
them for a source in your area.

BHI-Heel
P.O. Box 11280
Albuquerque, NM 87192
800-621-7644

This well-stocked homeopathic
pharmacy will send remedies on
request:

Santa Monica Drug
1513 Fourth Street
Santa Monica, CA 90401
310-395-1131

Herbal remedies:

Lifephase, Inc.
614 Venice Boulevard
Venice, CA 90291

BIBLIOGRAPHY

Abel, Ernest L., *Psychoactive Drugs and Sex.* New York, Plenum Press, 1985.

Abraham, Guy, M.D., and Ruth Rumley, EM.D., "The Role of Nutrition in Managing the Premenstrual Tension Syndromes." *Journal of Reproductive Medicine,* vol. 32, no. 6 (June 1987).

Adamson, G. D., "Management of Endometriosis, Pharmacologic Therapies." *The Female Patient,* vol. 16 (June 1991).

Allardice, Pamela, *Love Potions.* New York, Mallard Press, 1991.

Anand, Margo. *The Art of Sexual Ecstasy.* Los Angeles, Jeremy P. Tarcher. 1989.

Asthana, Rajiv, and M. K. Raina, "Pharmacology of Withaania Somerfera (LInn) Dunal—A Review." *Indian Drugs,* vol. 26, no. 5 (Feb. 1989).

Bach, Edward, M.D., and F. J. Wheeler, M.D., *The Bach Flower Remedies.* New Canaan, CT, Keats Publishing, 1931.

Bachmann, Gloria A., "Sexual Dysfunction in the Older Woman." *Medical Aspects of Human Sexuality,* Feb. 1991, 42.

————, "Sexual Changes and Dysfunction in the Older Woman." *Medical Aspects of Human Sexuality,* Aug. 1990.

Balch, James F., and Phyliss A., *Prescription for Nutritional Healing.* New York, Avery Publishing Group, 1990.

Barbach, Lonnie, *For Each Other: Sharing Sexual Intimacy.* New York, New American Library, 1984.

Barbo, D. M., "The Physiology of the Menopause." *Medical Clinics of North America,* vol. 71, no. 1 (Jan. 1987), 11.

Bennett, Alan H., "Nonprosthetic Surgical Treatment for Vasculogenic Impotence." *Medical Aspects of Human Sexuality,* special issue on Management of Impotence, vol. 23 (April 1989).

Bernstein, Gerald, "Counseling the Male Diabetic Patient with Erectile Dysfunction." Ibid.

Blackie, Margery, *Classical Homoeopathy.* Beaconsfield, Bucks, England, Beaconsfield Publishers, 1986.

Bloom, Floyd E., "Neuropeptides." *Scientific American,* Oct. 1981.

Boericke, William, *Materia Medica.* Philadelphia, Boericke and Tafel, 1927.

Brainum, Jerry, "Sexual Chemistry." *Muscle and Fitness,* July 1992.

Brauer, Alan P., and Donna J., *ESO, Extended Sexual Orgasm.* New York, Warner Books, 1983.

Brown, Donald J., "Phytotherapy Review and Commentary." *Townsend Letter for Doctors,* Feb./March 1992.

Bruyere, Rosalyn L., *Wheels of Light: A Study of the Chakras.* Sierra Madre, CA, Bon Productions, 1989.

Buffum, John, "Pharmacosexology: The Effects of Drugs on Sexual Function. A Review." *Journal of Psychoactive Drugs,* vol. 14, nos. 1–2 (Jan.–June 1982).

Burns, Minique, "Sex Drive: A User's Guide." *Essence,* vol. 21, no. 4 (Aug. 1990), 29.

Butler, Robert N., and Myrna I. Lewis, *Love and Sex After 60.* New York, HarperCollins, 1986.

Byyny, Richard L., *A Clinical Guide for the Care of Older Women.* Baltimore, Williams & Wilkins, 1990.

———, *The Biology of Aging.* Baltimore, Williams & Wilkins, 1990.

Callinan, Paul M. Sc., N.D., Hom. Ph.D., "Homeopathy." *Simply Living.* New York, HarperCollins, 1986.

Camphausen, Rufus C., *The Encyclopedia of Erotic Wisdom.* Rochester, VT, Inner Traditions International, 1991.

Carmichael, Marie S.; Richard Humbert; Jean Dixen; Glenn Palmisano; Walter Greenleaf; and Julian M. Davidson; "Plasma Oxytocin Increases in the Human Sexual Response." *Journal of Clinical Endocrinology and Metabolism,* vol. 64, no. 1 (1987), 27–31.

Carroll, Janell L., "Age-Related Changes in Hormones in Impotent Men." *Urology,* vol. 36, no. 1 (July 1990).

Castleman, Michael, *Sexual Solutions.* New York, Simon & Schuster, 1980.

Chancellar, Philip M., *Bach Flower Remedies,* New Canaan, CT, Keats Publishing, 1971.

Chang, Jolan, *The Tao of Love and Sex: The Ancient Chinese Way to Ecstasy.* New York, E. P. Dutton, 1977.

Chang, Stephen T., *The Tao of Sexology: The Book of Infinite Wisdom*. San Francisco, Tao Publishing, 1986.

Chia, Mantak, and Maneewan Chia, *Healing Love Through the Tao: Cultivating Female Sexual Energy*. New York, Healing Tao Books, 1986.

Chia, Mantak, and Michael Winn, *Taoist Secrets of Love: Cultivating Male Sexual Energy*. Santa Fe, Aurora Press, 1984.

Chopra, Deepak, *Quantum Healing*. New York, Bantam, 1989.

Copple, Cynthia, "Ayurvedic Massage." *Clarion Call* 2, no. 3 (1989).

Coulter, Catherine R., *Portraits of Homoeopathic Medicines*. Berkeley, North Atlantic Books, 1986.

Cowen, Ron, "Receptor Encounters: Untangling the Threads of the Serotonin System." *Science News*, Oct. 14, 1989.

Crawford, E. David, and Frank Mayer, "Organic Causes of Male Sexual Dysfunction: The Evaluation and Treatment of Impotence." *Modern Medicine*, vol. 59 (Sept. 1991).

Cutler, Winnifred B., *Love Cycles*. New York, Villard Books, 1991.

Dallo, J., T. T. Yen, and J. Knoll, "The Aphrodisiac Effect of Deprenyl in Male Rats." *Acta Physiologica Hungarica*, vol. 75 Supl. (1990).

Dean, Ward, and John Morgenthaler, *Smart Drugs and Nutrients*. Santa Cruz, CA, B and J Publications, 1990.

Dharmananda, Subhuti, *Foundations of Chinese Herb Prescribing*. Portland, OR, Subhuti Dharmananda, Institute for Traditional Medicine, 1989.

Dormont, Paul, "Life Events That Predispose to Erectile Dysfunction." *Medical Aspects of Human Sexuality*, special issue on Management of Impotence, vol. 23 (April 1989).

Dunn, M. E., and J. E. Trost, "Male Multiple Orgasms: A Descriptive Study." *Archives of Sexual Behavior*, vol. 18 (1989), 337.

Dunne, Lavon J., *Nutrition Almanac*, Third Edition. New York, McGraw-Hill, 1990.

DuPont, W.D., and D.L. Page, "Menopausal Estrogen Replacement Therapy and Breast Cancer." *Archives of Internal Medicine*, vol. 151 (Jan. 1991), 67.

Erasmus, Udo, *Fats and Oils*. Burnaby, B.C., Canada, Alive Books, 1986.

Feighner, J. P., M.D., et al., "Double Blind Comparison of Bupropion and Fluoxetine in Depressed Outpatients." *Journal of Clinical Psychiatry* 52 (1991), 329–335.

Fratkin, Jake, *Chinese Herbal Patient Formulas*. Portland, OR, Institute for Traditional Medicine, 1986.

Frawley, David, O.M.D., *Ayurvedic Healing.* Sandy, VT, Passage Press, 1989.

———, *The Yoga of Herbs.* Santa Fe, NM, Lotus Press, 1986.

Gambrell, R. Don, Jr., *Androgen Therapy* (a monograph).

Gardner, Elmer A., and J. Andrew Johnston. "Bupropion—An Antidepressant Without Sexual Pathophysiological Action." *Journal of Clinical Pharmacology,* vol. 5, no. 1 (1985).

Gessa, G. L., and A. Tagliamonte, "Role of Serotonin and Dopamine in Male Sexual Behavior." In *Sexual Behavior: Pharmacology and Biochemistry.* New York, Raven Press, 1975.

Gilman, A. G., L. S. Goodman, and A. Gilman, *The Pharmacologic Basis of Therapeutics.* New York, Macmillan, 1980.

Gise, L. H. "Premenstrual Syndrome: Which Treatments Help?" *Medical Aspects of Human Sexuality,* Feb. 1991.

Gould, Lawrence A., "Impact of Cardiovascular Disease on Male Sexual Function." *Medical Aspects of Human Sexuality,* special issue on Management of Impotence, vol. 23 (April 1989).

Green, James, Herbalist, *The Male Herbal Health Care for Men and Boys.* Freedom, CA, The Crossing Press, 1991.

Grof, Stanislav, *Beyond the Brain.* Albany, State University of New York Press, 1985.

Guillemin, Roger, and Roger Burgus, "The Hormones of the Hypothalamus." *Scientific American,* Nov. 1972.

———, "Peptides in the Brain: The New Endocrinology of the Neuron." *Science,* vol. 202 (Oct. 1978).

Gurudas, *Flower Essences and Vibrational Healing.* San Rafael, CA, Cassandra Press, 1983.

Halvorsen, John G., Michael E. Mertz, "Sexual Dysfunction, Part I: Classification, Etiology, and Pathogenesis." *Journal of the American Board of Family Practice,* vol. 5, no. 1 (Jan.–Feb. 1992).

Hamand, Jeremy, *Prostate Problems: The Complete Guide to Their Treatment.* London, Thorsons, 1991.

Hartman, W., and M. Fithian, *Any Man Can.* New York, St, Martin's Press, 1984.

Hayden, Naura, *How to Satisfy a Woman Every Time and Have Her Beg for More!.* New York, Bibli O'Phile Publishing Company, 1982.

Heinrich, Janet B., "The Postmenopausal Estrogen/Breast Cancer Controversy." *Journal of the American Medical Association,* vol. 268, no. 14 (Oct. 1992).

Hirsh, Roger C., "Chinese Herbal Aphrodisiacs: A Modern Approach." Unpublished paper.

Hutchens, Alma R., *Indian Herbalogy of North America.* Boston and London, Shambhala, 1973.

Iddenden, B., S.C., "Sexuality During the Menopause." *Medical Clinics of North America,* vol. 71, no. 1 (Jan. 1987).

Iverson, Leslie L., "The Chemistry of the Brain." *Scientific American,* Sept. 1979.

John, Da Free, *Love of the Two-Armed Form.* Clearlake, CA, The Dawn Horse Press, 1978.

Johnson, Kirk, "The Herbal Love Potions." *East/West Journal,* Feb. 1990.

Jouanny, Jacques, *The Essentials of Homeopathic Materia Medica.* Boiron, France, Laboratoires Boiron, 1984.

Kahn, Carol, "An Antiaging Aphrodisiac." *Longevity,* Dec. 1990.

Kaplan, Helen Singer, *The New Sex Therapy.* New York, Brunner Mazel, 1974.

Kaptchuk, Ted J., *The Web That Has No Weaver.* New York, Congdon and Weed, 1983.

Kennison, Robert D., and Luisa L. Fertitta, "Taking a Woman's Sexual History." *Medical Aspects of Human Sexuality,* Nov. 1990.

Kenton, Leslie, *Ageless Ageing.* New York, Grove Press, 1985.

Lee, William H., and Lynn, *Herbal Love Potions.* New Canaan, CT, Keats Publishing, 1991.

Leiblum, Sandra, Ph.D., et al., "Vaginal Atrophy in the Postmenopausal Woman: The Importance of Sexual Activity and Hormones." *Journal of the American Medical Association,* vol. 249, no. 16 (April 22/29, 1983).

Levine, Stephen B., et al., "Benefits and Problems with Intracavernosal Injections for the Treatment of Impotence." *Medical Aspects of Human Sexuality,* special issue on Management of Impotence, vol. 23 (April 1989).

Lizza, E. F., and R. Cricco-Lizza, "Impotence—Finding the Cause." *Medical Aspects of Human Sexuality,* Oct. 1990.

————, "Impotence: Know the Treatment Options." *Medical Aspects of Human Sexuality,* Nov. 1990.

Lloyd, L. Keith and Mark S. Soloway, *Emerging Trends in the Treatment of Benign Prostatic Hyperpiasia.* PRO Media Communications, Inc., 1992.

Lust, John, *The Herb Book.* New York, Bantam Books, 1974.

Marmar, Joel, "Nonsurgical Treatment of Impotence." *Medical Aspects of Human Sexuality*, special issue on Management of Impotence, vol. 23 (April 1989).

Marshall, Sumner, "Evaluation and Management of Simple Erectile Dysfunction in Office Practice." Ibid.

Masters, William H.; Virginia E. Johnson; and Robert C. Kolodny; *Masters and Johnson on Sex and Human Loving*. Boston, Little, Brown, 1982.

McKenna, Terence, *Food of the Gods*. New York, Bantam Books, 1992.

Medical Letter, Mark Abramwicz, editor, "Drugs That Cause Sexual Dysfunction: An Update." Vol. 34, issue 876 (Aug. 7, 1992).

———, "Finasteride for Benign Prostatic Hypertrophy." Vol. 34, issue 878 (Sept. 1992).

———, "Gamma Hydroxy Butyrate Poisoning." Vol. 33.

Medical World News, "Testosterone Replacement Looks Promising." Aug. 1992, 16.

Midgette, A. S., and J. A. Baron, "Cigarette Smoking and the Risk of Natural Menopause." *Epidemiology* 1990, vol. 1, no. 6.

Miller, Richard Alan, *The Magic and Ritual Use of Aphrodisiacs*. Rochester VT, Destiny Books, 1985.

Mookerjee, Ajit, *Kali the Feminine Force*. Rochester, VT, Destiny Books, 1988.

Moon, Thomas E., "Estrogens and Disease Prevention." *Archives of Internal Medicine*, vol. 151 (Jan. 1991), 17.

Morales, Alvaro, et al., "Nonhormonal Pharmacological Treatment of Organic Impotence." *Journal of Urology*, vol. 128 (July 1982).

Mowrey, Daniel B., *The Scientific Validation of Herbal Medicine*. New Canaan, CT, Keats Publishing, 1986.

Mulligan, Thomas, "Impotence in the Older Man." *Medical Aspects of Human Sexuality*, special issue on Management of Impotence, vol. 23 (April 1989).

Murphy, Michael R.; Jonathan R. Seckl; Steven Burton; Stuart A. Checkley; and Stafford L. Lightman, "Changes in Oxytocin and Vasopressin Secretion During Sexual Activity in Men." *Journal of Clinical Endocrinology and Metabolism*, vol. 65, no. 4 (1987), 738–741.

Nash, E. B., *Leaders in Homeopathic Therapeutics*. New Delhi, B. Jain Publishers, 1989.

National Women's Health Network. "Taking Hormones and Women's Health: Choices, Risks, Benefits," 1989.

Nemeroff, Charles B., "Chemical Messengers of the Brain." In *Geriatric Psychiatry*, E. W. Busse, M.D., and D. G. Blazer, Ph.D. Washington, D.C., American Psychiatric Press, 1989.

Notelovitz, Morris, M.D., "Gynecologic Problems of Menopausal Women: Part 3, Changes in Extragenital Tissues and Sexuality." *Geriatrics*, Oct. 1978.

Oesterling, Joseph E., *Benign Prostatic Hyperplasia.* Archives of Family Medicine, vol. 1 (Nov. 1992).

Ojha, J. K., *Chyavanaprashea: A Scientific Study.* Varanasi, Tara Publications, 1978.

Parker, Allan, *Sexual Energy Ecstasy.* Hacienda Heights, CA, Peak Skill Publishing, 1991.

Pearson, Durk, and Sandy Shaw, *Life Extention: A Practical Scientific Approach.* New York, Warner Books, 1982.

Pfau, Alphonse, M.D., "Sex and Recurrent UTI in Young Women." *Medical Aspects of Human Sexuality*, June 1991, 18–24, 34–39.

Radakovich, Anka, "Love Drugs." *Details*, Aug. 1992, 32.

Reamy, Kenneth Judson, and Eileen, "The Climacteric: Sexual Myths and Realities." *Medical Aspects of Human Sexuality*, Sept. 1991.

Reamy, Kenneth Judson, "A Management Guide to Postpartum Problems." *Medical Aspects of Human Sexuality*, Jan. 1991.

Roche, Max de, *The Foods of Love.* New York, Arcade Publishing, 1990.

Roth, Sanford H., "Arthritis and Impotence." *Medical Aspects of Human Sexuality*, special issue on Management of Impotence, vol. 23 (April 1989).

Rothenberg, Debra L., "Intimacy in the Wake of Surgery." *Self*, April 1991, 41–43.

Roy, J. B., R. L. Petrone, and S. I. Said, "A Clinical Trial of Intracavernous Vasoactive Intestinal Peptide to Induce Penile Erection." *Journal of Urology*, vol. 143 (Feb. 1990), 302.

Roylance, Frank D., "Ancient Notions on Healing Potions." *Los Angeles Times*, Sept. 13, 1992.

Rubinow, David R., "The Premenstrual Syndrome." *Journal of the American Medical Association*, vol. 268, no. 14, Oct. 14, 1992.

Sabinsa Corporation, "Ashwwaganda, A Herbal and Rejuvenating Tonic from Ayurvedic Medicine," 1991.

Sanderson, M. Olwen, and James W. Maddock, "Guidelines for Assessment and Treatment of Sexual Dysfunction." *Obstetrics and Gynecology*, vol. 73, no. 1 (Jan. 1989).

Sarrel, Philip M., "Sexuality in the Middle Years." *Obstetrics and Gynecology Clinics of North America*, vol. 14, no. 1 (March 1987).

Schover, Leslie, Ph.D., *Sexuality and Cancer*. American Cancer Society, 1988.

Seagraves, R. T., and K. B., "Sexual Function: Solutions to Evaluation and Treatment Dilemmas in Primary Care." *Modern Medicine*, vol. 59 (Feb. 1991).

Sherwin, Barbara B., Ph.D.; Morrie M. Gelfand, M.D.; and William Brender, "Androgen Enhances Sexual Motivation in Females: A Prospective, Crossover Study of Sex Steroid Administration in the Surgical Menopause." *Psychosomatic Medicine*, vol. 47, no. 4 (July/Aug. 1985).

Sherwin and Gelfand, "The Role of Androgen in the Maintenance of Sexual Functioning in Oophorectomized Women." *Psychosomatic Medicine*, vol. 49 (1987), 397–409.

Sherwin, "Sexuality in the Older Woman: New Hormonal Treatment." *Medical Aspects of Human Sexuality*, July 1990.

Shirai, Masofumi, et al., "Content and Distribution of Vasoactive Intestinal Peptide (VIP) in the Cavernous Tissue of Human Penis." *Urology*, vol. 35, no. 4 (April 1990), 360.

Shulgin, Alexander, and Ann, *Pihkal: A Chemical Love Story*. Berkeley, Transform Press, 1991.

Snyder, Solomon H., and David S. Bredt, "Biological Roles of Nitric Oxide." *Scientific American*, May 1992.

———, "Nitric Oxide: First in a New Class of Neurotransmitters?" *Science*, July 24, 1992.

Soloway, Mark S., M.D., "More Early Breast Cancers Being Detected." *Medical Aspects of Human Sexuality*, Sept. 1991, 41.

Spark, Richard F., *Male Sexual Health*. New York, Consumer Reports Books, 1991.

Stein, Diane, *The Natural Remedy Book for Women*. Freedom, CA, The Crossing Press, 1992.

Sternbach, George L., and Joseph Varon, " 'Designer Drugs,' Recognizing and Managing Their Toxic Effects." *Postgraduate Medicine*, vol. 91, no. 8 (June 1992).

Taberner, P. V., *Aphrodisiacs: The Science and the Myth*. London and Sydney, Croom Helm, 1985.

Teeguarden, Ron, *Chinese Tonic Herbs*. Briarcliff Manor, NY, Japan Publications, 1984.

Tierra, Michael, C.A., N.D., *Planetary Herbology*. Santa Fe, NM, Lotus Press, 1988.

Tilyard, Murray, W., "Treatment of Postmenopausal Osteoporsis with Calcitriol or Calcium." *New England Journal of Medicine*, vol. 326 (1992), 357.

U.S. News & World Report, "Where Emotions Come From." June 24, 1991.

Ullman, Dana, *The One Minute or So Healer*. Los Angeles, Jeremy P. Tarcher, 1991.

Vanderhoff, Bruce T., and Kevin H. Mosser, "Jimson Weed Toxicity: Management of Anticholinergic Plant Ingestion." *American Family Physician*, vol. 46, no. 2 (Aug. 1992).

Weiss, Dorothy Glasser, "The Cycles of Desire." *Glamour*, May 1990.

Weiss, Richard J., "Effects of Antihypertensive Agents on Sexual Function." *American Family Physician*, vol. 44, no. 6 (Dec. 1991).

Weiss, Rudolf Fritz, *Herbal Medicine*. Beaconsfield, Bucks, England, Beaconsfield Publishers, 1988.

Wells, Robert, "Hormone Replacement Before Menopause." *Postgraduate Medicine*, vol. 86, no. 6 (Nov. 1989), 61.

Werbach, Melvyn R., M.D., *Nutritional Influences on Illness*. Tarzana, CA, Third Line Press, 1987.

Whitehead, E. D., et al., "Diagnostic Evaluation of Impotence." *Post Graduate Medicine*, vol. 88, no. 2 (Aug. 1990).

———, "Treatment Alternatives for Impotence." *Post Graduate Medicine*, vol. 88, no. 2 (Aug. 1990).

Wilcox, Gisela, et al., "Oestrogenic Effects of Plant Foods in Postmenopausal Women." *British Medical Journal*, vol. 301 (Oct. 1990).

Wilson, Robert Anton, *Sex and Drugs*. Phoenix, AZ, Falcon Press, 1973.

Yates, Alayne, and Walter Wolman, "Aphrodisiacs: Myth and Reality." *Medical Aspects of Human Sexuality*, Dec. 1991.

Youngs, David D., "Common Misconceptions About Sex and Depression During Menopause. A Historical Perspective." *The Female Patient*, vol. 16 (Oct. 1991).

Zhang, Jun, et al., "Moderate Physical Activity and Bone Density Among Perimenopausal Women." *American Journal of Public Health*, vol. 82 (1992), 736.

Zorgniotti, Adrian W., "Physical Examination of the Patient with Impotence." *Medical Aspects of Human Sexuality*, Sept. 1991.

————, "Update on Pharmacologic Erection." *Medical Aspects of Human Sexuality*, Jan. 1991.

INDEX